William Dean Howells

The World of Chance

A Novel

William Dean Howells

The World of Chance
A Novel

ISBN/EAN: 9783744708425

Printed in Europe, USA, Canada, Australia, Japan

Cover: Foto ©Thomas Meinert / pixelio.de

More available books at **www.hansebooks.com**

THE WORLD OF CHANCE

A Novel

BY

W. D. HOWELLS

AUTHOR OF "A HAZARD OF NEW FORTUNES"
"THE QUALITY OF MERCY" ETC.

NEW YORK
HARPER & BROTHERS PUBLISHERS
1893

THE WORLD OF CHANCE.

I.

From the club where the farewell dinner was given him, Ray went to the depot of the East & West Railroad with a friend of his own age, and they walked up and down the platform talking of their lives and their loves, as young men do, till they both at once found themselves suddenly very drowsy. They each pretended not to be so; his friend made a show of not meaning to leave him till the through express should come along at two o'clock and pick up the sleeping-car waiting for it on the side track; and Ray feigned that he had no desire to turn in, but would much rather keep walking and talking.

They got rid of each other at last, and Ray hurried aboard his sleeper, and plunged into his berth as soon as he could get his coat and boots off. Then he found himself very wakeful. The soporific first effect of the champagne had passed, but it still sent the blood thumping in his neck and pounding in his ears as he lay smiling and thinking of the honor that had been done him, and the affection that had been shown him

by his fellow-townsmen.   In the reflected light of
these the future stretched brightly before him.   He
scarcely felt it a hardship any more that he should be
forced to leave Midland by the business change which
had thrown him out of his place on the Midland *Echo*,
and he certainly did not envy the friend who had just
parted from him, and who was going to remain with
the new owners.   His mind kept, in spite of him, a
sort of grudge toward the Hanks Brothers who had
bought the paper, and who had thought they must
reduce the editorial force as a first step towards making the property pay.   He could not say that they had
treated him unfairly or unkindly; they had been very
frank and very considerate with him; but he could not
conceal from himself the probability that if they had
really appreciated him they would have seen that it
would be a measure of the highest wisdom to keep
him.   He had given the paper standing and authority
in certain matters; he knew that; and he smiled to
think of Joe Hanks conducting his department.   He
hoped the estimation in which the dinner showed that
his fellow-citizens held him, had done something to
open the eyes of the brothers to the mistake they had
made; they were all three at the dinner, and Martin
Hanks had made a speech expressive of regard and
regret which did not reconcile Ray to them.   He now
tried to see them as benefactors in disguise, and when
he recalled the words of people who said that they
always thought he was thrown away on a daily paper,
he was willing to acknowledge that the Hankses had

probably, at least, not done him an injury. He had often been sensible himself of a sort of incongruity in using up in ephemeral paragraphs, and even leading articles, the mind-stuff of a man who had published poems in the *Century* Bric-à-brac and *Harper's* Drawer, and had for several years had a story accepted by the *Atlantic*, though not yet printed. With the manuscript of the novel which he was carrying to New York, and the four or five hundred dollars he had saved from his salary, he felt that he need not undertake newspaper work at once again. He meant to make a thorough failure of literature first. There would be time enough then to fall back upon journalism, as he could always do.

He counted a good deal upon his novel in certain moods. He knew it had weak points which he was not able to strengthen because he was too ignorant of life, though he hated to own it; but he thought it had some strong ones too; and he believed it would succeed if he could get a publisher for it.

He had read passages of it to his friend, and Sanderson had praised them. Ray knew he had not entered fully into the spirit of the thing, because he was merely and helplessly a newspaper mind, though since Ray had left the *Echo*, Sanderson had talked of leaving it too, and going on to devote himself to literature in New York. Ray knew he would fail, but he encouraged him because he was so fond of him; he thought now what a good, faithful fellow Sanderson was. Sanderson not only praised the novel to its

author, but he celebrated it to the young ladies. They
all knew that Ray had written it, and several of them
spoke to him about it; they said they were just dying
to see it. One of them had seen it, and when he
asked her what she thought of his novel, in the pretence that he did not imagine she had looked at the
manuscript, it galled him a little to have her say that
it was like Thackeray; he knew he had imitated
Thackeray, but he feigned that he did not know; and
he hoped no one else would see it. She recognized
traits that he had drawn from himself, and he did not
like that, either; in the same way that he feigned not
to know that he had imitated Thackeray, he feigned
not to know that he had drawn his own likeness. But
the sum of what she said gave him great faith in himself, and in his novel. He theorized that if its subtle-
ties of thought and its flavors of style pleased a girl
like her, and at the same time a fellow like Sanderson
was taken with the plot, he had got the two essentials
of success in it. He thought how delicately charming
that girl was; still he knew that he was not in love
with her. He thought how nice girls were, anyway;
there were lots of perfectly delightful girls in Midland,
and he should probably have fallen in love with some
of them if it had not been for that long passion of his
early youth, which seemed to have vastated him before
he came there. He was rather proud of his vastation,
and he found it not only fine, but upon the whole very
convenient, to be going away heart-free.

He had no embarrassing ties, no hindering obligations of any kind. He had no one but himself to look out for in seeking his fortune. His father, after long years of struggle, was very well placed in the little country town which Ray had come from to Midland; his brothers had struck out for themselves farther west; one of his sisters was going to be married; the other was at school. None of them needed his help, or was in anywise dependent upon him. He realized, in thinking of it all, that he was a very lucky fellow; and he was not afraid but he should get on if he kept trying, and if he did his best, the chances were that it would be found out. He lay in his berth, with a hopeful and flattered smile on his lips, and listened to the noises of the station: the feet on the platforms; the voices, as from some disembodied life; the clang of engine bells; the jar and clash and rumble of the trains that came and went, with a creaking and squealing of their slowing or starting wheels, while his sleeper was quietly side-tracked, waiting for the express to arrive and pick it up. He felt a sort of slight for the town he was to leave behind; a sort of contemptuous fondness; for though it was not New York, it had used him well; it had appreciated him, and Ray was not ungrateful. Upon the whole, he was glad that he had agreed to write those letters from New York which the Hanks Brothers had finally asked him to do for the *Echo*. He knew that they had asked him under a pressure of public sentiment, and because they had got it through them at last that other people thought he would be a loss to the paper. He liked well enough the notion of keeping the readers of the *Echo* in mind of him; if he failed to capture New York, Midland would always be a good point to fall back upon. He expected his novel to succeed, and then he should be independent. But till then, the five dollars a week which the Hanks Brothers proposed to pay him for his letters would be very convenient, though the sum was despicable in itself. Besides, he could give up the letters whenever he liked. He had his dreams of fame and wealth, but he knew very well that they were dreams, and he was not going to kick over his basket of glass till they had become realities.

A keen ray from one of the electric moons depending from the black roof of the depot suddenly pierced his window at the side of his drawn curtain; and he felt the car jolted backward. He must have been drowsing, for the express had come in unknown to him, and was picking up his sleeper. With a faint thrill of homesickness for the kindly town he was leaving, he felt the train pull forward and so out of its winking lamps into the night. He held his curtain aside to see the last of these lights. Then, with a luxurious sense of helplessness against fate, he let it fall; and Midland slipped back into the irrevocable past.

II.

THE next evening, under a rich, mild October sky, the train drew in towards New York over a long stretch of trestle-work spanning a New Jersey estuary. Ray had thriftily left his sleeper at the station where he breakfasted, and saved the expense of it for the day's journey by taking an ordinary car. He could be free with his dollars when he did not suppose he might need them; but he thought he should be a fool to throw one of them away on the mere self-indulgence of a sleeper through to New York, when he had no use for it more than half way. He experienced the reward of virtue in the satisfaction he felt at having that dollar still in his pocket; and he amused himself very well in making romances about the people who got on and off at different points throughout the day. He read a good deal in a book he had brought with him, and imagined a review of it. He talked with passengers who shared his seat with him, from time to time. He ate ravenously at the station where the train stopped twenty minutes for dinner, and he took little supernumerary naps during the course of the afternoon, and pieced out the broken and abbreviated slumbers of the night. From the last of these naps he woke with a sort of formless alarm, which he identified presently as the anxiety he must naturally feel at drawing so near the great, strange city which had his future in keeping. He was not so hopeful as he was when he left Midland; but he knew he had really no more cause now than he had then for being less so.

The train was at a station. Before it started, a brakeman came in and called out in a voice of formal warning: "This train express to Jersey City. Passengers for way stations change cars. This train does not stop between here and Jersey City."

He went out and shut the door behind him, and at the same time a young woman with a baby in her arms jumped from her seat and called out, "Oh, dear, what did he say?"

Another young woman, with another baby in her arms, rose and looked round, but she did not say anything. She had the place in front of the first, and their two seats were faced, as if the two young women were travelling together. Ray noted, with the interest that he felt in all young women as the elements both of love and of literature, that they looked a good deal alike, as to complexion and feature. The distraction of the one who rose first seemed to communicate itself to her dull, golden-brown hair, and make a wisp of it come loose from the knot at the back of her head, and stick out at one side. The child in her arms was fretful, and she did not cease to move it to and fro and up and down, even in the panic which brought her to her feet. Her demand was launched at the whole carful of passengers, but one old man answered for all:

"He said, this train doesn't stop till it gets to Jersey City."

The young woman said, "Oh!" and she and the other sat down again, and she stretched across the fretful child which clung to her, and tried to open her window. She could not raise it, and the old man who had answered her question lifted it for her. Then she sank back in her seat, and her sister, if it was her sister, leaned forward, and seemed to whisper to her. She put up her hand and thrust the loosened wisp of her hair back into the knot. To do this she gave the child the pocket-book which she seemed to have been holding, and she did not take it away again. The child stopped fretting, and began to pull at its plaything to get it open; then it made aimless dabs with it at the back of the car seat and at its mother's face. She moved her head patiently from side to side to escape the blows; and the child entered with more zest into the sport, and began to laugh and strike harder. Suddenly, mid-way of the long trestle-work, the child turned towards the window and made a dab at the sail of a passing sloop. The pocket-book flew from its hand, and the mother sprang to her feet again with a wail that filled the car.

"Oh, what shall I do! He's thrown my pocket-book out of the window, and it's got every cent of my money in it. Oh, couldn't they stop the train?"

The child began to cry. The passengers all looked out of the windows on that side of the aisle; and Ray could see the pocket-book drifting by in the water. A

brakeman whom the young woman's lamentation had
called to the rescue, passed through the car with a face
of sarcastic compassion, and spoke to the conductor
entering from the other end. The conductor shook
his head; the train kept moving slowly on. Of
course it was impossible and useless to stop. The
young women leaned forward and talked anxiously
together, as Ray could see from his distant seat; they
gave the conductor their tickets, and explained to him
what had happened; he only shook his head again.

When he came to get Ray's ticket, the young fellow
tried to find out something about them from him.

"Yes, I guess she told the truth. She had all her
money, ten dollars and some change, in that pocket-
book, and of course she gave it to her baby to play
with right by an open window. Just like a woman!
They're just about as *fit* as babies to handle money.
If they had to earn it, they'd be different. Some
poor fellow's week's work was in that pocket-book, like
as not. They don't look like the sort that would have
a great deal of money to throw out of the window, if
they was men."

"Do you know where they're going?" Ray asked.
"Are they going on any further?"

"Oh, no. They live in New York. 'Way up on
the East Side somewhere."

"But how will they get there with those two
babies? They can't walk."

The conductor shrugged. "Guess they'll have to
try it."

"Look here!" said Ray. He took a dollar note out of his pocket, and gave it to the conductor. "Find out whether they've got any change, and if they haven't, tell them one of the passengers wanted them to take this for car fares. Don't tell them which one."

"All right," said the conductor.

He passed into the next car. When he came back Ray saw him stop and parley with the young women. He went through the whole train again before he stopped for a final word with Ray, who felt that he had entered into the poetry of his intentions towards the women, and had made these delays and detours of purpose. He bent over Ray with a detached and casual air, and said:

"Every cent they had was in that pocket-book. Only wonder is they hadn't their tickets there, too. They didn't want to take the dollar, but I guess they had to. They live 'way up on Third Avenue about Hundred and First Street; and the one that gave her baby her money to hold looks all played out. They *couldn't* have walked it. I told 'em the dollar was from a lady passenger. Seemed as if it would make it kind of easier for 'em."

"Yes, that was right," said Ray.

III.

WHEN they stopped in Jersey City, Ray made haste out of the car to see what became of his beneficiaries, and he followed closely after them, and got near them on the ferry-boat. They went forward out of the cabin and stood among the people at the bow who were eager to get ashore first. They each held her heavy baby, and silently watched the New York shore, and scarcely spoke.

Ray looked at it too, with a sense of the beauty struggling through the grotesqueness of the huge panorama, and evoking itself somehow from the grossest details. The ferry-boats coming and going; the great barges with freight trains in sections on them; the canal-boats in tow of the river steamers; the shabby sloops slouching by with their sails half-filled by the flagging breeze; the ships lying at anchor in the stream, and wooding the shore with their masts, which the coastwise steamboats stared out of like fantastic villas, all window-shutters and wheel-houses; the mean, ugly fronts and roofs of the buildings beyond, and hulking high overhead in the further distance in vast bulks and clumsy towers, the masses of those ten-storied edifices which are the necessity of commerce and the despair of art, all helped to compose the brutal and stupid body of the thing, whose soul was collectively expressed in an incredible picturesqueness. Ray saw nothing amiss in it. This agglomeration of warring forms, feebly typifying the ugliness of the warring interests within them, did not repulse him. He was not afraid. He took a new grip of the travelling-bag where he had his manuscript, so that he should not be parted from it for a moment till it went into some publisher's keeping. He would not trust it to the trunk which he had checked at Midland, and which he now recognized among the baggage piled on a truck near him. He fingered the outside of his bag to make sure by feeling its shape that his manuscript was all right within. All the time he was aware of those two young women, each with her baby in her arms, which they amused with various devices, telling them to look at the water, the craft going by, and the horses in the wagon-way of the ferry-boat. The children fretted, and pulled the women's hair, and clawed their hats; and the passengers now and then looked censoriously at them. From time to time the young women spoke to each other spiritlessly. The one whose child had thrown her pocket-book away never lost a look of hopeless gloom, as she swayed her body half round and back, to give some diversion to the baby. Both were pretty, but she had the paleness and thinness of young motherhood; the other, though she was thin too, had the fresh color and firm texture of a young girl; she was at once less tragic and more serious than her sister, if it was her sister.

When she found Ray gazing fixedly at her, she turned discreetly away, after a glance that no doubt took in the facts of his neat, slight, rather undersized person; his regular face, with its dark eyes and marked brows; his straight fine nose and pleasant mouth; his sprouting black moustache, and his brown tint, flecked with a few browner freckles.

He was one of those men who have no vanity concerning their persons; he knew he was rather handsome, but he did not care; his mind was on other things. When he found those soft woman-eyes lingering a moment on him he had the wish to please their owner, of course, but he did not think of his looks, or the effect they might have with her. He fancied knowing her well enough to repeat poetry to her, or of reading some favorite author aloud with her, and making her sympathize in his admiration of the book. He permitted his fancy this liberty because, although he supposed her married, his fancy safely operated their intellectual intimacy in a region as remote from experience as the dreamland of sleep. She and her sister had both a sort of refinement; they were ladies, he felt, although they were poorly dressed, and they somehow did not seem as if they had ever been richly dressed. They had not the New Yorkeress air; they had nothing of the stylishness which Ray saw in the other women about him, shabby or splendid; their hats looked as if they had been trimmed at home, and their simple gowns as if their wearers had invented and made them up themselves, after no decided fashion, but after a taste of their own, which he thought good. He began to make phrases about them to himself, and he said there was something pathetically idyllic about them. The phrase was indefinite, but it was sufficiently clear for his purpose. The baby which had thrown away the pocket-book began to express its final dissatisfaction with the prospect, and its mother turned distractedly about for some new diversion, when there came from the ladies' cabin a soft whistle, like the warbling of a bird, low and rich and full, which possessed itself of the sense to the exclusion of all other sounds. Some of the people pressed into the cabin; others stood smiling in the benediction of the artless strain. Ray followed his idyllic sisters within, and saw an old negro, in the middle of the cabin floor, lounging in an easy pose, with his hat in one hand and the other hand on his hip, while his thick lips poured out those mellow notes, which might have come from the heart of some thrush-haunted wild wood. When the sylvan music ceased, and the old negro, with a roll of his large head, and a twist of his burly shape, began to limp round the circle, every one put something in his hat. Ray threw in a nickel, and he saw the sisters, who faced him from the other side of the circle, conferring together. The younger had the bill in her hand which Ray had sent them by the conductor to pay their car fares home. She parleyed a moment with the negro when he reached them, and he took some of the silver from his hat and changed the bill for her. She gave him a quarter back. He ducked his head, and said, " Thank yeh, miss," and passed on.

2

The transaction seemed to amuse some of the by-
standers, and Ray heard one of them, who stood near
him, say: "Well, that's the coolest thing I've seen yet.
I should have about as soon thought of asking the
deacon to change a bill for me when he came round
with the plate in church. Well, it takes all kinds to
make a world!"

He looked like a country merchant, on a first business visit to the city; his companion, who had an air
of smart ease, as of a man who had been there often,
said:

"It takes all kinds to make a town like New York.
You'll see queerer things than that before you get
home. If that old darkey makes much on that transaction, I'm no judge of human nature."

"Pshaw! You don't mean it wasn't a good bill?"

The two men lost themselves in the crowd now
pressing out of the cabin door. The boat was pushing into her slip. She bumped from one elastic side
to the other, and settled with her nose at the wharf.
The snarl of the heavy chains that held her fast was
heard; the people poured off and the hollow thunder
of the hoofs and wheels of the disembarking teams began. Ray looked about for a last glimpse of the two
young women and their babies; but he could not see
them.

IV.

Ray carried his bag himself when he left the elevated road, and resisted the offer of the small Italian dodging about his elbow, and proposing to take it, after he had failed to get Ray to let him black his boots. The young man rather prided himself on his thrift in denying the boy, whose naked foot came half through one of his shoes; he saw his tatters and nakedness with the indifference of inexperience, and with his country breeding he considered his frugality a virtue. His senses were not offended by the foulness of the streets he passed through, or hurt by their sordid uproar; his strong young nerves were equal to all the assaults that the city could make; and his heart was lifted in a dream of hope. He was going to a hotel that Sanderson had told him of, where you could get a room, on the European plan, for seventy-five cents, and then eat wherever you pleased; he had gone to an American hotel when he was in New York before, and he thought he could make a saving by trying Sanderson's. It had a certain gayety of lamps before it, but the splendor diminished within, and Ray's pride was further hurt by the clerk's exacting advance payment for his room from him. The clerk said he could not give him an outside room that night, but he would try

to change him in the morning; and Ray had either to
take the one assigned him or go somewhere else. But
he had ordered his trunk sent to this hotel by the express, and he did not know how he should manage
about that if he left; so he staid, and had himself
shown to his room. It seemed to be a large cupboard
in the wall of the corridor; but it had a window near
the bed, and the usual equipment of stand and bureau,
and Ray did not see why he should not sleep very well
there. Still, he was glad that his friends at Midland
could none of them see him in that room, and he resolved to leave the hotel as soon as he could the next
day. It did not seem the place for a person who had
left Midland with the highest social honors that could
be paid a young man. He hurried through the hotel
office when he came out, so as not to be seen by any
other Midlander that might happen to be there, and he
went down to the basement, where the clerk said the
restaurant was, and got his supper. When he had finished his oyster stew he started towards the street-door,
but was overtaken at the threshold by a young man
who seemed to have run after him, and who said,
" You didn't pay for your supper."

Ray said, " Oh, I forgot it," and he went back to
his table and got his check, and paid at the counter,
where he tried in vain to impress the man who took
his money with a sense of his probity by his profuse
apologies. Apparently they were too used to such
tricks at that restaurant. The man said nothing, but
he looked as if he did not believe him, and Ray was so

abashed that he stole back to his room, and tried to forget what had happened in revising the manuscript of his story. He was always polishing it; he had written it several times over, and at every moment he got he reconstructed sentences in it, and tried to bring the style up to his ideal of style; he wavered a little between the style of Thackeray and the style of Hawthorne, as an ideal. It made him homesick, now, to go over the familiar pages: they put him so strongly in mind of Midland, and the people of the kindly city. The pages smelt a little of Sanderson's cigar smoke; he wished that Sanderson would come to New York; he perceived that they had also a fainter reminiscence of the perfume he associated with that girl who had found him out in his story; and then he thought how he had been in the best society at Midland, and it seemed a great descent from the drawing-rooms where he used to call on all those nice girls to this closet in a fourth-rate New York hotel. His story appeared to share his downfall; he thought it cheap and poor; he did not believe now that he should ever get a publisher for it. He cowered to think how scornfully he had thought the night before of his engagement with the Hanks Brothers to write letters for the Midland *Echo;* he was very glad he had so good a basis; he wondered how far he could make five dollars a week go toward supporting him in New York; he could not bear to encroach upon his savings, and yet he probably must. In Midland, you could get very good board for five dollars a week.

He determined to begin a letter to the *Echo* at once; and he went to open the window to give himself some air in the close room; but he found that it would not open. He pulled down the transom over his door to keep from stifling in the heat of his gas-burner, and some voices that had been merely a dull rumbling before now made themselves heard in talk which Ray could not help listening to.

Two men were talking together, one very hopelessly, and the other in a vain attempt to cheer him from time to time. The comforter had a deep base voice, and was often unintelligible; but the disheartened man spoke nervously, in a high key of plangent quality, like that of an unhappy bell.

"No," he said; "I'd better fail, Bill. It's no use trying to keep along. I can get pretty good terms from the folks at home, there; they all know me, and they know I done my best. I can pay about fifty cents on the dollar, I guess, and that's more than most business men could, if they stopped; and if I ever get goin' again, I'll pay dollar for dollar; they know that."

The man with the deep voice said something that Ray did not catch. The disheartened man seemed not to have caught it either; he said, "What say?" and when the other repeated his words, he said: "Oh yes! I know. But I been dancing round in a quart cup all my life there; and now it's turning into a pint cup, and I guess I better get out. The place did grow for a while, and we got all ready to be a city as soon as

the railroad come along. But when the road come, it
didn't do all we expected of it. We could get out into
the world a good deal easier than we could before, and
we had all the facilities of transportation that we could
ask for. But we could get away so easy that most of
our people went to the big towns to do their trading,
and the facilities for transportation carried off most of
our local industries. The luck was against us. We
bet high on what the road would do for us, and we
lost. We paid out nearly our last dollar to get the
road to come our way, and it came, and killed us. We
subscribed to the stock, and we've got it yet; there
ain't any fight for it anywhere else; we'd let it go
without a fight We tried one while for the car shops,
but they located them further up the line, and since
that we ha'n't even wiggled. What say? Yes; but,
you see, I'm part of the place. I've worked hard all
my life, and I've held out a good many times when
ruin stared me in the face, but I guess I sha'n't hold
out this time. What's the use? Most every business
man I know has failed some time or other; some of
'em three or four times over, and scrambled up and
gone on again, and I guess I got to do the same. Had
a kind of pride about it, m' wife and me; but I guess
we got to come to it. It does seem, sometimes, as if
the very mischief was in it. I lost pretty heavy, for
a small dealer, on Fashion's Pansy, alone — got left
with a big lot of 'em. What say? It was a bustle.
Women kept askin' for Fashion's Pansy, till you'd 'a'
thought every last one of 'em was going to live and be

buried in it. Then all at once none of 'em wanted it
— wouldn't touch it. That and butter begun it. You
know how a country merchant's got to take all the
butter the women bring him, and he's got to pay for
sweet butter, and sell it for grease half the time. You
can tell a woman she'd better keep an eye on her
daughter, but if you say she don't make good butter,
that's the last of that woman's custom. But what's
finally knocked me out is this drop in bric-à-brac. If
it hadn't been for that, I guess I could have pulled
through. Then there was such a rush for Japanese
goods, and it lasted so long, that I loaded up all I
could with 'em last time I was in New York, and now
nobody wants 'em; couldn't give 'em away. Well, it's
all a game, and you don't know any more how it's
comin' out — you can't bet on it with any more certainty — than you can on a trottin' match. My! I
wish I was dead."

The deep-voiced man murmured something again,
and the high-voiced man again retorted :

"What say? Oh, it's all well enough to preach;
and I've heard about the law of demand and supply
before. There's about as much of a law to it as there
is to three-card monte. If it wasn't for my poor wife,
I'd let 'em take me back on ice. I would that."

The deep-voiced man now seemed to have risen;
there was a shuffling of feet, and presently a parley at
the open door about commonplace matters; and then
the two men exchanged adieux, and the door shut
again, and all was silent in the room opposite Ray's.

He felt sorry for the unhappy man shut in there; but he perceived no special significance in what he had overheard. He had no great curiosity about the matter; it was one of those things that happened every day, and for tragedy was in no wise comparable to a disappointment in first love, such as he had carefully studied for his novel from his own dark experience. Still it did suggest something to Ray; it suggested a picturesque opening for his first New York letter for the Midland *Echo*, and he used it in illustration of the immensity of New York, and the strange associations and juxtapositions of life there. He treated the impending failure of the country storekeeper from an overstock of Japanese goods rather humorously: it was not like a real trouble, a trouble of the heart; and the cause seemed to him rather grotesquely disproportionate to the effect. In describing the incident as something he had overheard in a hotel, he threw in some touches that were intended to give the notion of a greater splendor than belonged to the place.

He made a very good start on his letter, and when he went to bed the broken hairs that pierced his sheet from the thin mattress did not keep him from falling asleep, and they did prove that it was a horse-hair mattress.

V.

IN the morning, Ray determined that he would not breakfast at the restaurant under the hotel, partly because he was ashamed to meet the people who, he knew, suspected him of trying to beat them out of the price of his supper, and partly because he had decided that it was patronized chiefly by the country merchants who frequented the hotel, and he wanted something that was more like New York. He had heard of those foreign eating-houses where you got a meal served in courses at a fixed price, and he wandered about looking for one. He meant to venture into the first he found, and on a side street he came on a hotel with a French name, and over the door in an arch of gilt letters the inscription, Restaurant Français. There was a large tub on each side of the door, with a small evergreen tree in it; some strings or wires ran from these tubs to the door-posts and sustained a trailing vine that formed a little bower on either hand; a Maltese cat in the attitude of a sphinx dozed in the thicket of foliage, and Ray's heart glowed with a sense of the foreignness of the whole effect. He had never been abroad, but he had read of such things, and he found himself at home in an environment long familiar to his fancy.

The difference of things was the source of his romance, as it is with all of us, and he looked in at the window of this French restaurant with the feelings he would have had in the presence of such a restaurant in Paris, and he began to imagine gay, light-minded pictures about it. At the same time, while he was figuring inside at one of the small tables, *vis-à-vis* with a pretty actress whom he invented for the purpose, he was halting on the sidewalk outside, wondering whether he could get breakfast there so early as eight o'clock, and doubtful whether he should not betray his strangeness to New York hours if he tried. When he went in there was nobody there but one white-aproned waiter, who was taking down some chairs from the middle table where they had been stacked with their legs in the air while he was sweeping. But he did not disdain to come directly to Ray, where he had sat down, with a plate and napkin and knife and fork, and exchange a good-morning with him in arranging them before him. Then he brought half a yard of French bread and a tenuous, translucent pat of American butter; and asked Ray whether he would have chops or beefsteak with his coffee. The steak came with a sprig of water-cress on it, and the coffee in a pot; and the waiter, who had one eye that looked at Ray, and another of uncertain focus, poured out the coffee for him, and stood near, with a friendly countenance, and a cordial interest in the young fellow's appetite. By this time a neat *dame de comptoir*, whom Ray knew for a *dame de comptoir* at once, though he had never

seen one before, took her place behind a little desk in
the corner, and the day had begun for the Restaurant
Français.

Ray felt that it was life, and he prolonged his meal
to the last drop of the second cup of coffee that his
pot held, and he wished that he could have Sanderson
with him to show him what life really was in New
York. Sanderson had taken all his meals in the basement of that seventy-five cent hotel, which Ray meant
to leave at once. Where he was he would not have
been ashamed to have any of the men who had given
him that farewell dinner see him. He was properly
placed, as a young New York literary man ; he was
already a citizen of that great Bohemia which he had
heard and read so much of. He was sure that artists
must come there, and actors, but of course much later
in the day. His only misgiving was lest the taxes of
Bohemia might be heavier than he could pay, and he
asked the waiter for his account somewhat anxiously.
It was forty cents, and his ambition leaped at the possibility of taking all his meals at that place. He
made the occasion of telling the cross-eyed waiter to
keep the change out of the half-dollar he gave him,
serve for asking whether one could take board there by
the week, and the waiter said one could for six dollars :
a luncheon like the breakfast, but with soup and wine,
and a dinner of fish, two meats, salad, sweets, and
coffee. "On Sundays," said the waiter, "the dinner
is something splendid. And there are rooms ; oh, yes,
it is a hotel."

"Yes, I knew it was a hotel," said Ray.

The six dollars did not seem to him too much; but he had decided that he must live on ten dollars a week in order to make his money last for a full experiment of New York, or till he had placed himself in some permanent position of profit. The two strains of prudence and of poetry were strongly blended in him; he could not bear to think of wasting money, even upon himself, whom he liked so well, and whom he wished so much to have a good time. He meant to make his savings go far; with those five hundred dollars he could live a year in New York if he helped himself out on dress and incidental expenses with the pay for his Midland *Echo* letters. He would have asked to see some of the rooms in the hotel, but he was afraid it was too early, and he decided to come to dinner and ask about them. On his way back to the place where he had lodged he rapidly counted the cost, and he decided, at any rate, to try it for awhile; and he shut himself into his cupboard at the hotel, and began to go over some pages of his manuscript for the last time, with a lightness of heart which decision, even a wrong decision, often brings.

It was still too soon to go with the story to a publisher; he could not hope to find any one in before ten o'clock, and he had a whole hour yet to work on it. He was always putting the last touches on it; but he almost wished he had not looked at it, now, when the touches must really be the last. It seemed to suffer a sort of disintegration in his mind. It fell into witless

and repellent fragments; it lost all beauty and coher-
ence, so that he felt ashamed and frightened with it,
and he could not think what the meaning of it had
once so clearly been. He knew that no publisher
would touch it in the way of business, and he doubted
if any would really have it read or looked at. It
seemed to him quite insane to offer it, and he had to
summon an impudently cynical courage in nerving
himself to the point. The best way, of course, would
have been to get the story published first as a serial, in
one of the magazines that had shown favor to his
minor attempts; and Ray had tried this pretty fully.
The manuscript had gone the rounds of a good many
offices; and returned, after a longer or shorter sojourn,
bearing on some marginal corner the hieroglyphic or
numerical evidence that it had passed through the
reader's hand in each. Ray innocently fancied that he
suppressed the fact by clipping this mark away with
the scissors; but probably no one was deceived. In
looking at it nòw he was not even deceived himself;
the thing had a desperately worn and battered air; it
was actually dog's-eared; but he had still clung to the
hope of getting it taken somewhere, because in all the
refusals there was proof that the magazine reader had
really read it through; and Ray argued that if this
were so, there must be some interest or property in it
that would attract the general reader if it could ever
be got to his eye in print.

He was not wrong; for the story was fresh and new,
in spite of its simple-hearted, unconscious imitations of

the style and plot of other stories, because it was the soul if not the body of his first love. He thought that he had wrapped this fact impenetrably up in so many travesties and disguises that the girl herself would not have known it if she had read it; but very probably she would have known it. Any one who could read between the lines could penetrate through the innocent psychical posing and literary affectation to the truth of conditions strictly and peculiarly American, and it was this which Ray had tried to conceal with all sorts of alien splendors of make and manner. It seemed to him now, at the last moment, that if he could only uproot what was native and indigenous in it, he should make it a strong and perfect thing. He thought of writing it over again, and recoloring the heroine's hair and the hero's character, and putting the scene in a new place; but he had already rewritten it so many times that he was sick of it; and with all his changing he had not been able to change it much. He decided to write a New York novel, and derive the hero from Midland, as soon as he could collect the material; the notion for it had already occurred to him; the hero should come on with a play; but first of all it would be necessary for Ray to get this old novel behind him, and the only way to do that was to get it before the public.

VI.

RAY put his manuscript back into its covering, and took it under his arm. He meant to make a thorough trial of the publishers, and not to be discouraged by his failures as long as a publisher was left untried. He knew from his experience with the magazine editors that it would be a slow affair, and he must have patience. Some of the publishers, even if they did not look at his story, would keep it for days or weeks with the intention or the appearance of reading it, and if they did read it they would of course want time for it. He expected this, and he calculated that it might very well take his manuscript six months to go the rounds of all the houses in New York. Yet he meant, if he could, to get it through sooner, and he was going to use his journalistic connection to make interest for it. He would have given everything but honor to have it known that he had written some things for *Harper's* and the *Century;* he did not wish, or he said to himself and stood to it that he did not wish, any favor shown his novel because he had written those things. At the same time he was willing the fact that he was the correspondent of the Midland *Echo* should help him to a prompt examination of his manuscript if it could ; and he meant to let it be known that he was a journalist before he let it be known that he was an author.

. He formulated some phrases introducing himself in his newspaper character, as he walked up Broadway with his manuscript held tight under his arm, and with that lifting and glowing of the heart which a young man cannot help feeling if he walks up Broadway on a bright October morning. The sun was gay on the senseless façades of the edifices, littered with signs of the traffic within, and hung with effigies and emblems of every conceit and color, from the cornice to the threshold, where the show-cases crowded the passengers toward the curbstones, and to the cellarways that overflowed the sidewalks with their wares. The frantic struggle and jumble of these appeals to curiosity and interest jarred themselves to an effect of kaleidoscopic harmony, just as the multitudinous noises of the hoofs and wheels and feet and tongues broke and bruised themselves to one roar on the ear; and the adventurer among them found no offence in their confusion. He had his stake, too, in the tremendous game that all were playing, some fair and some foul, and shrieking out their bets in these strident notes; and he believed so much he should win that he was ready to take the chances of losing. From the stainless blue sky overhead the morning sun glared down on the thronged and noisy street, and brought out all its details with keen distinctness; but Ray did not feel its anarchy. The irregularity of the buildings, high and low, as if they were parts of a wall wantonly hacked

and notched, here more and here less, was of the same
moral effect to him as the beautiful spire of Grace
Church thrilling heavenward like a hymn.

He went along, wondering if he should happen to
meet either of those young women whom he had be-
friended the evening before.   He had heard that you
were sure to meet somebody you knew whenever you
stepped out on Broadway, and he figured meeting them,
in fancy.   He had decided to put them into his story
of New York life, and he tried to imagine the character he should assign them, or rather one of them;
the one who had given the old darkey a quarter out of
his dollar.   He did not quite know what to do with
the child; something could be made of the child if it
were older, but a mere baby like that would be difficult
to manage in such a story as Ray meant to write.   He
wondered if it would do to have her deserted by her
husband, and have the hero, a young literary adventurer, not at all like himself, fall in love with her,
and then have them both die when the husband, a
worthless, drunken brute, came back in time to prevent their marriage.   Such a scheme would give scope
for great suffering; Ray imagined a scene of renunciation between the lovers, who refused each other even
a last kiss; and he felt a lump rise in his throat.   It
could be made very powerful.

He evolved a character of reckless generosity for
her from her beneficence to the old negro in the ferry-
boat.   Under that still, almost cold exterior, he made
her conceal a nature of passionate impulse, because

the story required a nature of that sort. He did not know whether to have the husband finally die, and the lovers marry, or whether to have the lovers killed in an accident. It would be more powerful to have them killed; it would be so conventional and expected to have them happily married; but he knew the reader liked a novel that ended well. It would be at once powerful and popular to have them elope together. Perhaps the best thing he could do would be to have them elope; there was a fascination in the guilty thought; he could make such a *dénoument* very attractive; but upon the whole he felt that he must not, for very much the same reason that he must not himself run off with his neighbor's wife.

All the time that this went on in his mind, Ray was walking up Broadway, and holding fast to the novel under his arm, which the novel in his brain was eclipsing. His inner eye was fixed on the remembered face of that strange girl, or woman, whom he was fashioning into a fictitious heroine, but his outward vision roved over the women faces it encountered, and his taste made its swift selection among them, and his ambidextrous fancy wove romances around such as he found pretty or interesting enough to give his heart to. They were mostly the silly or sordid faces that women wear when they are shopping, and they expressed such emotions as are roused by the chase of a certain shade of ribbon, or the hope of getting something rich and fashionable for less than its worth. But youth is not nice, or else its eyes are

keener than those of after-life; and Ray found many
beautiful and stylish girls where the middle-aged witness would have seen a long procession of average
second-rate young women. He admired their New-
Yorky dash; he saw their difference in look and carriage from the Midland girls; and he wondered what
they would be like, if he knew them. He reflected
that he did not know any one in New York; but he
expected soon to be acquainted. If he got his novel
taken he would very soon be known, and then his
acquaintance would be sought. He saw himself
launched upon a brilliant social career, and he suddenly had a difficulty presented to him which he had
not foreseen a moment before; he had to choose between
a brilliant marriage with a rich and well-born girl and
fealty to the weird heroine of his story. The unexpected
contingency suggested a new ending to his original
story. The husband could die and the lovers be about
to marry, when they could become aware that the rich
girl was in love with the hero. They could renounce
each other, and the hero could marry the rich girl; and
shortly after the heroine could die. An ending like
that could be made very powerful; and it would be
popular, too.

Ray found himself in a jam of people who had begun suddenly to gather at the corner he was approaching. They were looking across at something on the
other corner, and Ray looked too. Trunks and trav-
elling-bags had overflowed from a store in the basement there, and piled themselves on the sidewalk and

up the house wall; and against the background they formed stood two figures. One was a decent-looking young man in a Derby hat, and wearing spectacles, which gave him a sort of scholarly air; he remained passive in the grip of another, probably the shopman, who was quite colorless with excitement, and who clung fast to the shoulder of the first, as if his prisoner were making violent efforts to escape. A tall young policeman parted the crowd, and listened a moment to the complaint the shopman made, with many gestures toward his wares. Then he turned to the passive captive, and Ray heard the click of the handcuffs as they snapped on the wrists of this scholarly-looking man; and the policeman took him by the arm and led him away.

The intrusion of such a brutal fact of life into the tragic atmosphere of his revery made the young poet a little sick, but the young journalist avidly seized upon it. The poet would not have dreamed of using such an incident, but the journalist saw how well it would work into the scheme of that first letter he was writing home to the *Echo*, where he treated of the surface contrasts of life in New York as they present themselves to the stranger. A glad astonishment at the profusion of the material for his letters possessed him; at this rate he should have no trouble in writing them; he could make them an indispensable feature; they would be quoted and copied, and he could get a rise out of Hanks Brothers on the price.

He crossed to the next corner, where the shopman

was the centre of a lessening number of spectators, and found him willing to prolong the interest he had created in the public mind. He said the thief had priced a number of bags in the place below, and on coming up had made a grab at one and tried to get off with it; but he was onto him like lightning. He showed Ray which bag it was, and turned it round and upside down as if with a fresh sense of its moral value. He said he should have to take that bag into court, and he set it aside so that he should not forget it.

"I suppose," said a tall, elderly gentleman, who seemed to have been listening to Ray's dialogue with the shopman, "you wouldn't be willing to sell me that bag?" He spoke slowly with a thick, mellow voice, deep in his throat.

"Money wouldn't buy that bag; no sir," said the shopman; but he seemed uneasy.

"You know," urged the soft-voiced stranger, "you could show some other bag in court that was just like it."

"I couldn't swear to no other bag," said the shopman, daunted, and visibly relenting.

"That is true," said the stranger. "But you could swear that it was exactly like this. Still, I dare say you're quite right, and it's better to produce the *corpus delicti*, if possible."

He glanced at Ray with a whimsical demand for sympathy; Ray smiled, and they walked off together, leaving the shopman in dubious study of his eventful bag. He was opening it, and scrutinizing the inside.

VII.

THE stranger skipped into step with Ray more lightly than would have been expected from one of his years. He wore a soft felt hat over locks of silken silver that were long enough to touch his beautiful white beard. He wore it with an effect of intention, as if he knew it was out of character with the city, but was so much in character with himself that the city must be left to reconcile itself to the incongruity or not, as it chose. For the same reason, apparently, his well-fitting frock-coat was of broadcloth, instead of modern diagonal; a black silk handkerchief tied in an easy knot at his throat strayed from under his beard, which had the same waviness as his hair; he had black trousers, and drab gaiters showing themselves above wide, low shoes. In his hands, which he held behind him, he dangled a stick with an effect of leisure and ease, enhanced somehow by the stoop he made towards the young fellow's lower stature, and by his refusal to lift his voice above a certain pitch, whatever the uproar of the street about them. Ray screamed out his words, but the stranger spoke in what seemed his wonted tone, and left Ray to catch the words as he could.

"I didn't think," he said, after a moment, and with

some misgiving, that this stranger who had got into step with him might be some kind of confidence man — "I didn't think that fellow looked like a thief much."

"You are a believer in physiognomy?" asked the stranger, with a philosophic poise. He had himself a regular face, with gay eyes, and a fine pearly tint; lips that must have been beautiful shaped his branching mustache to a whimsical smile.

"No," said Ray. "I wasn't near enough to see his face. But he looked so decent and quiet, and he behaved with so much dignity. Perhaps it was his spectacles."

"Glasses can do much," said the stranger, "to redeem the human countenance, even when worn as a protest against the presence of one's portrait in the rogues' gallery I don't say you're wrong; I'm only afraid the chances are that you'll never be proved right. I should prefer to make a speculative approach to the facts on another plane. As you suggest, he had a sage and dignified appearance; I observed it myself; he had the effect — how shall I express it? — of some sort of studious rustic. Say he was a belated farm youth, working his way through a fresh-water college, who had great latent gifts of peculation, such as might have won him a wide newspaper celebrity as a defaulter later in life, and under more favorable conditions. He finds himself alone in a great city for the first time, and is attracted by the display of the trunk-dealer's cellarway. The opportunity seems favorable to the acquisition of a neat travelling-bag; perhaps he has never owned one, or he wishes to present it to the object of his affections, or to a sick mother; he may have had any respectable motive: but his outlook has been so restricted that he cannot realize the difference between stealing a travelling-bag and stealing, say, a street; though I believe Mr. Sharp only bought Broadway of those who did not own it, and who sold it low; but never mind, it may stand for an illustration. If this young man had stolen a street, he would not have been arrested and handcuffed in that disgraceful way and led off to the dungeon-keep of the Jefferson Market Police Court — I presume that is the nearest prison, though I won't be quite positive — but he would have had to be attacked and exposed a long time in the newspapers; and he would have had counsel, and the case would have been fought from one tribunal to another, till at last he wouldn't have known whether he was a common criminal or a public benefactor. The difficulty in his case is simply an inadequate outlook."

The philosophic stranger lifted his face and gazed round over Ray's head, but he came to a halt at the same time with the young fellow. "Well, sir," he said, with bland ceremony, "I must bid you good-morning. As we go our several ways let us remember the day's lesson, and when we steal, always steal enough."

He held out his hand, and Ray took it with a pleasure in his discourse which he was wondering how he should express to him. He felt it due himself to

say something clever in return, but he could not think
of anything. "I'm sure I shall remember your inter-
pretation of it," was all he could get out.

"Ah, well, don't act upon that without due reflection," the stranger said; and he gave Ray's hand a
final and impressive downward shake. "Dear me!"
he added, for Ray made no sign of going on. "Are
we both stopping here — two spiders at the parlor of
the same unsuspecting fly? But perhaps you are
merely a buyer, not a writer, of books? After you,
sir!"

The stranger promoted a little polite rivalry that
ensued between them; he ended it by passing one hand
through the young man's arm, and with the other
pressing open the door which they had both halted at,
and which bore on either jamb a rounded metallic plate
with the sign, "H. C. Chapley & Co., Publishers."
Within, he released Ray with a courteous bow, as if
willing to leave him now to his own devices. He went
off to a distant counter in the wide, low room, and
occupied himself with the books on it; Ray advanced
and spoke to a clerk, who met him half-way. He
asked for Mr. Chapley, and the clerk said he was not
down yet — he seldom got down so early; but Mr.
Brandreth would be in almost any minute now. When
Ray said he had a letter for the firm, and would wait
if the clerk pleased, the clerk asked if he would not
take a chair in Mr. Brandreth's room.

Ray could not help thinking the civility shown him
was for an imaginable customer rather than a concealed

author, but he accepted it all the same, and sat looking
out into the salesroom, with its counters of books, and
its shelves full of them around its walls, while he
waited. Chapley & Co. were of the few old-fashioned
publishers who had remained booksellers too, in a day
when most publishers have ceased to be so. They
were jobbers as well as booksellers; they took orders
and made terms for public and private libraries; they
had customers all over the country who depended on
them for advice and suggestion about forth-coming
books, and there were many booksellers in the smaller
cities who bought through them. The bookseller in
Midland, who united bookselling with a stationery and
music business, was one of these, and he had offered
Ray a letter to them.

"If you ever want to get a book published," he said,
with a touch on the quick that made the conscious
author wince, "they're your men."

Ray knew their imprint and its relative value better
than the Midland bookseller, stationer, and music-
dealer; and now, as he sat in the junior partner's neat
little den, with the letter of introduction in his hand,
it seemed to him such a crazy thing to think of having
his book brought out by them that he decided not to
say anything about it, but to keep to that character of
literary newspaper man which his friend gave him in
his rather florid letter. He had leisure enough to
make this decision and unmake it several times while
he was waiting for Mr. Brandreth to come. It was so
early that, with all the delays Ray had forced, it was

still only a little after nine, and no one came in for a
quarter of an hour. The clerks stood about and chatted
together. The bookkeepers, in their high-railed en-
closure, were opening their ledgers under the shaded
gas-burners that helped out the twilight there. Ray
could see his unknown street friend scanning the books
on the upper shelf and moving his person from side to
side, and letting his cane rise and fall behind him as
if he were humming to himself and keeping time to the
tune.

VIII.

THE distant street door opened at last, and a gentleman came in. His entrance caused an indefinite sensation in the clerks, such as we all feel in the presence of the man who pays our wages. At the sound of his step, Ray's street friend turned about from his shelf, but without offering to leave it.

"Ah, good-morning, good-morning!" he called out; and the other called back, "Ah, good-morning, Mr. Kane!" and pushed on up towards a door near that of Ray's retreat. A clerk stopped him, and after a moment's parley he came in upon the young fellow. He was a man of fifty-five or sixty, with whiskers slightly frosted, and some puckers and wrinkles about his temples and at the corners of his mouth, and a sort of withered bloom in his cheeks, something like the hardy self-preservation of the late-hanging apple that people call a frozen-thaw. He was a thin man, who seemed once to have been stouter; he had a gentle presence and a somewhat careworn look.

"Mr. Brandreth?" Ray said, rising.

"No," said the other; "Mr. Chapley."

"Oh, I beg your pardon," said Ray. "They showed me into Mr. Brandreth's room, and I thought" —

"It's quite right, quite right," said Mr. Chapley.
"Mr. Brandreth will be in almost any moment if you
wish to see him personally." Mr. Chapley glanced at
the parcel in Ray's hand.

"Oh no; I have a letter for the firm," and Ray
gave it to Mr. Chapley, who read it through and then
offered his hand, and said he was glad to meet Mr.
Ray. He asked some questions of commonplace
friendliness about his correspondent, and he said, with
the kind of melancholy which seemed characteristic of
him: "So you have come to take a hand in the great
game here. Well, if there is anything I can do to
serve you, I shall be very glad."

Ray answered promptly, in pursuance of his plan:
"You are very kind, Mr. Chapley. I'm going to
write letters to the paper I've been connected with in
Midland, and I wish to give them largely a literary
character. I shall be obliged to you for any literary
news you have."

Mr. Chapley seemed relieved of a latent dread. A
little knot of anxiety between his eyes came untied;
he did not yet go to the length of laying off his light
overcoat, but he set his hat down on Mr. Brandreth's
desk, and he loosed the grip he had kept of his cane.

"Why, Mr. Brandreth rather looks after that side
of the business. He's more in touch with the younger
men — with what's going on, in fact, than I am. He
can tell you all there is about our own small affairs,
and put you in relations with other publishers, if you
wish."

"Thank you — " Ray began.

"Not at all; it will be to our advantage, I'm sure. We should be glad to do much more for any friend of our old friends " — Mr. Chapley had to refer to the letter-head of the introduction before he could make sure of his old friends' style — " Schmucker & Wills. I hope they are prospering in these uncertain times ? "

Ray said they were doing very well, he believed, and Mr. Chapley went on.

"So many of the local booksellers are feeling the competition of the large stores which have begun to deal in books as well as everything else under the sun, nowadays. I understand they have completely disorganized the book trade in some of our minor cities; completely! They take hold of a book like *Robert Elsmere,* for instance, as if it were a piece of silk that they control the pattern of, and run it at a price that is simply ruinous; besides doing a large miscellaneous business in books at rates that defy all competition on the part of the regular dealers. But perhaps you haven't suffered from these commercial monstrosities yet in Midland ? "

"Oh, yes," said Ray; "We have our local Stewart's or Macy's, whichever it is; and I imagine Schmucker & Wills feel it, especially at the holidays." He had never had to buy any books himself, because he got the copies sent to the *Echo* for review; and now, in deference to Mr. Chapley, he was glad that he had not shared in the demoralization of the book trade. "But I think," he added, cheerfully, "that they are holding their own very well."

"I am very glad to hear it, very glad, indeed," said Mr. Chapley. "If we can only get this international copyright measure through and dam up the disorganizing tide of cheap publications at its source, we may hope to restore the tone of the trade. As it is, we are ourselves constantly restricting our enterprise as publishers. We scarcely think now of looking at the manuscript of an unknown author."

Mr. Chapley looked at the manuscript of the unknown author before him, as if he divined it through its wrappings of stiff manilla paper. Ray had no reason to think that he meant to prevent a possible offer of manuscript, but he could not help thinking so, and it cut him short in the inquiries he was going to make as to the extent of the demoralization the book trade had suffered through the competition of the large variety stores. He had seen a whole letter for the *Echo* in the subject, but now he could not go on. He sat blankly staring at Mr. Chapley's friendly, pensive face, and trying to decide whether he had better get himself away without seeing Mr. Brandreth, or whether he had better stay and meet him, and after a cold, formal exchange of civilities, shake the dust of Chapley & Co.'s publishing house from his feet forever. The distant street door opened again, and a small light figure, much like his own, entered briskly. Mr. Kane turned about at the new-comer's step as he had turned at Mr. Chapley's, and sent his cheerful hail across the book counters as before. "Ah, good-morning, good-morning!"

"Good-morning, Mr. Kane; magnificent day," said the gentleman, who advanced rapidly towards Ray and Mr. Chapley, with a lustrous silk hat on his head, and a brilliant smile on his face. His overcoat hung on his arm, and he looked fresh and warm as if from a long walk. "Ah, good-morning," he said to Mr. Chapley; "how are you this morning, sir?" He bent his head inquiringly towards Ray, who stood a moment while Mr. Chapley got himself together and said:

"This is Mr. — ah — Ray, who brings a letter from our old friends" — he had to glance at the letter-head — "Schmucker & Wills, of — Midland."

"Ah! Midland! yes," said Mr. Brandreth, for Ray felt it was he, although his name had not been mentioned yet. "Very glad to see you, Mr. Ray. When did you leave Midland? Won't you sit down? And you, Mr. Chapley?"

"No, no," said Mr. Chapley, nervously. "I was going to my own room. How is poor Bella this morning?"

"Wonderfully well, wonderfully! I waited for the doctor's visit before I left home, so as to report reliably, and he says he never saw a better convalescence. He promises to let her go out in a fortnight or so, if the weather's good."

"You must be careful! Don't go too fast!" said Mr. Chapley. And the — child?"

"Perfectly splendid! He slept like a top last night, and we could hardly get him awake for breakfast."

4

"Poor thing!" said Mr. Chapley. He offered Ray his hand, and said that he hoped they should see him often; he must drop in whenever he was passing. "Mr. Ray," he explained, "has come on to take up his residence in New York. He remains connected with one of the papers in — Midland; and I have been referring him to you for literary gossip, and that kind of thing."

"All right, sir, all right!" said Mr. Brandreth. He laughed out after Mr. Chapley had left them, and then said: "Excuse me, Mr. Ray. You mustn't mind my smiling rather irrelevantly. We've had a great event at my house this week — in fact, we've had a boy."

"Indeed!" said Ray. He had the sort of contempt a young man feels for such domestic events; but he easily concealed it from the happy father, who looked scarcely older than himself.

"An eight-pounder," said Mr. Brandreth. "I have been pretty anxious for the last few weeks, and — I don't know whether you married or not, Mr. Ray?"

"No."

"Well, then you wouldn't understand." Mr. Brandreth arrested himself reluctantly, Ray thought, in his confidences. "But you will, some day; you will, some day," he added, gayly; "and then you'll know what it is to have an experience like that go off well. It throws a new light on everything." A clerk came in with a pile of opened letters and put them on Mr. Brandreth's desk, with some which were still sealed;

Ray rose again. "No, don't go. But you won't mind my glancing these over while we talk. I don't know how much talk you've been having with Mr. Chapley — he's my father-in-law, you know?"

Ray owned that he did not.

"Yes; I came into the firm and into the family a a little over a year ago. But if there are any points I can give you, I'm quite at your service."

"Thank you," said Ray. "Mr. Chapley was speaking of the effect of the competition of the big variety stores on the regular booksellers."

Mr. Brandreth slitted the envelope of one of the letters with a slim paper-knife, and glanced the letter over. "Well, that's a little matter I differ with Mr. Chapley about. Of course, I know just how he feels, brought up the way he was, in the old traditions of the trade. It seems to him we must be going to the bad because our books are sold over a counter next to a tin-ware counter, or a perfume and essence counter, or a bric-à-brac counter. I don't think so. I think the great thing is to sell the books, and I wish we could get a book into the hands of one of those big dealers; I should be glad of the chance. We should have to make him a heavy discount; but look at the discounts we have to make to the trade, now! Forty per cent., and ten cents off for cash; so that a dollar and a half book, that it costs twenty-five cents or thirty cents to make, brings you in about seventy cents. Then, when you pay the author his ten per cent. copyright, how far will the balance go towards

(advertising, rent, clerk hire and sundries? If you
want to get a book into the news companies, you have
got to make them a discount of sixty per cent. out of
{ hand."

"Is it possible?" asked Ray. "I'd no idea it was
anything like that!"

"No; people haven't. They think publishers are
rolling in riches at the expense of the author and the
reader. And some publishers themselves believe that
if we could only keep up the old system of letting the
regular trade have the lion's share on long credit, their
prosperity would be assured. I don't, myself. If we
could get hold of a good, breezy, taking story, I'd like
to try my chance with it in the hands of some large
dry-goods man."

Ray's heart thrilled. His own story had often
seemed to him good and taking; whether it was
breezy or not, he had never thought. He wished he
knew just what Mr. Brandreth meant by breezy; but
he did not like to ask him. His hand twitched nerve-
lessly on the manuscript in his lap, and he said,
timidly: "Would it be out of the way for me to refer
to some of these facts — they're not generally known
— in my letters? Of course not using your name."

"Not at all! I should be very glad to have them
understood," said Mr. Brandreth.

"And what do you think is the outlook for the
winter trade, Mr. Brandreth?"

"Never better. I think we're going to have a *good*
trade. We've got a larger list than we've had for a

great many years. The fact is," said Mr. Brandreth,
and he gave a glance at Ray, as if he felt the trust the
youthful gravity of his face inspired in most people —
"the fact is, Chapley & Co. have been dropping too
much out of sight, as publishers; and I've felt, ever
since I've been in the firm, that we ought to give the
public a sharp reminder that we're not merely booksellers and jobbers. I want the house to take its old
place again. I don't mean it's ever really lost caste,
or that its imprint doesn't stand for as much as it did
twenty years ago. I'll just show you our list if you
can wait a moment." Mr. Brandreth closed a pair of
wooden mandibles lying on his desk; an electric bell
sounded in the distance, and a boy appeared. "You
go and ask Miss Hughes if she's got that list of announcements ready yet." The boy went, and Mr.
Brandreth took up one of the cards of the firm. "If
you would like to visit some of the other houses, Mr.
Ray, I'll give you our card," and he wrote on the card,
"Introducing Mr. Ray, of the Midland *Echo*. P.
Brandreth," and handed it to him. "Not Peter, but
Percy," he said, with a friendly smile for his own
pleasantry. "But for business purposes it's better to
let them suppose it's Peter."

Ray laughed, and said he imagined so. He said he
had always felt it a disadvantage to have been named
Shelley; but he could not write himself P. B. S. Ray,
and he usually signed simply S. Ray.

"Why, then, we really have the same first name,"
said Mr. Brandreth. "It's rather an uncommon

name, too. I'm very glad to share it with you, Mr. Ray." It seemed to add another tie to those that already bound them in the sympathy of youth, and the publisher said, " I wish I could ask you up to my house ; but just now, you know, it's really a nursery."

"You are very kind," said Ray. " I couldn't think of intruding on you, of course."

Their exchange of civilities was checked by the return of the boy, who said Miss Hughes would have the list ready in a few minutes.

" Well, just ask her to bring it here, will you?" said Mr. Brandreth. " I want to speak to her about some of these letters."

" I'm taking a great deal of your time, Mr. Brandreth," Ray said.

" Not at all, not at all. I'm making a kind of holiday week of it, anyway. I'm a good deal excited," and Mr. Brandreth smiled so benevolently that Ray could not help taking advantage of him.

The purpose possessed him almost before he was aware of its activity; he thought he had quelled it, but now he heard himself saying in a stiff unnatural voice, "I have a novel of my own, Mr Brandreth, that I should like to submit to you."

IX.

"Oh, indeed!" said Mr. Brandreth, with a change in his voice, too, which Ray might well have interpreted as a tone of disappointment and injury. "Just at present, Mr. Ray, trade is rather quiet, you know."

"Yes, I know," said Ray, though he thought he had been told the contrary. He felt very mean and guilty; the blood went to his head, and his face burned.

"Our list for the fall trade is full, as I was saying, and we couldn't really touch anything till next spring."

"Oh, I didn't suppose it would be in time for the fall trade," said Ray, and in the sudden loss of the easy terms which he had been on with the publisher, he could not urge anything further.

Mr. Brandreth must have felt their estrangement too, for he said, apologetically: "Of course it's our business to examine manuscripts for publication, and I hope it's going to be our business to publish more and more of them, but an American novel by an unknown author, as long as we have the competition of these pirated English novels — If we can only get the copyright bill through, we shall be all right."

Ray said nothing aloud, for he was busy reproaching himself under his breath for abusing Mr. Brandreth's hospitality.

"What is the — character of your novel?" asked
Mr. Brandreth, to break the painful silence, apparently,
rather than to inform himself.

"The usual character," Ray answered, with a listlessness which perhaps passed for careless confidence
with the young publisher, and piqued his interest.
"It's a love-story."

"Of course. Does it end well? A great deal depends upon the ending with the public, you know."

"I suppose it ends badly. It ends as badly as it
can," said the author, feeling that he had taken the bit
in his teeth. "It's unrelieved tragedy."

"That isn't so bad, sometimes," said Mr. Brandreth.
"That is, if the tragedy is intense enough. Sometimes
a thing of that kind takes with the public, if the love
part is good and strong. Have you the manuscript
here in New York with you?"

"I have it here in my lap with me," said Ray, with
a desperate laugh.

Mr. Brandreth cast his eye over the package.
"What do you call it? So much depends upon a title
with the public."

"I had thought of several titles : the hero's name
for one; the heroine's for another. Then I didn't
know but *A Modern Romeo* would do. It's very
much on the lines of the play."

"Indeed!" said Mr. Brandreth, with a sudden interest that flattered Ray with fresh hopes. "That's
very curious. I once took part in an amateur performance of *Romeo* myself. We gave it in the open
air. The effect was very novel."

"I should think it might be," said Ray. He hastened to add, "My story deals, of course, with
American life, and the scene is laid in the little village
where I grew up."

"Our play," said Mr. Brandreth, "was in a little
summer place in Massachusetts. One of the ladies
gave us her tennis-ground, and we made our exits and
our entrances through the surrounding shrubbery.
You've no idea how beautiful the mediæval dresses
looked in the electric light. It was at night."

"It must have been beautiful," Ray hastily admitted.
"My Juliet is the daughter of the village doctor, and
my Romeo is a young lawyer, who half kills a cousin
of hers for trying to interfere with them."

"That's good," said Mr. Brandreth. "I took the
part of Romeo myself, and Mrs. Brandreth — she was
Miss Chapley, then — was cast for Juliet; but another
girl who had refused the part suddenly changed her
mind and claimed it, and we had the greatest time
to keep the whole affair from going to pieces. I beg
your pardon; I interrupted you."

"Not at all," said Ray. "It must have been
rather difficult. In my story there has been a feud
between the families of the lovers about a land boun-
dary; and both families try to break off the engagement."

"That's very odd," said Mr. Brandreth. "The
play nearly broke off my acquaintance with Mrs.
Brandreth. Of course she was vexed — as anybody
would be — at having to give up the part at the

eleventh hour, when she'd taken so much trouble with
it; but when she saw my suffering with the other girl,
who didn't know half her lines, and walked through
it all like a mechanical doll, she forgave me. *Romeo*
is my favorite play. Did you ever see Julia Marlowe
in it?"

"No."

"Then you never *saw* Juliet! I used to think
Margaret Mather was about the loveliest Juliet, and
in fact she has a great deal of passion " —

"My Juliet," Ray broke in, "is one of those impassioned natures. When she finds that the old people are inexorable, she jumps at the suggestion of a
secret marriage, and the lovers run off and are married, and come back and live separately. They meet
at a picnic soon after, where Juliet goes with her
cousin, who makes himself offensive to the husband,
and finally insults him. They happen to be alone together near the high bank of a river, and the husband,
who is a quiet fellow of the deadly sort, suddenly
throws the cousin over the cliff. The rest are dancing " —

"We introduced a minuet in our theatricals," Mr.
Brandreth interposed, "and people said it was the best
thing in it. I *beg* your pardon!"

"Not at all. It must have been very picturesque.
The cousin is taken up for dead, and the husband goes
into hiding until the result of the cousin's injuries can
be ascertained. They are searching for the husband
everywhere, and the girl's father, who has dabbled in

hypnotism, and has hypnotized his daughter now and then, takes the notion of trying to discover the husband's whereabouts by throwing her into a hypnotic trance and questioning her: he believes that she knows. The trance is incomplete, and with what is left of her consciousness the girl suffers tremendously from the conflict that takes place in her. In the midst of it all, word comes from the room where the cousin is lying insensible that he is dying. The father leaves his daughter to go to him, and she lapses into the cataleptic state. The husband has been lurking about, intending to give himself up if it comes to the worst. He steals up to the open window — I forgot to say that the hypnotization scene takes place in her father's office, a little building that stands apart from the house, and of course it's a ground floor — and he sees her stretched out on the lounge, all pale and stiff, and he thinks she is dead."

Mr. Brandreth burst into a laugh. "I *must* tell you what our Mercutio said — he was an awfully clever fellow, a lawyer up there, one of the natives, and he made simply a *perfect* Mercutio. He said that our Juliet was magnificent in the sepulchre scene; and if she could have played the part as a dead Juliet throughout, she would have beat us all!"

"Capital!" said Ray. "Ha, ha, ha!"

"Well, go on," said Mr. Brandreth.

"Oh! Well, the husband gets in at the window and throws himself on her breast, and tries to revive her. She shows no signs of life, though all the time

she is perfectly aware of what is going on, and is struggling to speak and reassure him. She recovers herself
just at the moment he draws a pistol and shoots himself through the heart. The shot brings the father
from the house, and as he enters the little office, his
daughter lifts herself, gives him one ghastly stare, and
falls dead on her husband's body."

"That is strong," said Mr. Brandreth. "That is a
very powerful scene."

"Do you think so?" Ray asked. He looked flushed
and flattered, but he said: "Sometimes I've been
afraid it was overwrought, and improbable — weak.
It's not, properly speaking, a novel, you see. It's
more in the region of romance."

"Well, so much the better. I think people are getting tired of those commonplace, photographic things.
They want something with a little more imagination,"
said Mr. Brandreth.

"The motive of my story might be called psychological," said the author. "Of course I've only given
you the crudest outline of it, that doesn't do it justice" —

"Well, they say that *roman psychologique* is superseding the realistic novel in France. Will you allow
me?"

He offered to take the manuscript, and Ray eagerly
undid it, and placed it in his hands. He turned over
some pages of it, and dipped into it here and there.

"Yes," he said. "Now I'll tell you what we'll do,
Mr. Ray. You leave this with us, and we'll have our

readers go over it, and report to us, and then we'll
communicate with you about it. What did you say
your New York address was?"

"I haven't any yet," said Ray; but I'll call and
leave it as soon as I've got one." He rose, and the
young publisher said:

"Well, drop in any time. We shall always be glad
to see you. Of course I can't promise you an immediate decision."

"Oh, no; I don't expect that. I can wait. And
I can't tell you how much — how much I appreciate
your kindness."

"Oh, not at all. Ah!" The boy came back with
a type-written sheet in his hand; Mr. Brandreth took
it and gave it to Ray. "There! You can get some
idea from that of what we're going to do. Take it
with you. It's manifolded, and you can keep this
copy. Drop in again when you're passing."

They shook hands, but they did not part there. Mr.
Brandreth followed Ray out into the store, and asked
him if he would not like some advance copies of their
new books; he guessed some of them were ready. He
directed a clerk to put them up, and then he said, "I'd
like to introduce you to one of our authors. Mr.
Kane!" he called out to what Ray felt to be the gentleman's expectant back, and Mr. Kane promptly
turned about from his bookshelf and met their advance half-way. "I want to make you acquainted
with Mr. Ray."

"Fortune," said Mr. Kane, with evident relish of

his own voice and diction, "had already made us friends, in the common interest we took in a mistaken fellow-man whom we saw stealing a bag to travel with instead of a road to travel on. Before you came in, we were street intimates of five minutes' standing, and we entered your temple of the Muses together. But I am very glad to know my dear friend by name." He gave Ray the pressure of a soft, cool hand. "My name is doubtless familiar to you, Mr. Ray. We spell it a little differently since that unfortunate affair with Abel; but it is unquestionably the same name, and we are of that ancient family. Am I right," he said, continuing to press the young man's hand, but glancing at Mr. Brandreth for correction, with ironical deference, "in supposing that Mr. Ray is *one* of us? I was sure," he said, letting Ray's hand go, with a final pressure, "that it must be so from the first moment! The signs of the high freemasonry of letters are unmistakable!"

"Mr. Ray," said Mr. Brandreth, "is going to cast his lot with us here in New York. He is from Midland, and he is still connected with one of the papers there."

"Then he is a man to be cherished and avoided," said Mr. Kane. "But don't tell me that he has no tenderer, no more sacred tie to literature than a meretricious newspaper connection!"

Ray laughed, and said from his pleased vanity, "Mr. Brandreth has kindly consented to look at a manuscript of mine."

"Poems?" Mr. Kane suggested.

"No, a novel," the author answered, bashfully.

"The great American one, of course?"

"We are going to see," said the young publisher, gaily.

"Well, that is good. It is pleasant to have the old literary tradition renewed in all the freshness of its prime, and to have young Genius coming up to New York from the provinces with a manuscript under its arm, just as it used to come up to London, and I've no doubt to Memphis and to Nineveh, for that matter; the indented tiles must have been a little more cumbrous than the papyrus, and were probably conveyed in an ox-cart. And when you offered him your novel, Mr. Ray, did Mr. Brandreth say that the book trade was rather dull, just now?"

"Something of that kind," Ray admitted, with a laugh; and Mr. Brandreth laughed too.

"I'm glad of that," said Mr. Kane. "It would not have been perfect without that. They always say that. I've no doubt the publishers of Memphis and Nineveh said it in their day. It is the publishers' way with authors. It makes the author realize the immense advantage of getting a publisher on any terms at such a disastrous moment, and he leaves the publisher to fix the terms. It is quite right. You are launched, my dear friend, and all you have to do is to let yourself go. You will probably turn out an ocean greyhound; we expect no less when we are launched. In that case, allow an old water-logged derelict to hail you, and

wish you a prosperous voyage to the Happy Isles."
Mr. Kane smiled blandly, and gave Ray a bow that
had the quality of a blessing.

"Oh, that book of yours is going to do well yet, Mr.
Kane," said Mr. Brandreth, consolingly. "I believe
there's going to be a change in the public taste, and
good literature is going to have its turn again."

"Let us hope so," said Mr. Kane, devoutly. "We
will pray that the general reader may be turned from
the error of his ways, and eschew fiction and cleave to
moral reflections, But not till our dear friend's novel
has made its success!" He inclined himself again
towards Ray. "Though, perhaps," he suggested, "it
is a novel with a purpose?"

"I'm afraid hardly" — Ray began; but Mr. Brandreth interposed.

"It is a psychological romance — the next thing on
the cards, *I* believe!"

"Indeed!" said Mr. Kane. "Do you speak by the
card, now, as a confidant of fate; or is this the exuberant optimism of a fond young father? Mr. Ray, I
am afraid you have taken our friend when he is all
molten and fluid with happiness, and have abused his
kindness for the whole race to your single advantage!"

"No, no! Nothing of the kind, I assure you!"
said Mr. Brandreth, joyously. "Everything is on a
strict business basis with me, always. But I wish you
could see that little fellow, Mr. Kane. Of course it
sounds preposterous to say it of a child only eight days
old, but I believe he begins to notice already."

"You must get him to notice your books. Do get
him to notice mine! He is beginning young, but perhaps not *too* young for a critic," said Mr. Kane, and he
abruptly took his leave, as one does when he thinks he
has made a good point, and Mr. Brandreth laughed the
laugh of a man who magnanimously joins in the mirth
made at his expense.

Ray stayed a moment after Mr. Kane went out, and
Brandreth said, "There is one of the most puzzling
characters in New York. If he could put himself into
a book, it would make his fortune. He's a queer
genius. Nobody knows how he lives; but I fancy he
has a little money of his own; his book doesn't sell
fifty copies in a year. What did he mean by that
about the travelling-bag?"

Ray explained, and Mr. Brandreth said: "Just like
him! He must have spotted you in an instant. He
has nothing to do, and he spends most of his time wandering about. He says New York is his book, and he
reads it over and over. If he could only work up that
idea, he could make a book that everybody would want.
But he never will. He's one of those men whose talk
makes you think he could write anything; but his
book is awfully dry — perfectly crumby. Ever see it?
Hard Sayings? Well, good-by! I *wish* I could ask
you up to my house; but you see how it is!"

"Oh, yes! I see," said Ray. "You're only too
good as it is, Mr. Brandreth."

5

X.

RAY's voice broke a little as he said this; but he hoped Mr. Brandreth did not notice, and he made haste to get out into the crowded street, and be alone with his emotions. He was quite giddy with the turn that Fortune's wheel had taken, and he walked a long way up town before he recovered his balance. He had never dreamt of such prompt consideration as Mr. Brandreth had promised to give his novel. He had expected to carry it round from publisher to publisher, and to wait weeks, and perhaps whole months, for their decision. Most of them he imagined refusing to look at it at all; and he had prepared himself for rebuffs. He could not help thinking that Mr. Brandreth's different behavior was an effect of his goodness of heart, and of his present happiness. Of course he was a little ridiculous about that baby of his; Ray supposed that was natural, but he decided that if he should ever be a father he would not gush about it to the first person he met. He did not like Mr. Brandreth's interrupting him with the account of those amateur theatricals when he was outlining the plot of his story; but that was excusable, and it showed that he was really interested. If it had not been for the accidental fact that Mr. Brandreth had taken the part of

Romeo in those theatricals, he might not have caught on to the notion of *A Modern Romeo* at all. The question whether he was not rather silly himself to enter so fully into his plot, helped him to condone Mr. Brandreth's weakness, which was not incompatible with shrewd business sense. All that Mr. Brandreth had said of the state of the trade and its new conditions was sound; he was probably no fool where his interest was concerned. Ray resented for him the cruelty of Mr. Kane in turning the baby's precocity into the sort of joke he had made of it; but he admired his manner of saying things, too. He would work up very well in a story; but he ought to be made pathetic as well as ironical; he must be made to have had an early unhappy love-affair; the girl either to have died, or to have heartlessly jilted him. He could be the hero's friend at some important moment; Ray did not determine just at what moment; but the hero should be about to wreck his happiness, somehow, and Mr. Kane should save him from the rash act, and then should tell him the story of his own life. Ray recurred to the manuscript he had left with Mr. Brandreth, and wondered if Mr. Brandreth would read it himself, and if he did, whether he would see any resemblance between the hero and the author. He had sometimes been a little ashamed of that mesmerization business in the story, but if it struck a mood of the reading public, it would be a great piece of luck; and he prepared himself to respect it. If Chapley & Co. accepted the book, he was going to write all that passage over, and strengthen it.

He was very happy; and he said to himself that he
must try to be very good and to merit the fortune that
had befallen him.   He must not let it turn his head, or
seem more than it really was; after all it was merely a
chance to be heard that he was given.   He instinctively strove to arrest the wheel which was bringing
him up, and must carry him down if it kept on moving.
With an impulse of the old heathen superstition lingering in us all, he promised his god, whom he imagined
to be God, that he would be very grateful and humble
if He would work a little miracle for him, and let the
wheel carry him up without carrying him over and
down.   In the unconscious selfishness which he had
always supposed morality, he believed that the thing
most pleasing to his god would be some immediate
effort in his own behalf, of prudent industry or frugality; and he made haste to escape from the bliss of his
high hopes as if it were something that was wrong in
itself, and that he would perhaps be punished for.

He went to the restaurant where he had breakfasted,
and bargained for board and lodging by the week.   It
was not so cheap as he had expected to get it; with an
apparent flexibility, the landlord was rigorous on the
point of a dollar a day for the room; and Ray found
that he must pay twelve dollars a week for his board
and lodging instead of the ten he had set as a limit.
But he said to himself that he must take the risk, and
must make up the two dollars, somehow.   His room
was at the top of the house, and it had a view of the
fourth story of a ten-story apartment-house opposite;

but it had a southerly exposure, and there was one
golden hour of the day when the sun shone into it,
over the shoulder of a lower edifice next to the apartment-house, and round the side of a clock tower beyond
the avenue. He could see a bit of the châlet-roof of
an elevated railroad station; he could see the tops of
people's heads in the street below if he leaned out of
his window far enough, and he had the same bird's-eye
view of the passing carts and carriages. He shared it
with the sparrows that bickered in the window-casing,
and with the cats that crouched behind the chimneys
and watched the progress of the sparrows' dissensions
with furtive and ironical eyes.

Within, the slope of the roof gave a picturesque
slant to the ceiling. The room was furnished with an
American painted set; there was a clock on the little
shelf against the wall that looked as if it were French;
but it was not going, and there was no telling what
accent it might tick with if it were wound up. There
was a little mahogany table in one corner-near the
window to write on, and he put his books up on the
shelf on each side of the clock.

It was all very different from the dignified housing
of his life at Midland, where less than the money he
paid here got him a stately parlor, with a little chamber
out of it, at the first boarding-house in the place. But
still he would not have been ashamed to have any one
from Midland see him in his present quarters. They
were proper to New York in that cosmopolitan phase
which he had most desired to see. He tried writing at

the little table, and found it very convenient. He forced himself, just for moral effect, and to show himself that he was master of all his moods, to finish his letter to the *Echo*, and he pleased himself very well with it. He made it light and lively, and yet contrived to give it certain touches of poetry and to throw in bits of description which he fancied had caught something of the thrill and sparkle of the air, and imparted some sense of such a day as he felt it to be. He fancied different friends turning to the letter the first thing in the paper; and in the fond remembrance of the kindness he had left behind there, he became a little homesick.

XI

RAY would have liked to go again that day, and give Mr. Brandreth his new address in person ; but he was afraid it would seem too eager, and would have a bad effect on the fortunes of his book. He mastered himself so far that even the next day he did not go, but sent it in a note. Then he was sorry he had done this, for it might look a little too indifferent ; that is, he feigned that it might have this effect ; but what he really regretted was that it cut him off from going to see Mr. Brandreth as soon as he would have liked. It would be absurd to run to him directly after writing. He languished several days in the heroic resolution not to go near Chapley & Co. until a proper time had passed ; then he took to walking up and down Broadway, remote from their place at first, and afterwards nearer, till it came to his pacing slowly past their door, and stopping at their window, in the hope that one or other of the partners would happen upon him in some of their comings or goings. But they never did, and he had a faint, heart-sick feeling of disappointment, such as he used to have when he hung about the premises of his first love in much the same fashion and to much the same effect.

He cajoled himself by feigning interviews, now with

Mr. Chapley and now with Mr. Brandreth; the publishers accepted his manuscript with transport, and
offered him incredible terms. The good old man's
voice shook with emotion in hailing Ray as the heir of
Hawthorne; Mr. Brandreth had him up to dinner, and
presented him to his wife and baby; he named the
baby for them jointly. As nothing of this kind really
happened, Ray's time passed rather forlornly. Without being the richer for it, he won the bets he made
himself, every morning, that he should not get a letter
that day from Chapley & Co., asking to see him at
once, or from Mr. Brandreth hoping for the pleasure of
his company upon this social occasion or that. He
found that he had built some hopes upon Mr. Brandreth's hospitable regrets; and as he did not know how
long it must be after a happiness of the kind Mrs.
Brandreth had conferred upon her husband before her
house could be set in order for company, he was perhaps too impatient. But he did not suffer himself to
be censorious; he was duly grateful to Mr. Brandreth
for his regrets; he had not expected them; but for
them he would not have expected anything.

He did what he could to pass the time by visiting
other publishers with Mr. Brandreth's card. He perceived sometimes, or fancied that he perceived, a
shadow of anxiety in the gentlemen who received him
so kindly, but it vanished, if it ever existed, when he
put himself frankly on the journalistic ground, and satisfied them that he had no manuscript lurking about
him. Then he found some of them willing to drop

into chat about the trade, and try to forecast its nearer
future, if not to philosophize its conditions. They
appeared to think these were all right; and it did not
strike Ray as amiss that a work of literary art should
be regarded simply as a merchantable or unmerchant-
able commodity, or as a pawn in a game, a counter
that stood for a certain money value, a risk which the
player took, a wager that he made.

" You know it's really that," one publisher explained
to Ray. "*No* one can tell whether a book will succeed or not; no one knows what makes a book succeed.
We have published things that I've liked and respected
thoroughly, and that I've taken a personal pride and
pleasure in pushing. They've been well received and
intelligently praised by the best critics from the Atlantic to the Pacific, and cultivated people have talked
about them everywhere; and they haven't sold fifteen
hundred copies   Then we've tried trash — decent
trash, of course; we always remember the cheek of the
Young Person — and we've all believed that we had
something that would hit the popular mood, and would
leap into the tens of thousands; and it's dropped dead
from the press. Other works of art and other pieces
of trash succeed for no better reason than some fail.
You can't tell anything about it. If I were to trust
my own observation, I should say it was *luck*, pure and
simple, and mostly bad luck. Ten books fail, and
twenty books barely pay, where one succeeds. Nobody can say why. Can't I send you some of our new
books?" He had a number of them on a table near

him, and he talked them over with Ray, while a clerk
did them up; and he would not let Ray trouble himself
to carry them away with him. They were everywhere
lavish of their publications with him, and he had so
many new books and advance sheets given him that if
he had been going to write his letters for the *Echo*
about literature alone, he would have had material for
many weeks ahead.

The letters he got at this time were some from
home: a very sweet one from his mother, fondly con-
jecturing and questioning about his comfort in New
York, and cautioning him not to take cold; a serious
one from his father, advising him to try each week to
put by something for a rainy day. There was also a
letter from Sanderson, gay with news of all the goings
on in Midland, and hilariously regretful of his absence.
Sanderson did not say anything about coming to New
York to seek his fortune, and the effect of his news
was to leave Ray pining for the society of women,
which had always been the sweetest thing in life to
him, and next to literature the dearest. If he could
have had immediate literary success, the excitement of
it might have made him forget the privilege he had enjoyed at Midland of going every evening to call on
some lovely young girl, and of staying as long as he
liked. What made him feel still more lonesome and
dropped out was Sanderson's telling of several engagements among the girls they knew in Midland; it
appeared to him that he only was destined to go love-
less and mateless through life.

There were women enough in his hotel, but after the first interest of their strangeness, and the romantic effect of hearing them speak in their foreign tongues as if they were at home in them, he could not imagine a farther interest in those opaque Southern blondes, who spoke French, or the brunettes with purple-ringed vast eyes, who coughed out their Spanish gutturals like squirrels. He was appointed a table for his meals in a dining-room that seemed to be reserved for its inmates, as distinguished from the frequenters of the restaurant, who looked as if they were all Americans; and he was served by a shining black waiter weirdly ignorant of English. He gazed wistfully across into the restaurant at times, and had half a mind to ask if he might not eat there; but he liked the glances of curiosity and perhaps envy which its frequenters now and then cast at him in the hotel dining-room. There were no young ladies among them, that he ever saw, but sometimes there were young men whom he thought he would have liked to talk with. Some of them came in company, and at dinner they sat long, discussing matters which he could overhear by snatches were literary and artistic matters. They always came late, and rarely sat down before seven, when Ray was finishing his coffee. One night these comrades came later than usual and in unusual force, and took a large table set somewhat apart from the rest in the bay of a deep window which had once looked out into the little garden of the dwelling that the hotel had once been. They sat down, with a babble of questions and an-

swers, as of people who had not all met for some time,
and devoured the little radishes and olives and ancho-
vies, with which the table had been prefatorily furnished, in apparent patience till all the places but the
head of the table had been taken; then they began to
complain and to threaten at the delay of the dinner.
Ray was not aware just how a furious controversy suddenly began to rage between two of them. As nearly
as he could make out, amidst the rapid thrust and parry
of the principals, and the irregular lunges of this one
or that of the company which gave it the character of
a free fight, it turned upon a point of æsthetics, where
the question was whether the moral aspect ought or
ought not to be sought in it. In the heat of the
debate the chiefs of the discussion talked both at once,
interrupted each other, tried which should clamor
loudest and fastest, and then suddenly the whole uproar fell to silence. The two parties casually discovered that they were of exactly the same mind, but
each had supposed the other thought differently. Some
one came in during the lull that followed, and took the
seat at the head of the table.

It was Mr. Kane, and Ray's heart leaped with the
hope that he would see him and recognize him, but out
of self-respect he tried to look as if it were not he, but
perhaps some one who closely resembled him. He
perceived that it was a club dinner of some literary
sort; but because he could not help wishing that he
were one of the company, he snubbed his desires with
unsparing cruelty. He looked down at his plate, and

shunned the roving glance which he felt sure Mr.
Kane was sending into the room where he now sat
almost alone; and he did his best to be ashamed of
overhearing the talk now and then. He grew very
bitter in his solitude, and he imagined himself using
Mr. Kane with great hauteur, after *A Modern Romeo*
had succeeded. He was not obliged to go out that
way, when he left the dining-room, but he feigned
that he must, and in spite of the lofty stand he had
taken with Mr. Kane in fancy, he meanly passed
quite near him. Kane looked up, and called out,
"Ah, good-evening, good-evening!" and rose and shook
hands with him, and asked him how in the world he
happened to have found out that restaurant, and he
was astonished to hear that Ray was staying in the
hotel; he said that was very *chic*. He introduced him
to the company generally, as his young friend Mr. Ray,
of Midland, who had come on to cast in his literary
lot with them in New York; and then he presented
him personally to the nearest on either hand. They
were young fellows, but their names were known to
Ray with the planetary distinctness that the names of
young authors have for literary aspirants, though they
are all so nebulous to older eyes. .

Mr. Kane asked Ray to sit down and take his coffee
with them; Ray said he had taken his coffee; they all
urged that this was no reason why he should not take
some more; he stood out against them, like a fool —
as he later called himself with gnashing teeth. He
pretended he had an engagement, and he left the pleas-

ant company he was hungering so to join, and went
out and walked the streets, trying to stay himself with
the hope that he had made a better impression than if
he had remained and enjoyed himself. He was so
lonesome when he came back, and caught the sound of
their jolly voices on his way up stairs, that he could
hardly keep from going in upon them, and asking if
they would let him sit with them.   In his room he
could not work; he wanted to shed tears in his social
isolation.   He determined to go back to Midland, at
any cost to his feelings or fortunes, or even to the
little village where his family lived, and where he had
been so restless and unhappy till he could get away
from it.   Now, any place seemed better than this
waste of unknown hundreds of thousands of human
beings, where he had not a friend, or even an enemy.

XII.

In the morning Ray woke resolved to brace up against the nerveless suspense he had been in ever since he had left his manuscript with Mr. Brandreth, and go and present the letters that some people in Midland had given him to their friends in New York. At least he need not suffer from solitude unless he chose; he wondered if it would do to present his letters on Sunday.

He breakfasted in this question. Shortly after he went back to his room, there was a knock at his door, and when he shouted "Come in!" it was set softly ajar, and Mr. Kane showed his face at the edge of it.

"I suppose you know," he said, ignoring Ray's welcome, "or if you haven't been out, you don't know, that this is one of those Sunday mornings which make you feel that it has been blessed and hallowed above all the other days of the week. But I dare say," he added, coming inside, "that the Mohammedans feel exactly so about a particularly fine Friday."

He glanced round the little room with an air of delicate impartiality, and asked leave to look from Ray's window. As he put his head out, he said to the birds in the eaves, "Ah, sparrows!" as if he knew them personally, before he began to make com-

pliments to the picturesque facts of the prospect.
Then he stood with his back to Ray, looking down
into the street, and praising the fashion of the shadow
and sunshine in meeting so solidly there, at all sorts
of irregular points and angles. Once he looked round
and asked, with the sun making his hair all a shining
silver:

"Has any one else been shown this view? No?
Then let me be the first to utter the stock imbecility
that it ought to inspire you if anything could." He
put out his head again, and gave a glance upward at
the speckless heaven, and then drew it in. "Yes,"
he said, thoughtfully, "a partially clouded sky is better
for us, no doubt. Why didn't you sit down with us
last night? I saw that you wished to do so." He
faced Ray benignly, with a remote glimmer of mock-
ing in his eye.

Ray felt it safest to answer frankly. "Yes, I did
want to join you awfully. I overheard a good deal
you were saying where I was sitting, but I couldn't
accept your invitation. I knew it was a great chance,
but I couldn't."

"Don't you know," Mr. Kane asked, "that the
chances have a polite horror of iteration? Those men
and those moods may never be got together again.
You oughtn't to have thrown such a chance away!"

"I know," said Ray. "But I had to."

Mr. Kane leaned back in the chair he had taken,
and murmured as if to himself: "Ah, youth, youth!
Yes, it has to throw chances away. Waste is a condi-

tion of survival. Otherwise we should perish of mere fruition. But could you," he asked, addressing Ray more directly, "without too much loss to the intimacies that every man ought to keep sacred, could you tell me just *why* you had to refuse us your company?"

"Oh, yes," said Ray, with the self-scorn which Mr. Kane's attitude enabled him to show. "I was so low-spirited that I couldn't rise to the hands that offered to pull me out of my Slough of Despond. I felt that the slightest exertion would sink me over head and ears. I had better stay as I was."

"I understand," said Mr. Kane. "But why should a man of your age be in low spirits?"

"Why? Nobody can tell why he's in low spirits exactly. I suppose I got to thinking the prospect for my book wasn't very gay. It's hard to wait."

"Was that all?"

"I was a little homesick, too. But wasn't the other enough?"

"I can't say. It's a long time since I was your age. But shall I tell you what I first thought your unhappiness was, when you confessed it just now?"

"Yes, by all means."

"I wonder if I'd better! I supposed it was not such as any *man* could inflict. Excuse me!" He kept his eyes smilingly on the young fellow's face, as if to prevent his taking the audacity in bad part. "I don't know why I should say this to you, except that it really went through my mind, and I did you the wrong to wonder why you should mention it."

6

"I can forgive the wrong; it's so very far from the fact"—Ray began.

"Ah, you've already noticed *that!*" Mr Kane interrupted.

"Noticed what?"

"That we can forgive people. their injurious conjectures when they're wrong rather than when they're right?"

"No, I hadn't noticed," Ray confessed; and he added, "I was only thinking how impossible that was for me in a place where I haven't spoken to a woman yet."

If Mr. Kane tasted the bitterness in a speech which Ray tried to carry off with a laugh, his words did not confess it. "It wasn't a reasoned conjecture, and I don't defend it; I'm only too glad to escape from it without offence. When I was of your age, a slight from a woman was the only thing that could have kept me from any pleasure that offered itself. But I understand that now youth is made differently."

"I don't see why," said Ray, and he quelled a desire he had to boast of his wounds; he permitted himself merely to put on an air of gloom.

"Why, I've been taught that modern society and civilization generally has so many consolations for unrequited affection that young men don't suffer from that sort of trouble any more, or not deeply."

Ray was sensible that Mr. Kane's intrusiveness was justifiable upon the ground of friendly interest; and he was not able to repel what seemed like friendly interest. "It may be as you say, in New York; I've not been here long enough to judge."

. "But in Midland things go on in the old way? Tell me something about Midland, and why any one should ever leave Midland for New York?"

"I can't say, generally speaking," answered Ray, with pleasure in Kane's pursuit, "but I think that in my case Midland began it."

"Yes?"

Ray was willing enough to impart as much of his autobiography as related to the business change that had thrown him out of his place on the *Echo*. Then he sketched with objective airiness the sort of life one led in Midland, if one was a young man in society; and he found it no more than fair to himself to give some notion of his own local value in a graphic little account of the farewell dinner.

"Yes," said Mr. Kane, "I can imagine how you should miss all that, and I don't know that New York has anything so pleasant to offer. I fancy the conditions of society are incomparably different in Midland and in New York. You seem to me a race of shepherds and shepherdesses out there; your pretty world is like a dream of my own youth, when Boston was still only a large town, and was not so distinctly an aoristic Athens as it is now."

"I had half a mind to go to Boston with my book first," said Ray. "But somehow I thought there were more chances in New York."

"There are certainly more publishers," Kane admitted. " Whether there are more chances depends upon how much independent judgment there is among the publishers. Have you found them very judicial?"

" I don't quite understand what you mean."

" Did any one of them seem to be a man who would give your novel an unprejudiced reading if you took it to him and told him honestly that it had been rejected by all the others?"

" No, I can't say any of them did. But I don't know that I could give my manuscript an unprejudiced reading myself under the same circumstances. I certainly shouldn't blame any publisher who couldn't. Should you?"

" I? I blame nobody, my dear friend," said Kane. " That is the way I keep my temper. I should not blame you if Chapley & Co. declined your book, and you went to the rest of the trade carefully concealing from each publisher, the fact that he was not the first you had approached with it."

Ray laughed, but he winced, too. " I suppose that's what I should have to do. But Chapley & Co. haven't declined it yet."

" Ah, I'm glad of that. Not that you could really impose upon any one. There would be certain infallible signs in your manuscript that would betray you : an air of use; little private marks and memoranda of earlier readers ; the smell of their different brands of tobacco and sachet powder."

" I shouldn't try to impose upon any one," Ray began, with a flush of indignation, which ended in shame. " What would *you* do under the same circumstances ? " he demanded, with desperation.

" My dear friend! My dear boy," Mr. Kane protested. " I am not censuring you. It's said that Bismarck found it an advantage to introduce truth even into diplomacy. He discovered there was nothing deceived *like* it; *nobody* believed him. Some successful advertisers have made it work in commercial affairs. You mustn't expect me to say what I should do under the same circumstances ; the circumstances couldn't be the same. I am not the author of a manuscript novel with a potential public of tens of thousands. But you can imagine that as the proprietor of a volume of essays which has a certain sale — Mr. Brandreth used that fatal term in speaking of my book, I suppose ? "

" No, I don't remember that he did," said Ray.

" He was kinder than I could have expected. It is the death-knell of hope to the devoted author when his publisher tells him that his book will always have a certain sale ; he is expressing in a pitying euphemism of the trade that there is no longer any chance for it, no happy accident in the future, no fortuity ; it is dead. As the author of a book with a certain sale, I feel myself exempt from saying what I should do in your place. But I'm very glad it hasn't come to the ordeal with you. Let us hope you won't be tempted. Let us hope that Messrs. Chapley & Co. will be equal to the golden opportunity offered them, and gradually — snatch it."

Kane smiled, and Ray laughed out. He knew that

he was being played upon, but he believed the touch was kindly, and even what he felt an occasional cold cynicism in it had the fascination that cynicism always has for the young when it does not pass from theory to conduct; when it does that, it shocks. He thought that Mr. Kane was something like Warrington in *Pendennis*, and again something like Coverdale in *Blithedale Romance*. He valued him for that; he was sure he had a history ; and when he now rose, Ray said : "Oh, must you go?" with eager regret.

"Why, I had thought of asking you to come with me. I'm going for a walk in the Park, and I want to stop on the way for a moment to see an old friend of mine " — he hesitated, and then added — "a man whom I was once intimately associated with in some joint hopes we had for reconstructing the world. I think you will be interested in him, as a type, even if you don't like him."

Ray professed that he should be very much interested, and they went out together.

XIII.

The streets had that Sunday sense which is as unmistakable as their week-day effect. Their noises were subdued almost to a country quiet; as he crossed with his friend to the elevated station, Ray noted with a lifting heart the sparrows that chirped from the knots and streamers of red Virginia-creeper hanging here and there from a porch roof or over a bit of garden wall; overhead the blue air was full of the jargoning of the blended church bells.

He tried to fit these facts with phrases in the intervals of his desultory talk with Kane, and he had got two or three very good epithets by the time they found seats together in an up-town train. It was not easy to find them, for the cars were thronged with work-people going to the Park for one of the last Sundays that could be fine there.

Kane said: "The man we are going to see belongs to an order of thinking and feeling that one would have said a few years ago had passed away forever, but of late its turn seems to be coming again; it's curious how these things recur. Do you happen to hate altruism in any of its protean forms?"

Ray smiled with the relish for the question which

Kane probably meant him to feel. "I can't say that I have any violent feeling against it."

"It is usually repulsive to young people," Kane went on, "and I could very well conceive your loathing it. My friend has been an altruist of one kind or another all his life. He's a man whom it would be perfectly useless to tell that the world is quite good enough for the sort of people there are in it; he would want to set about making the people worthy of a better world, and he would probably begin on *you*. You have heard of Brook Farm, I suppose?"

"Of course," Ray answered, with a show of resentment for such a question. "*Blithedale Romance* — I think it's the best of Hawthorne's books."

"Blithedale," said Mr. Kane, ignoring the literary interest, "is no more Brook Farm than — But we needn't enter upon that! My friend's career as an altruist began there; and since then there's hardly been a communistic experiment in behalf of Man with a capital and without capital that he hasn't been into and out of."

"I should like immensely to see him," said Ray. "Any man who was at Brook Farm — Did he know Hollingsworth and Zenobia, and Priscilla and Coverdale? Was it at Brook Farm that you met?"

Kane shook his head. "I think no one knew them but Hawthorne. I don't speak positively; Brook Farm was a little before my day, or else I should have been there too, I dare say. But I've been told those characters never were."

Then it was doubly impossible that Hawthorne should have studied Miles Coverdale from Kane; Ray had to relinquish a theory he had instantly formed upon no ground except Kane's sort of authority in speaking of Brook Farm; what was worse he had to abandon an instant purpose of carrying forward the romance and doing *The Last Days of Miles Coverdale;* it would have been an attractive title.

"I met David Hughes," Kane continued, "after the final break-up of the community, when I was beginning to transcendentalize around Boston, and he wanted me to go into another with him, out West. He came out of his last community within the year; he founded it himself, upon a perfectly infallible principle. It was so impregnable to the logic either of metaphysics or events, that Hughes had to break it up himself, I understand. At sixty-nine he has discovered that his efforts to oblige his fellow-beings ever since he was twenty have been misdirected. It isn't long for an error of that kind in the life of the race, but it hasn't exactly left my old friend in the vigor of youth. However, his hope and good-will are as athletic as ever."

"It's rather pathetic," Ray suggested.

"Why, I don't know — I don't know! Is it so? He hasn't found out the wrong way without finding the right way at the same time, and he's buoyantly hopeful in it, though he's not only an old man; he's a sick man, too. Of course, he's poor. He never was a fellow to do things by halves, and when he dispersed

his little following he divided nearly all his substance
among his disciples. He sees now that the right way
to universal prosperity and peace is the political way;
and if he could live long enough, we should see him in
Congress — if *we* lived long enough. Naturally, he is
paving the way with a book he's writing." Kane
went on to speak of his friend at length ; he suddenly
glanced out of the car window, and said : " Ah, we're
just there. This is our station."

The avenue had been changing its character as they
rushed along. It had ceased to be a street of three or
four story houses, where for the most part the people
lived over their shops, and where there was an effect
of excessive use on everything, a worn-out and shabby
look, rather than a squalid look. The cross-streets of
towering tenement-houses, had come and gone, and
now the buildings were low again, with greater or less
gaps between them, while the railroad had climbed
higher, and was like a line drawn through the air
without reference to the localities which the train left
swiftly behind. The houses had begun to be of wood
here and there, and it was at a frame of two stories
that Mr. Kane stopped with Ray, when they clambered
down the long iron staircase of the station to the foot-
way below. They pulled a bell that sounded faintly
somewhere within, and the catch of the lock clicked
as if it were trying to release itself; but when they
tried the door it was still fast, and Mr. Kane rang
again. Then a clatter of quick, impatient feet sounded
on the stairs ; the door was pulled sharply open, and

they confronted a tall young man, with a handsome pale face, who bent on them a look of impartial gloom from clouded blue eyes under frowning brows. A heavy fringe of dull yellow hair almost touched their level with its straight line, which the lower lip of the impassioned mouth repeated.

"Ah, Denton!" said Mr. Kane. "Good-morning, good-morning! This is my friend, Mr. Ray." The young men shook hands with a provisional civility, and Mr. Kane asked, "Are you all at home?"

"We are, at the moment," said the other. "I'm just going out with the babies; but father will be glad to see you. Come in."

He had a thick voice that came from his throat by nervous impulses; he set the door open and twisted his head in the direction of the stairs, as if to invite them to go up. They found he had a perambulator in the narrow hall behind the door, and two children facing each other in it. He got it out on the sidewalk without further attention to them, and shut the door after him. But in the light which his struggles to get out had let into the entry they made their way up the stairs, where a woman's figure stood silhouetted against an open door-way behind her.

"Ah, Mrs. Denton, how do you do?" said Kane, gaily.

The figure answered gaily back, "Oh, Mr. Kane!" and after Kane's presentation of Ray, set open a door that opened from the landing into the apartment. "Father will be so glad to see you. Please walk in."

Ray found himself in what must be the principal room of the apartment; its two windows commanded an immediate prospect of the elevated road, with an effect of having their sills against its trestle work. Between them stood a tall, gaunt old man, whose blue eyes flamed under the heavy brows of age, from a face set in a wilding growth of iron-gray hair and beard. He was talking down upon a gentleman whom Ray had black against the light, and he was saying: "No, Henry, no! Tolstoï is mistaken. I don't object to his theories of non-resistance; the Quakers have found them perfectly practicable for more than two centuries; but I say that in quitting the scene of the moral struggle, and in simplifying himself into a mere peasant, he begs the question as completely as if he had gone into a monastery. He has struck out some tremendous truths, I don't deny that, and his examination of the conditions of civilization is one of the most terrifically searching studies of the facts that have ever been contributed to the science of sociology; but his conclusions are as wrong as his premises are right. If I had back the years that I have wasted in a perfectly futile effort to deal with the problem of the race at a distance where I couldn't touch it, I would have nothing to do with eremitism in any of its forms, either collectively as we have had it in our various communistic experiments, or individually on the terms which Tolstoï apparently advises."

"But I don't understand him to advise eremitism," the gentleman began.

"It amounts to the same thing," said the other, cutting himself short in hollow cough, so as not to give up the word. "He would have us withdraw from the world, as if, where any man was, the world was not there in the midst of him!"

"Poor Tolstoï," said Mr. Kane, going up and shaking hands with the others, "as I understand it, is at present able only to rehearse his rôle, because his family won't consent to anything else. He's sold all he has in order to give to the poor, but his wife manages the proceeds."

"It's easy enough to throw ridicule on him," said the gentleman against the window, who now stood up.

"*I* throw no ridicule upon him," said the tall, gaunt man. "He has taught me at least this, that contempt is of the devil — I beg your pardon, Kane — and I appreciate to the utmost the spiritual grandeur of the man's nature. But practically, I don't follow him. We shall never redeem the world by eschewing it. Society is not to be saved by self-outlawry. The body politic is to be healed politically. The way to have the golden age is to elect it by the Australian ballot. The people must vote themselves into possession of their own business, and intrust their economic affairs to the same faculty that makes war and peace, that frames laws, and that does justice. What I object to in Tolstoï is his utter unpracticality. I cannot forgive any man, however good and great, who does not measure the means to the end. If there is anything in my own life that I can regard with entire

satisfaction it is that at every step of my career I have
invoked the light of common-sense. Whatever my
enemies may say against me, they cannot say that I
have not instantly abandoned any project when I found
it unpractical. I abhor dreamers ; they have no place
in a world of thinking and acting." Ray saw Kane
arching his eyebrows, while the other began again : " I
tell you " —

" I want to introduce my young friend Mr. Ray,"
Mr. Kane broke in.

The old man took Ray's hand between two hot
palms, and said, " Ah ! " with a look at him that was
benign, if somewhat bewildered.

" You know Mr. Ray, Chapley," Kane pursued,
transferring him to the other, who took his hand in
turn.

" Mr. Ray ? " he queried, with the distress of the
elderly man who tries to remember.

" If you forget your authors in the green wood so
easily, how shall it be with them in the dry ? " Kane
sighed ; and now the publisher woke up to Ray's
identity.

" Oh, yes, yes, yes ! Of course ! Mr. Ray, of —
of — Mr. Ray, of " —

" Midland," Ray suggested, perspiring.

" Why, certainly ! " Mr. Chapley pressed his hand
with as much apologetic entreaty as he could intimate
in that way, and assured him that he was glad to see
him ; and then he said to the old man, whose name
Kane had not mentioned to Ray in presenting him, but

whom Ray knew to be Hughes, "Well, I must be going now. I'm glad to find you looking so much better this morning."

"Oh; I'm quite a new man — quite a new man!"

"You were always that!" said Mr. Chapley, with a certain fondness. He sighed, "I wish I knew your secret."

"Stay, and let him expound it to us all!" Kane suggested. "I've no doubt he would."

"No; I must be going," said Mr. Chapley. "Good-by." He shook hands with the old man. "Good-by, Kane. Er — good-morning, Mr. — er — Ray. You must drop in and see us, when you can find time."

Ray bubbled after him some incoherencies about being afraid he could find only too much time. Apparently Mr. Chapley did not hear. He pottered out on the landing, and Ray heard him feeling his way carefully down stairs. It was an immense relief for him to have met Mr. Chapley there. It stamped his own presence in the place with propriety; he was fond of adventure and hungry for experience, but he wished all his adventures and experiences to be respectable. He had a young dread of queerness and irregularity; and he could not conceal from himself that but for Mr. Chapley his present environment was not in keeping with his smooth Philistine traditions. He had never been in an apartment before, much less a mere tenement; at Midland every one he knew lived in his own house; most of the people he knew lived in handsome houses of their own, with large grass-plots and shade-trees about them. But if Mr. Chapley were here, with this old man who called him by his first name, and with whom he and Mr. Kane seemed to have the past if not the present in common, it must be all right.

XIV.

Ray woke from his rapid mental formulation of this comforting reassurance to find the old man saying to him, " What is the nature of the work that Chapley has published for you ? I hope something by which you intend to advance others, as well as yourself: something that is to be not merely the means of your personal aggrandizement in fame and fortune. Nothing, in my getting back to the world, strikes me as more shamelessly selfish than the ordinary literary career. I don't wonder the art has sunk so low ; its aims are on the business level."

Mr. Kane listened with an air of being greatly amused, and even gratified, and Ray thought he had purposely let the old man go on as if he were an author who had already broken the shell. Before he could think of some answer that should at once explain and justify him, Kane interposed:

" I hope Mr. Ray is no better than the rest of us ; but he may be ; you must make your arraignment and condemnation conditional, at any rate. He's an author *in petto*, as yet; Chapley may never publish him."

" Then why," said the old man, irascibly, " did you speak of him as you did to Chapley ? It was misleading."

" In the world you've come back to, my dear friend,"

7

said Kane, "you'll find that we have no time to refine
upon the facts. We can only sketch the situation in
large, bold outlines. Perhaps I wished to give Mr.
Ray a hold upon Chapley by my premature recognition
of him as an author, and make the wicked publisher
feel that there was already a wide general impatience
to see Mr. Ray's book."

"That would have been very corrupt, Kane," said
the other. "But I owe Mr. Ray an apology."

Ray found his tongue. "Perhaps you won't think
so when you see my novel."

"A novel! Oh, I have no time to read novels!"
the old man burst out. "A practical man "—

"Nor volumes of essays," said Kane, picking up a
book from the table at his elbow. "Really, as a
measure of self-defence, I must have the leaves of my
presentation copies cut, at any rate. I must sacrifice
my taste to my vanity. Then I sha'n't know when
the grateful recipients haven't opened them."

"   e no time to read books of any kind "— the old
man   gan again.

" 'ou ought to set up reviewer," Kane interposed
again.

"Oh, I've looked into your essays, Kane, here and
there. The literature is of a piece with the affectation
of the uncut dges: something utterly outdated and
superseded. It's all as impe   t as the demand you
make that the reader should do the work of a book-
binder, and cut your leaves."

"Do you know that I'm re"ly hurt — not for my-

self, but for you! — by what you say of my uncut
edges? You descend to the level of a Brandreth,"
said Kane.

"A Brandreth? What is a Brandreth?"

"It is a publisher: Chapley's son-in-law and partner."

"Oh, yes, yes," said Hughes.

"I spent many hours," said Kane, plaintively,
"pleading with him for an edition with uncut edges.
He contended that the public would not buy it if the
edges were not cut; and I told him that I wished to
have that fact to fall back upon, in case they didn't
buy it for some other reason. And I was right. The
edition hasn't sold, and the uncut edges have saved me
great suffering until now. Why not have confined
your own remarks, my dear friend, to the uncut edges?
I might have agreed with you."

"Because" said the old man, "I cannot have
patience with a man of your age who takes the mere
dilettante view of life — who regards the world as
something to be curiously inspected and neatly com-
mented, instead of toiled for, sweated for, suffered for!"

"It appears to me that there is toiling and sweating
and suffering enough for the world already," said
Kane, with a perverse levity. "Look at the poor
millionnaires, struggling to keep their employés in
work! If you've come back to the world for no better purpose than to add to its perseverance and perspiration, I could wish for your own sake that you had
remained in some of our communities — or all of
them, for that matter."

The other turned half round in his chair, and looked hard into Kane's smiling face. "You are a most unserious spirit, Kane, and you always were! When will you begin to be different? Do you expect to continue a mere frivolous maker of phrases to the last? Your whole book there is just a bundle of phrases — labels for things. Do you ever intend to *be* anything?"

"I intend to be an angel, some time — or some eternity," said Kane. "But, in the meanwhile, have you ever considered that perhaps you are demanding, in your hopes of what you call the redemption of the race from selfishness, as sheer and mere an impossibility as a change of the physical basis of the soul?"

"What do you mean?"

"I mean — or, I won't put it affirmatively; I will put it interrogatively."

"Yes, that was always your way!"

"I will merely ask you," Kane went on, without heeding the interruption, "what reason you have to suppose the altruistic is not eternally conditioned in the egoistic, just as the spiritual is conditioned in the animal?"

"What jargon is that?" demanded the old man, throwing one leg over the other, and smoothing the upper one down with his hand, as he bent forward to glower at Kane.

"It is the harmony of the spheres, my dear David; it is a metaphysical variation of the pleasing air that the morning stars sang together; it is the very truth.

The altruistic can no more shake off the egoistic in this world than the spiritual can shake off the animal. As soon as man ceases to get hungry three times a day, just so soon will he cease to eat his fellow-man."

"There is the usual trivial truth in what you say," Hughes replied, "and the usual serious impiety. You probably are not aware that your miserable paradox accuses the Creative Intelligence."

"Ah, but use another word! Say Nature, and then where is the impiety?"

"But I decline to use the other word," Hughes retorted.

"And I insist upon it; I must. It is Nature that I accuse; not the divine nature, or even human nature, but brute nature, that commits a million blunders, and destroys myriads of types, in order to arrive at such an imperfect creature as man still physically is, after untold ages of her blind empiricism. If the human intelligence could be put in possession of the human body, we should have altruism at once. We should not get hungry three times a day; instead of the crude digestive apparatus which we have inherited with apparently no change whatever from the cave-dweller, we should have an organ delicately adjusted to the exigencies of modern life, and responsive to all the emotions of philanthropy. But no! The stomach of the nineteenth century remains helplessly in the keeping of primeval nature, who is a—mere—Bourbon; who learns nothing and forgets nothing. She obliges us to struggle on with a rude arrangement developed from the mollusk, and adapted at best to the conditions of the savage; imperative and imperfect; liable to get out of order with the carefulest management, and to give way altogether with the use of half a lifetime. No, David! You will have to wait until man has come into control of his stomach, and is able to bring his ingenuity to bear upon its deficiencies. Then, and not till then, you will have the Altruistic Man. Until then the egoistic man will continue to eat his brother, and more or less indigest him — if there is such a verb."

Ray listened with one ear to them. The other was filled with the soft murmur of women's voices from the further end of the little apartment; they broke now and then from a steady flow of talk, and rippled into laughter, and then smoothed themselves to talk again. He longed to know what they were talking about, laughing about.

"No, David," Kane went on, "when you take man out of the clutches of Nature, and put Nature in the keeping of man, we shall have the millennium. I have nothing to say against the millennium, *per se*, except that it never seems to have been on time. I am willing to excuse its want of punctuality; there may have always been unavoidable delays; but you can't expect me to have as much faith in it as if it had never disappointed people. Now with you I admit it's different. You've seen it come a great many times, and go even oftener."

"Young man!" the other called so abruptly to Ray

that it made him start in his chair, "I wish you would step out into the room yonder, and ask one of my daughters to bring me my whiskey and milk. It's time for it," and he put down a watch which he had taken from the table beside him.

He nodded toward a sort of curtained corridor at one side of the room, and after a glance of question at Kane, who answered with a reassuring smile, Ray went out through this passage. The voices had suddently fallen silent, but he found their owners in the little room beyond; they were standing before their chairs as if they had jumped to their feet in a feminine dismay which they had quelled. In one he made out the young Mrs. Denton, whose silhouette had received him and Kane; the other looked like her, but younger, and in the two Ray recognized the heroines of the pocket-book affair on the train.

He trembled a little inwardly, but he said, with a bow for both: "I beg your pardon. Your father wished me to ask you for his" —

He faltered at the queerness of it all, but the younger said, simply and gravely: "Oh, yes, I'll take it in. I've got it ready here," and she took up a tumbler from the hearth of the cooking-stove keeping itself comfortable at one side of a little kitchen beyond the room where they were, and went out with it.

Ray did not know exactly what to do, or rather how he should do what he wished. He hesitated, and looked at Mrs. Denton, who said, "Won't you sit down — if it isn't too hot here?"

XV

"Oh, it isn't at all hot," said Ray, and in fact the air was blowing freely in through the plants at the open window. Then he sat down, as if to prove that it was not too hot; there was no other reason that he could have given for staying, instead of going back to Kane and her father.

"We can keep the windows open on this side," said Mrs. Denton, "but the elevated makes too much noise in front. When we came here first, it was warm weather; it was stifling when we shut the windows, and when we opened them, it seemed as if the trains would drive us wild. It was like having them in the same room with us. But now it's a little cooler, and we don't need the front windows open; so it's very pleasant."

Ray said it was delightful, and he asked, "Then you haven't been in New York long?"

"No; only since the beginning of September. We thought we would settle in New Jersey first, and we did take a house there, in the country; but it was too far from my husband's work, and so we moved in. Father wants to meet people; he's more in the current here."

As she talked, Mrs. Denton had a way of looking

down at her apron, and smoothing it across her knees
with one hand, and now and then glancing at Ray out
of the corner of her eye, as if she were smiling on
the further side of her face.

"We went out there a little while ago to sell off the
things we didn't want to keep. The neighbors took
them." She began to laugh, and Ray laughed, too,
when she said, "We found they had taken *some* of
them before we got there. They might as well have
taken all, they paid us so little for the rest. I didn't
suppose there would be such a difference between first-
hand and second-hand things. But it was the first
time we had ever set up housekeeping for ourselves,
and we had to make mistakes. We had always lived
in a community."

She looked at him for the impression of this fact,
and Ray merely said, "Yes ; Mr. Kane told me something of the kind."

"It's all very different in the world. I don't know
whether you've ever been in a community?"

"No," said Ray.

"Well," she went on, "we've had to get used to all
sorts of things since we came out into the world. The
very day we left the community, I heard some people
in the seat just in front of me, in the car, planning
how they should do something to get a living; it
seemed ridiculous and dreadful. It fairly frightened
me."

Ray was struck with the literary value of the fact.
He said : "I suppose it would be startling if we could

any of us realize it for the first time. But for most of us there never is any first time."

Mrs. Denton said: "No, but in the community we never had to think how we should get things to eat and wear, any more than how we should get air to breathe. You know father believes that the world can be made like the Family, in that, and everybody be sure of a living, if he is willing to work."

She glanced at Ray with another of her demure looks, which seemed inquiries both as to his knowledge of the facts and his opinion of them.

"I didn't know just what your father's ideas were," he said; and she went on:

"Yes; he thinks all you've got to do is to have patience. But it seems to me you've got to have money too, or you'll starve to death before your patience gives out."

Mrs. Denton laughed, and Ray sat looking at her with a curious mixture of liking and misgiving: he would have liked to laugh with her from the poet in him, but his civic man could not approve of her irresponsibility. In her quality of married woman, she was more reprehensible than she would have been as a girl; as a girl, she might well have been merely funny. Still, she was a woman, and her voice, if it expressed an irresponsible nature, was sweet to hear. She seemed not to dislike hearing it herself, and she let it run lightly on. "The hardest thing for us, though, has been getting used to money, and the care of it. It seems to be just as bad with a little as a great deal

—the care does; and you have to be thinking about it all the time; we never had to think of it at all in the Family. Most of us never saw it, or touched it; only the few that went out and sold and bought things."

" That's very odd," said Ray, trying the notion if it would not work somewhere into literature; at the same time he felt the charm of this pretty young woman, and wondered why her sister did not come back. He heard her talking with Kane in the other room; now and then her voice, gentle and clear and somewhat high, was lost in Kane's laugh, or the hoarse plunge of her father's bass.

" Yes," Mrs. Denton went on, " I think I feel it more than my husband or my sister does; they just have to earn the money, but I have to take care of it, and see how far I can make it go. It's perfectly distracting; and sometimes when I forget, and do something careless!" She let an impressive silence follow, and Ray laughed.

" Yes, that's an anxious time for us, even if we're brought up with the advantages of worldly experience."

" Anxious!" Mrs. Denton repeated; and her tongue ran on. " Why, the day I went out to New Jersey with my sister to settle up our 'estate' out there, we each of us had a baby to carry — my children are twins, and we couldn't leave them here with father; it was bad enough to leave him! and my husband was at work; and on the train coming home I forgot and

gave the twins my pocket-book to play with; and just
then a kind old gentleman put up the car window for
me, and the first thing I knew they threw it out into
the water — we were crossing that piece of water before
you get to Jersey City. It had every cent of my
money in it; and I was so scared when they threw
my pocket-book away — we always say *they,* because
they're so much alike we never can remember which
did a thing — I was so scared that I didn't know what
I was doing, and I just screamed out all about it."
Ray listened restively; he felt as if he were eaves-
dropping; but he did not know quite how, or when, or
whether, after all, to tell her that he had witnessed the
whole affair; he decided that he had better not; and
she went on : "My sister said it was just as if I had
begged of the whole carful; and I suppose it was. I
don't suppose that a person who was more used to
money would have given it to a baby to play with."

She stopped, and Ray suddenly changed his mind;
he thought he ought not to let her go on as if he
knew nothing about it; that was hardly fair.

"The conductor," he said, "appeared to think *any*
woman would have done it."

Mrs. Denton laughed out her delight. "It *was* you,
then. My sister was sure it was, as soon as she saw
you at Mr. Chapley's."

"At Mr. Chapley's?"

"Yes; his store. That is where she works. You
didn't see her, but she saw you," said Mrs. Denton;
and then Ray recalled that Mr. Brandreth had sent to

a Miss Hughes for the list of announcements she had given him.

"We saw you noticing us in the car, and we saw you talking with the conductor. Did he say anything else about us?" she asked, significantly.

"I don't know exactly what you mean," Ray answered, a little consciously, and coloring slightly.

"Why," Mrs. Denton began; but she stopped at sight of her sister, who came in with the empty tumbler in her hand, and set it down in the room beyond. "Peace!" she called to her, and the girl came back reluctantly, Ray fancied. He had remained standing since her reappearance, and Mrs. Denton said, introducing them, "This is my sister, Mr. Ray;" and then she cried out joyfully, "It *was* Mr. Ray!" while he bowed ceremoniously to the girl, who showed an embarrassment that Mrs. Denton did not share. "The conductor told him that any woman would have given her baby her pocket-book to play with; and so you see I wasn't so very bad, after all. But when one of these things happens to me, it seems as if the world had come to an end; I can't get over it. Then we had another experience! One of the passengers that heard me say all our money was in that pocket-book, gave the conductor a dollar for us, to pay our car-fares home. We had to take it; we *couldn't* have carried the children from the ferry all the way up here; but I never knew before that charity hurt so.—It was dreadful!"

A certain note made itself evident in her voice which

Ray felt as an appeal. " Why, I don't think you need
have considered it as charity. It was what might have
happened to any lady who had lost her purse."

" It wasn't like that," Miss Hughes broke in. " It
would have been offered then so that it could be returned. We were to blame for not making the conductor say who gave it. But we were so confused!"

" I think the giver was to blame for not sending his
address with it. But perhaps he was confused too,"
said Ray.

" The conductor told us it was a lady," said Mrs.
Denton, with a sudden glance upward at Ray.

They all broke into a laugh together, and the girl
sprang up and went into another room. She came
back with a bank-note in her hand, which she held out
toward Ray.

He did not offer to take it. " I haven't pleaded
guilty yet."

" No," said Mrs. Denton ; " but we know you did
it. Peace always thought you did ; and now we've
got you in our power, and you *must* take it back."

" But you didn't use it all. You gave a quarter to
the old darkey who whistled. You're as bad as I am.
You do charity, too."

" No ; he earned his quarter. You paid him something yourself," said the girl.

" He did whistle divinely," Ray admitted. " How
came you to think of asking him to change your bill ?
I should have thought you'd have given it all to him."

They had a childlike joy in his railery, which they

laughed simply out. "We did want to," Mrs. Denton
said; "but we didn't know how we could get home."

"I don't see but that convicts me." Ray put out
his hand as if to take the note, and then withdrew it.
"I suppose I ought to take it," he began. "But if I
did, I should just spend it on myself. And the fact is,
I had saved it on myself, or else, perhaps, I shouldn't
have given it to the conductor for you." He told
them how he had economized on his journey, and they
laughed together at the picture he gave of his satisfaction in his self-denial.

"Oh, I know that *good* feeling!" said Mrs. Denton.

"Yes, but you can't imagine how *superior* I felt
when I handed my dollar over to the conductor. *Good*
is no name for it; and I've simply gloated over my
own merit ever since. Miss Hughes, you must keep
that dollar, and give it to somebody who needs it!"

This was not so novel as it seemed to Ray; but the
sisters glanced at each other as if struck with its origi-
nality.

Then the girl looked at him steadily out of her
serene eyes a moment, as if thinking what she had
better do, while Mrs. Denton cooed her pleasure in the
situation.

"I knew just as *well*, when the conductor said it
was a lady passenger sent it! He said it like a sort of
after-thought, you know; he turned back to say it just
after he left us."

"Well, I will do that," said the girl to Ray; and
she carried the money back to her room.

"Do sit down!" said Mrs. Denton to Ray when
she came back. The community of experience, and
the wonder of the whole adventure, launched them indefinitely forward towards intimacy in their acquaintance. "We were awfully excited when my sister
came home and said she had seen you at Mr. Chapley's." Her sister did not deny it; but when Mrs.
Denton added the question, "Are you an author?"
she protested — "Jenny!"

"I wish I were," said Ray; "but I can't say I am,
yet. That depends upon whether Mr. Chapley takes
my book."

He ventured to be so frank because he thought Miss
Hughes probably knew already that he had offered a
manuscript; but if she knew, she made no sign of
knowing, and Mrs. Denton said:

"Mr. Chapley gives my sister all the books he pub-
lishes. Isn't it splendid? And he lets her bring
home any of the books she wants to, out of the store.
Are you acquainted in his family?"

"No; I only know Mr. Brandreth, his son-in-law."

"My sister says he's very nice. Everybody likes
Mr. Brandreth. Mr. Chapley is an old friend of
father's. I should think his family would come to see
us, some of them. But they haven't. Mr. Chaplev
comes ever so much."

Ray did not know what to say of a fact which Mrs.
Denton did not suffer to remain last in his mind. She
went on, as if it immediately followed.

"We are reading Browning now. But my husband

likes Shelley the best of all. Which is your favorite
poet?"

Ray smiled. "I suppose Shelley ought to be. I
was named after him." When he had said this he
thought it rather silly, and certainly superfluous. So
he added, "My father was a great reader of him when
he was a young man, and I got the benefit of his taste,
if it's a benefit."

"Why, do you hate to be named Shelley?" Mrs.
Denton asked.

"Oh, no; except as I should hate to be named
Shakespeare; it suggests comparisons."

"Yes; but it's a very pretty name." As if it
recalled him, she said, "My husband was just going
out with the twins when you came in with Mr. Kane.
He was taking them over to the Park. Do you like
cats?" She leaned over and lugged up into her lap a
huge Maltese from the further side of her. "My sister doesn't because they eat sparrows." She passed
her hand slowly down the cat's smooth flank, which
snapped electrically, while the cat shut its eyes to a
line of gray light.

"If your cat's fond of sparrows, he ought to come
and live with me," said Ray. "I've got a whole col-
ony of them outside of my dormer-window."

Mrs. Denton lifted the cat's head and rubbed her
cheek on it. "Oh, we've got plenty of sparrows here,
too. Where do you live? Down town? Mr. Kane
does."

Ray gave a picturesque account of his foreign hotel;
8

but he had an impression that its strangeness was
thrown away upon his hearers, who seemed like children in their contact with the world; it was all so
strange that nothing was stranger than another to
them. They thought what he told them of life in
Midland as queer as life in New York.

The talk went on without sequence or direction,
broken with abrupt questions and droll comments; and
they laughed a good deal. They spoke of poems and
of dreams. Ray told of a fragment of a poem he had
made in a dream, and repeated it; they thought it
was fine, or at least Mrs. Denton said she did. Her
sister did not talk much, but she listened, and now
and then she threw in a word. She sat against the
light, and her face was in shadow to Ray, and this
deepened his sense of mystery in her; her little head,
so distinctly outlined, was beautiful. Her voice, which
was so delicate and thin, had a note of childish inno-
cence in it. Mrs. Denton cooed deep and low. She
tried to make her sister talk more, and tell this and
that. The girl did not seem afraid or shy, but only
serious. Several times they got back to books, and at
one of these times it appeared that she knew of Ray's
manuscript, and that it was going through the hands of
the readers.

"And what is the name of your story?" Mrs. Denton asked, and before he could tell her she said, "Oh,
yes; I forgot," and he knew that they must have
talked of it together. He wondered if Miss Hughes
had read it. "Talking of names," Mrs. Denton went

on, "I think my sister's got the queerest one: Peace.
Isn't it a curious name?"

"It's a beautiful name," said Ray. "The Spanish
give it a great deal, I believe."

"Do they? It was a name that mother liked; but
she had never heard of it, although there were so
many Faiths, Hopes, and Charities. She died just a
little while after Peace was born, and father gave her
the name."

Ray was too young to feel the latent pathos of the
lightly treated fact. "It's a beautiful name," he said
again.

"Yes," said Mrs. Denton, "and it's so short you
can't *nick* it. There can't be anything shorter than
Peace, can there?"

"Truce," Ray suggested, and this made them laugh.

The young girl rose and went to the window, and
began looking over the plants in the pots there. Ray
made bold to go and join her.

"Are you fond of flowers?" she asked gently, and
with a seriousness as if she really expected him to say
truly.

"I don't know. I've never thought," he answered,
thinking how pretty she was, now he had her face
where he could see it fully. Her hair was of the indefinite blonde tending to brown, which most people's
hair is of; her sensitive face was cast in the American
mould that gives us such a high average of good looks
in our women; her eyes were angelically innocent.
When she laughed, her lip caught on her upper teeth,

and clung there; one of the teeth was slightly broken; and both these little facts fascinated Ray. She did not laugh so much as Mrs. Denton, whose talk she let run on with a sufferance like that of an older person, though she was the younger. She and Ray stood awhile there playing the game of words in which youth hides itself from its kind, and which bears no relation to what it is feeling. The charm of being in the presence of a lovely and intelligent girl enfolded Ray like a caressing atmosphere, and healed him of all the hurts of homesickness, of solitude. Their talk was intensely personal, because youth is personal, and they were young; they thought that it dealt with the different matters of taste they touched on, but it really dealt with themselves, and not their preferences in literature, in flowers, in cats, in dress, in country and city. Ray was aware that they were discussing these things in a place very different from the parlors where he used to enjoy young ladies' society in Midland; it was all far from the Midland expectation of his career in New York society. He recalled how, before the days of his social splendor in Midland, he had often sat and watched his own mother and sisters about their household work, which they did for themselves, while they debated the hopes and projects of his future, or let their hearts out in jest and laughter. Afterwards, he would not have liked to have this known among the fashionable people in Midland, with whom he wished to be so perfectly *comme il faut*.

From time to time Mrs. Denton dropped the cat out

of her lap, and ran out to pull the wire which operated the latch of the street door; and then Ray heard her greeting some comer and showing him into the front room, where presently he heard him greeting her father. At last there was a sound below as of some one letting himself in with a latch-key, and then came the noises of the perambulator wheels bumping from step to step as it was pulled up. Mrs. Denton sat still, and kept on talking to Ray, but her sister went out to help her husband; and reappeared with a sleeping twin in her arms, and carried it into the room adjoining. The husband, with his pale face flushed from his struggle with the perambulator, came in with the other, and when he emerged from the next room again, Mrs. Denton introduced him to Ray.

"Oh, yes," he said; "I saw you with Mr. Kane." He sat down a moment at the other window, and put his bare head out for the air. "It has grown warm," he said.

"Was the Park very full?" his wife asked.

"Crowded. It's one of their last chances for the year."

"I suppose it made you homesick."

"Horribly," said the husband, with his head still half out of the window. He took it in, and listened with the tolerance of a husband while she explained him to Ray.

"My husband's so homesick for the old Family place — it *was* a pretty place! — that he almost dies when he goes into the Park; it brings it all back so. Are you homesick, too, Mr. Ray?"

"Well, not exactly for the country," said Ray "I've been homesick for the place 1 came from — for Midland, that is."

"Midland?" Denton repeated. "I've been there. I think those small cities are more deadly than New York. They're still trying to get rid of the country, and New York is trying to get some of it back. If I had my way, there wouldn't be a city, big or little, on the whole continent." He did not wait for any reply from Ray, but he asked his wife, "Who's come?"

She mentioned a number of names, ten or twelve, and he said, "We'd better go in," and without further parley he turned toward the curtained avenue to the front room.

XVI.

In the front room the little assemblage had the effect of some small religious sect. The people were plainly dressed in a sort of keeping with their serious faces; there was one girl who had no sign of a ribbon or lace about her, and looked like a rather athletic boy in her short hair and black felt hat, and her jacket buttoned to her throat. She sat with her hands in the side pockets of her coat, and her feet pushed out beyond the hem of her skirt. There were several men of a foreign type, with beards pointed and parted; an American, who looked like a school-master, and whose mouth worked up into his cheek at one side with a sort of mechanical smile when he talked, sat near a man who was so bald as not to have even a spear of hair anywhere on his head. The rest were people who took a color of oddity from these types; a second glance showed them to be of the average humanity; and their dress and its fashion showed them to be of simple condition. They were attired with a Sunday consciousness and cleanliness, though one gentleman, whose coat sleeves and seams were brilliant with long use, looked as if he would be the better for a little benzining, where his moustache had dropped soup and coffee on his waistcoat; he had prominent eyes, with a straining, near-sighted look.

Kane sat among them with an air at once alert and aloof; his arms were folded, and he glanced around from one to another with grave interest. They were all listening, when Ray came in, to a young man who was upholding the single-tax theory, with confidence and with eagerness, as something which, in its operation, would release the individual energies to free play and to real competition. Hughes broke in upon him:

"That is precisely what I object to in your theory. I don't *want* that devil released. Competition is the Afreet that the forces of civilization have bottled up after a desperate struggle, and he is always making fine promises of what he will do for you if you will let him out. The fact is he will do nothing but mischief, because that is his nature. He is Beelzebub, he is Satan; in the Miltonic fable he attempted to compete with the Almighty for the rule of heaven; and the fallen angels have been taking the consequence ever since. Monopoly is the only prosperity. Where competition is there can be finally nothing but disaster and defeat for one side or another. That is self-evident. Nothing succeeds till it begins to be a monopoly. This holds good from the lowest to the highest endeavor — from the commercial to the æsthetic, from the huckster to the artist. As long, for instance, as an author is young and poor " — Ray felt, looking down, that the speaker's eye turned on him — " he must compete, and his work must be deformed by the struggle; when it becomes known that he alone can do his kind of work, he monopolizes and prospers in the full measure of his powers; and he realizes his ideal unrestrictedly. ⎨Competition enslaves, monopoly liberates. We must, therefore, have the greatest possible monopoly; one that includes the whole people economically as they are now included politically. Try to think of competition in the political administration as we now have it in the industrial. It isn't thinkable! Or, yes! They do have it in those Eastern countries where the taxes are farmed to the highest bidder, and the taxpayer's life is ground out of him."

"I think," said the school-masterly-looking man, "we all feel this instinctively. The trusts and the syndicates are doing our work for us as rapidly as we could ask."

A voice, with a German heaviness of accent, came from one of the foreigners. "But they are not doing it for our sake, and they mean to stop distinctly short of the whole-people trust. As far back as Louis Napoleon's rise we were expecting the growth of the corporate industries to accomplish our purposes for us. But between the corporation and the collectivity there is a gulf — a chasm that has never yet been passed."

"We must bridge it!" cried Hughes.

A young man, with a clean-cut, English intonation, asked, "Why not fill it up with capitalists?"

"No," said Hughes, "our cause should recognize no class as enemies."

"I don't think it matters much to them whether we recognize them or not, if we let them have their own

w'y," said the young man, whose cockney origin betrayed itself in an occasional vowel and aspirate.

" We shall not let them have their own way unless
it is the way of the majority, too," Hughes returned.
" From my point of view they are simply and purely a
part of the movement, as entirely so as the proletariat."

" The difficulty will be to get them to take your
point of view," the young man suggested.

" It isn't necessary they should,"·Hughes answered,
" though some of them do already. Several of the
best friends of our cause are capitalists; and there are
numbers of moneyed people who believe in the nation-
alization of the telegraphs, railroads, and expresses."

" Those are merely the first steps," urged the young
man, " which may lead now'ere."·

" They are the first steps," said Hughes, " and they
are not to be taken over the bodies of men. We must
advance together as brothers, marching abreast, to the
music of our own heart-beats."

" Good!" said Kane. Ray did not know whether
he said it ironically or not. It made the short-haired
girl turn round and look at him where he sat behind
her.

" We, in Russia," said another of the foreign-look-
ing people, " have seen the futility of violence. The
only force that finally prevails is love; and we must
employ it with those that can feel it best — with the
little children. The adult world is hopeless ; but with
the next generation we may do something — everything. The highest office is the teacher's, but we must

become as little children if we would teach them, who are of the kingdom of heaven. We must begin by learning of them."

"It appears rather complicated," said the young Englishman, gayly; and Ray heard Kane choke off a laugh into a kind of snort.

"Christ said He came to call sinners to repentance," said the man who would have been the better for benzining. "He evidently thought there was some hope of grown-up people if they would cease to do evil."

"And several of the disciples were elderly men," the short-haired girl put in.

"Our Russian friend's idea seems to be a version of our Indian policy," said Kane. "Good adults, dead adults."

"No, no. You don't understand, all of you," the Russian began, but Hughes interrupted him.

"How would you deal with the children?"

"In communities here, at the heart of the trouble, and also in the West, where they could be easily made self-supporting."

"I don't believe in communities," said Hughes. "If anything in the world has thoroughly failed, it is communities. They have failed all the more lamentably when they have succeeded financially, because that sort of success comes from competition with the world outside. A community is an aggrandized individual; it is the extension of the egoistic motive to a large family, which looks out for its own good against other families, just as a small family does. I have had enough of communities. The family we hope to found must include all men who are willing to work; it must recognize no aliens except the drones, and the drones must not be suffered to continue. They must either cease to exist by going to work, or by starving to death. But this great family — the real human family — must be no agglutinated structure, no mere federation of trades-unions; it must be a natural growth from indigenous stocks, which will gradually displace individual and corporate enterprises by pushing its roots and its branches out under and over them, till they have no longer earth or air to live in. It will then slowly possess itself of the whole field of production and distribution."

"*Very* slowly," said the young Englishman; and he laughed.

The debate went on, and it seemed as if there were almost as many opinions as there were people present. At times it interested Ray, at times it bored him; but at all times he kept thinking that if he could get those queer zealots into a book, they would be amusing material, though he shuddered to find himself personally among them. Hughes coughed painfully in the air thickened with many breaths, and the windows had to be opened for him; then the rush of the elevated trains filled the room, and the windows were shut again. After one of these interludes, Ray was aware of Hughes appealing to some one in the same tone in which he had asked him to go and send in his whiskey and milk; he looked up, and saw that Hughes was appealing to him.

"Young man, have you nothing to say on all these questions? Is it possible that you have not thought of them?"

Ray was so startled that for a moment he could not speak. Then he said, hardily, but in the frank spirit of the discussion, "No, I have never thought of them at all."

"It is time you did," said Hughes. "All other interests must yield to them. We can have no true art, no real literature, no science worthy the name, till the money-stamp of egoism is effaced from success, and it is honored, not paid."

The others turned and stared at Ray; old Kane arched his eyebrows at him, and made rings of white round his eyes; he pursed his mouth as if he would like to laugh. Ray saw Mrs Denton put her hand on her mouth; her husband glowered silently; her sister sat with downcast eyes.

Hughes went on: "I find it easier to forgive enmity than indifference; he who is not for us is against us in the worst sense. Our cause has a sacred claim upon all generous and enlightened spirits; they are recreant if they neglect it. But we must be patient, even with indifference; it is hard to bear, but we cannot fight it, and we must bear it. Nothing has astonished me more, since my return to the world, than to find the great mass of men living on, as when I left it, in besotted indifference to the vital interests of the hour. I find the politicians still talking of the tariff, just as they used to talk; low tariff and cheap clothes for the

working-man ; high tariff and large wages for the working-man. Whether we have high tariff or low, the
working-man always wins. But he does not seem to
prosper. He is poor; he is badly fed and housed;
when he is out of work he starves in his den till he is
evicted with a ruthlessness unknown in the history of
Irish oppression. Neither party means to do anything
for the working-man, and he hasn't risen himself yet
to the conception of anything more philosophical than
more pay and fewer hours."

A sad-faced man spoke from a corner of the room.
"We must have time to think, and something to eat
to-day. We can't wait till to-morrow."

"That is true," Hughes answered. "Many must
perish by the way. But we must have patience."

His son-in-law spoke up, and his gloomy face dark-
ened. "I have no heart for patience. When I see
people perishing by the way, I ask myself how they
shall be saved, not some other time, but now. Some
one is guilty of the wrong they suffer. How shall the
sin be remitted?" His voice shook with fanatical passion.

"We must have patience," Hughes repeated. "We
are all guilty."

"It would be a good thing," said the man with a
German accent, "if the low-tariff men would really cut
off the duties. The high-tariff men don't put wages
up because they have protection, but they would surely
put them down if they didn't have it. Then you would
see labor troubles everywhere."

"Yes," said Hughes; "but such hopes as that would make me hate the cause, if anything could. Evil that good may come? Never! Always good, and good for evil, that the good may come more and more! We must have the true America in the true American way, by reasons, by votes, by laws, and not otherwise."

The spirit which he rebuked had unlocked the passions of those around him. Ray had a vision of them in the stormy dispute which followed, as waves beating and dashing upon the old man; the head of the bald man was like a buoy among the breakers, as it turned and bobbed about, in his eagerness to follow all that was said.

Suddenly the impulses spent themselves, and a calm succeeded. One of the men looked at his watch; they all rose one after another to go.

Hughes held them a little longer. "I don't believe the good time is so far off as we are apt to think in our indignation at wrong. It is coming soon, and its mere approach will bring sensible relief. We must have courage and patience."

Ray and Kane went away together. Mrs. Denton looked at him with demure question in her eyes when they parted; Peace imparted no feeling in her still glance. Hughes took Ray's little hand in his large, loose grasp, and said:

"Come again, young man; come again!"

XVII.

"If ever I come again," Ray vowed to himself, when he got into the street, "I think I shall know it!" He abhorred all sorts of social outlandishness; he had always wished to be conformed, without and within, to the great world of smooth respectabilities. If for the present he was willing to Bohemianize a little, it was in his quality of author, and as part of a world-old tradition. To have been mixed up with a lot of howling dervishes like those people was intolerable. He tingled with a sense of personal injury from Hughes's asking him to take part in their discussion; and he was all the angrier because he could not resent it, even to Kane, on account of that young girl, who could not let him see that it distressed her, too; he felt bound to her by the tie of favor done which he must not allow to become painful.

He knew, as they walked rapidly down the avenue, crazy with the trains hurtling by over the jingling horse-cars and the clattering holiday crowds, that old Kane was seeking out his with eyes brimming with laughter, but he would not look at him, and he would not see any fun in the affair. He would not speak, and he held his tongue the more resolutely because he believed Kane meant to make him speak first.

He had his way; it was Kane who broke the silence, after they left the avenue and struck into one of the cross-streets leading to the Park. Piles of lumber and barrels of cement blocked two-thirds of its space, in front of half-built houses, which yawned upon it from cavernous depths. Boys were playing over the boards and barrels, and on the rocky hill-side behind the houses, where a portable engine stood at Sunday rest, and tall derricks rose and stretched their idle arms abroad. At the top of the hill a row of brown-stone fronts looked serenely down upon the havoc thrown up by the blasting, as if it were a quiet pleasance.

"Amiable prospect, isn't it?" said Kane. "It looks as if Hughes's Afreet has got out of his bottle, and had a good time here, holding on for a rise, and then building on spec. But perhaps we oughtn't to judge of it at this stage, when everything is in transition. Think how beautiful it will be when it is all solidly built up here as it is down-town!" He passed his hand through Ray's lax arm, and leaned affectionately toward him as they walked on, after a little pause he made for this remark on the scenery. "Well, my dear young friend, what do you think of my dear old friend?"

"Of Mr. Hughes?" Ray asked; and he restrained himself in a pretended question.

"Of Mr. Hughes, and of Mr. Hughes's friends."

Ray flashed out upon this. "I think his friends are a lot of cranks."

"Yes; very good; very excellent good! They *are* a lot of cranks. Are they the first you have met in New York?"
9

"No; the place seems to be full of them."

"Beginning with the elderly gentleman whom you met the first morning?"

"Beginning with the young man who met the elderly gentleman."

Kane smiled with appreciation. "Well, we won't be harsh on those two. We won't call *them* cranks. They are philosophical observers, or inspired dreamers, if you like. As I understand it, we are all dreamers. If we like a man's dream, we call him a prophet; if we don't like his dream, we call him a crank. Now, what is the matter with the dreams, severally and collectively, of my dear old friend and his friends? Can you deny that any one of their remedies, if taken faithfully according to the directions blown on the bottle, would cure the world of all its woes inside of six months?"

The question gave Ray a chance to vent his vexation impersonally. "What is the matter with the world?" he burst out. "I don't see that the world is so very sick. Why isn't it going on very well? I don't understand what this talk is all about. I don't see what those people have got to complain of. All any one can ask is a fair chance to show how much his work is worth, and let the best man win. What's the trouble? Where's the wrong?"

"Ah," said Kane, "what a pity you didn't set forth those ideas when Hughes called upon you!"

"And have all that crew jump on me? Thank you!" said Ray.

"You would call them a crew, then? Perhaps they were a crew," said Kane. "I don't know why a reformer should be so grotesque; but he is, and he is always the easy prey of caricature. I couldn't help feeling to-day how very like the burlesque reformers the real reformers are. And they are always the same, from generation to generation.) For all outward difference, those men and brethren of both sexes at poor David's were very like a group of old-time abolitionists conscientiously qualifying themselves for tar and feathers. Perhaps you don't like being spoken to in meeting?"

"No, I don't," said Ray, bluntly.

"I fancied a certain reluctance in you at the time, but I don't think poor David meant any harm. He preaches patience, but I think he secretly feels that he's got to hurry, if he's going to have the kingdom of heaven on earth in his time; and he wants every one to lend a hand."

For the reason, or from the instinct, that forbade Ray to let out his wrath directly against Hughes, he now concealed his pity. He asked stiffly: "Couldn't he be got into some better place? Where he wouldn't be stunned when he tried to keep from suffocating?"

"No, I don't know that he could," said Kane, with a pensive singleness rare in him. "Any help of that kind would mean dependence, and David Hughes is proud."

They had passed through lofty ranks of flats, and they now came to the viaduct carrying the northern

railways ; one of its noble arches opened before them
like a city gate, and the viaduct in its massy extent
was like a wall that had stood a hundred sieges. Beyond they found open fields, with the old farm fences
of stone still enclosing them, but with the cellars of
city blocks dug out of the lots. In one place there
was a spread of low sheds, neighbored by towering
apartment-houses ; some old cart-horses were cropping
the belated grass ; and comfortable companies of hens
and groups of turkeys were picking about the stable-
yard ; a shambling cottage fronted on the avenue next
the park, and drooped behind its dusty, leafless vines.

"He might be got into that," said Kane, whimsically, "at no increase of rent, and at much increase of
comfort and quiet — at least till the Afreet began to
get in his work."

"Wouldn't it be rather too much like that eremitism
which he's so down on ? " asked Ray, with a persistence
in his effect of indifference.

"Perhaps it would, perhaps it would," Kane consented, as they struck across into the Park. The grass
was still very green, though here and there a little sal-
low ; the leaves, which had dropped from the trees in
the October rains, had lost their fire, and lay dull and
brown in the little hollows and at the edges of the
paths and the bases of the rocks ; the oaks kept theirs,
but in death ; on some of the ash-trees and lindens the
leaves hung in a pale reminiscence of their summer
green.

"I understood the son-in-law to want a hermitage

somewhere — a co-operative hermitage, I suppose,"
Ray went on. He did not feel bound to spare the
son-in-law, and he put contempt into his tone.

" Ah, yes," said Kane. " What did you make of
the son-in-law ? "

" I don't know. He's a gloomy sprite. What is
he, anyway ? His wife spoke of his work."

" Why, it's rather a romantic story, I believe," said
Kane. " He was a young fellow who stopped at the
community on his way to a place where he was going
to find work; he's a wood-engraver. I believe he's
always had the notion that the world was out of kilter,
and it seems that he wasn't very well himself when he
looked in on the Family to see what they were doing
to help it. He fell sick on their hands, and the
Hugheses took care of him. Naturally, he married
one of them when he got well enough, and naturally
he married the wrong one."

" Why the wrong one?" demanded Ray, with an
obscure discomfort.

" Well, I don't know! But if it isn't evident to you
that Mrs. Denton is hardly fitted to be the guide,
philosopher, and friend of such a man " —

Ray would not pursue this branch of the inquiry.
" *His* notion of what the world wanted was to have its
cities eliminated. Then he thought it would be all
serene."

" Ah, that wouldn't do," said Kane. " Cities are a
vice, but they are essential to us now. We could not
live without them; perhaps we are to be saved by

them. But it is well to return to Nature from time
to time."

"I thought I heard you saying some rather dis-
paraging things of Nature a little while ago," said
Ray, with a remaining grudge against Kane, and with
a young man's willingness to convict his elder of any
inconsistency, serious or unserious.

"Oh, primeval Nature, yes. But I have nothing
but praise for this kind — the kind that man controls
and guides. It is outlaw Nature that I object to, the
savage survival from chaos, the mother of earthquakes
and cyclones, blizzards and untimely frosts, inunda-
tions and indigestions. But ordered Nature — the
Nature of the rolling year; night and day, and seed-
time and harvest " —

"The seasons," Ray broke in scornfully, from the
resentment still souring in his soul, "turn themselves
upside down and wrong end to, about as often as
financial panics occur, and the farmer that has to rely
on them is as apt to get left as the husbandman that
sows and reaps in Wall Street."

"Ah!" sighed Kane. "That was well said. I
wish I had thought of it for my second series of *Hard
Sayings*."

"Oh, you're welcome to it!"

"Are you so rich in paradoxes? But I will con-
trive to credit it somehow to the gifted author of *A
New Romeo*. Is that what you call it?"

Ray blushed and laughed, and Kane continued:

"It's a little beyond the fact, but it's on the lines of

truth. I don't justify Nature altogether. She is not free from certain little foibles, caprices ; perhaps that's why we call her *she*. But I don't think that, with all her faults, she's quite so bad as Business. In that we seem to have gone to Nature for her defects. Why copy her weakness and bad faith ? Why not study her steadfastness, her orderliness, her obedience, in laying the bases of civilization ? We don't go to her for the justification of murder, incest, robbery, gluttony, though you can find them all in her. We have our little prejudice against these things, and we seem to derive it from somewhere outside of what we call Nature. Why not go to that Somewhere for the law of economic life ? But come," Kane broke off, gayly, " let us babble of green fields ; as for God, God, I hope we have no need to think of such things yet. Please Heaven, our noses are not as sharp as pens, by a long way. I don't wonder you find it a beautiful and beneficent world, in spite of our friends yonder, who want to make it prettier and better, in their way." Kane put his arm across Ray's shoulder, and pulled him affectionately towards him. "Are you vexed with me for having introduced you to those people ? I have been imagining something of the kind."

"Oh, no " — Ray began.

" I didn't really mean to stay for Hughes's conventicle," said Kane. " Chapley was wise, and went in time, before he could feel the wild charm of those visionaries ; it was too much for me ; when they began to come, I *couldn't* go. I forgot how repugnant the golden age has always been to the heart of youth, which likes the nineteenth century much better. The fact is, I forgot that I had brought you till it was too late to take you away."

He laughed, and Ray, more reluctantly, laughed with him.

"I have often wondered," he went on, "how it is we lose the youthful point of view. We have it some night, and the next morning we haven't it; and we can hardly remember what it was. I don't suppose you could tell me what the youthful point of view of the present day is, though I should recognize that of forty years ago. I " —

He broke off to look at a party of horsemen pelting by on the stretch of the smooth hard road, and dashing into a bridle-path beyond. They were heavy young fellows, mounted on perfectly groomed trotters, whose round haunches trembled and dimpled with their hard pace.

"Perhaps *that* is the youthful point of view now: the healthy, the wealthy, the physically strong, the materially rich. Well, I think ours was better; pallid and poor in person and in purse as we imagined the condition of the ideal man to be. There is something," said Kane, "a little more expressive of the insolence of money in one of those brutes than in the most glittering carriage and pair. I think if I had in me the material for really hating a fellow-man, I should apply it to the detestation of the rider of one of those animals. But I haven't. I am not in prospective need even, and I am at the moment no hungrier than a gentleman ought to be who is going to lunch with a lady in the Mandan Flats. By-the-way! Why shouldn't you come with me? They would be delighted to see you. A brilliant young widow, with a pretty step-daughter, is not to be lunched with every day, and I can answer for your welcome."

Ray freed himself. " I'm sorry I can't go. But I can't. You must excuse me; I really couldn't; I am very much obliged to you. But " —

" You don't trust me ! "

" Oh, yes, I do. But I don't feel quite up to meeting people just now; I'll push on down town. I'm rather tired. Good-by."

Kane held his hand between both his palms. " I wonder what the real reason is! Is it grudge, or pride, or youth ? "

" Neither," said Ray. " It's — clothes. My boots are muddy, and I've got on my second-best trousers."

" Ah, now you are frank with me, and you give me a real reason. Perhaps you are right. I dare say I should have thought so once."

XVIII.

RAY did not go to deliver any of his letters that afternoon ; he decided now that it would be out of taste to do so on Sunday, as he had already doubted that it would be, in the morning. He passed the afternoon in his room, trying from time to time to re-duce the turmoil of his reveries to intelligible terms in verse, and in poetic prose. He did nothing with them ; in the end, though, he was aware of a new ideal, and he resolved that if he could get his story back from Chapley & Co., he would rewrite the pas-sages that characterized the heroine, and make it less like the every-day, simple prettiness of his first love. He had always known that this did not suit the character he had imagined ; he now saw that it re-quired a more complex and mystical charm. But he did not allow himself to formulate these volitions and perceptions, any more than his conviction that he had now a double reason for keeping away from Mr. Brandreth and from Miss Hughes. He spent the week in an ecstasy of forbearance. On Saturday afternoon he feigned the necessity of going to ask Mr. Brandreth how he thought a novel in verse, treating a strictly American subject in a fantastic way, would succeed. He really wished to learn something without seeming to wish it, about his manuscript, but he called so late in the afternoon that he found Mr. Brandreth putting his desk in order just before starting home. He professed a great pleasure at sight of Ray, and said he wished he would come part of the way home with him; he wanted to have a little talk.

As if the word home had roused the latent forces of hospitality in him, he added, "I want to have you up at my place, some day, as soon as we can get turned round. Mrs. Brandreth is doing first-rate, now; and that boy — well, sir, he's a perfect Titan. I wish you could see him undressed. He's just like the figure of the infant Hercules strangling the serpent when he grips the nurse's finger. I know it sounds ridiculous, but I believe that fellow recognizes me, and dis- tinguishes between me and his mother. I suppose it's my hat — I come in with my hat on, you know, just to try him; and when he catches sight of that hat, you ought to see his arms go!"

The paternal rhapsodies continued a long time after they were in the street, and Ray got no chance to bring in either his real or pretended business. He listened with mechanical smiles and hollow laughter, alert at the same time for the slightest vantage which Mr. Brandreth should give him. But the publisher said of his own motion:

"Oh, by-the-way, you'll be interested to know that our readers' reports on your story are in."

"Are they?" Ray gasped. He could not get out any more.

Mr. Brandreth went on : " I didn't examine the reports very attentively myself, but I think they were favorable, on the whole. There were several changes suggested : I don't recall just what. But you can see them all on Monday. We let Miss Hughes go after lunch on Saturdays, and she generally takes some work home with her, and I gave them to her to put in shape for you. I thought it would be rather instructive for you to see the different opinions in the right form. I believe you can't have too much method in these things."

" Of course," said Ray, in an anguish of hope and fear. The street seemed to go round ; he hardly knew where he was. He bungled on inarticulately before he could say : " I believe in method, too. But I'm sorry I couldn't have had the reports to-day, because I might have had Sunday to think the suggestions over, and see what I could do with them."

" Well, I'm sorry, too. She hadn't been gone half an hour when you came in. If I'd thought of your happening in ! Well, it isn't very long till Monday ! She'll have them ready by that time. I make it a rule myself to put all business out of my mind from 2 P. M. on Saturday till Monday 9 A. M., and I think you'll find it an advantage, too. I won't do business, and I won't talk business, and I won't think business after two o'clock on Saturday. I believe in making Sunday a day of rest and family enjoyment. We have an early dinner ; and then I like to have my wife read or play to me, and now we have in the baby, and that amuses us."

Ray forced himself to say that as a rule he did not believe in working on Sunday either; he usually wrote letters. He abruptly asked Mr. Brandreth how he thought it would do for him to go and ask Miss Hughes for a sight of the readers' reports in the rough.

Mr. Brandreth laughed. "You *are* anxious! Do you know where she lives?"

"Oh, yes; I stopped there last Sunday with Mr. Kane on our way to the Park. I saw Mr. Chapley there."

"Oh!" said Mr. Brandreth, with the effect of being arrested by the last fact in something he might otherwise have said. It seemed to make him rather unhappy. "Then you saw Miss Hughes's father?"

"Yes; and all his friends," Ray answered, in a way that evidently encouraged Mr. Brandreth to go on.

"Yes? What did you think of them?"

"I thought they were mostly harmless; but one or two of them ought to have been in the violent wards."

"Did Mr. Chapley meet them?"

"Oh, no; he went away before any of them came in. As Mr. Kane took me, I had to stay with him."

Mr. Brandreth got back a good deal of his smiling complacency, which had left him at Ray's mention of Mr. Chapley in connection with Hughes. "Mr. Chapley and Mr. Hughes are old friends."

"Yes; I understood something of that kind."

"They date back to the Brook Farm days together."

"Mr. Hughes is rather too much of the Hollings-worth type for my use," said Ray. He wished Mr. Brandreth to understand that he had no sympathy with Hughes's wild-cat philosophy, both because he had none, and because he believed it would be to his interest with Mr. Brandreth to have none.

"I've never seen him," said Mr. Brandreth. "I like Mr. Chapley's loyalty to his friends — it's one of his fine traits; but I don't see any necessity for my taking them up. He goes there every Sunday morning to see Mr. Hughes, and they talk — political economy together. You knew Mr. Chapley has been a good deal interested in this altruistic agitation."

"No, I didn't," said Ray.

"Yes. You can't very well keep clear of it altogether. I was mixed up in it myself at one time : our summer place is on the outskirts of a manufacturing town in Massachusetts, and we had our *Romeo and Juliet* for the benefit of a social union for the workpeople; we made over two hundred dollars for them. Mr. Chapley was a George man in '86. Not that he agreed with the George men exactly; but he thought there ought to be some expression against the way things are going. You know a good many of the nicest kind of people went the same way at that time. I don't object to that kind of thing as long as it isn't carried too far. Mr. Chapley used to see a good deal of an odd stick of a minister at our summer place that had got some of the new ideas in a pretty crooked kind of shape; and then he's read Tolstoï a good deal, and he's been influenced by him. I think Hughes is a sort of safety valve for Mr. Chapley, and that's what I tell the family. Mr. Chapley isn't a fool, and he's always had as good an eye for the main chance as anybody. That's all."

Ray divined that Mr. Brandreth would not have entered into this explanation of his senior partner and father-in-law, except to guard against the injurious inferences which he might draw from having met Mr. Chapley at Hughes's, but he did not let his guess appear in his words. "I don't wonder he likes Mr. Hughes," he said. "He's fine, and he seems a light of sanity and reason among the jack-a-lanterns he gathers round him. He isn't at all Tolstoïan."

"He's a gentleman, born and bred," said Mr. Brandreth, "and he was a rich man for the days before he began his communistic career. And Miss Hughes is a perfect lady. She's a cultivated girl, too, and she reads a great deal. I'd rather have her opinion about a new book than half the critics' I know of, because I know I could get it honest, and I know it would be intelligent. Well, if you're going up there, you'll want to be getting across to the avenue to take the elevated." He added, "I don't mean to give you the impression that we've made up our minds about your book, yet. We haven't. A book is a commercial venture as well as a literary venture, and we've got to have a pow-wow about that side of it before we come to any sort of conclusion. You understand?"

"Oh, yes, I understand that," said Ray, "and I'll

try not to be unreasonably hopeful," but at the same
moment his heart leaped with hope.

"Well, that's right," said Mr. Brandreth, taking his
hand for parting. He held it, and then he said, with
a sort of desperate impulse, "By-the-way, why not
come home with me, now, and take dinner with us?"

XIX.

Ray's heart sank. He was so anxious to get at those opinions; and yet he did not like to refuse Mr. Brandreth; a little thing might prejudice the case; he ought to make all the favor at court that he could for his book. "I — I'm afraid it mightn't be convenient — at such a time — for Mrs. Brandreth "—

"Oh, yes it would," said Mr. Brandreth in the same desperate note. "Come along. I don't know that Mrs. Brandreth will be able to see you, but I want you to see my boy; and we can have a bachelor bite together, anyway."

Ray yielded, and the stories of the baby began again when he moved on with Mr. Brandreth. It was agony for him to wrench his mind from his story, which he kept turning over and over in it, trying to imagine what the readers had differed about, and listen to Mr. Brandreth saying, "Yes, sir, I believe that child knows his grandmother and his nurse apart, as well as he knows his mother and me. He's got his likes and his dislikes already: he cries whenever his grandmother takes him. By-the-way, you'll see Mrs. Chapley at dinner, I hope. She's spending the day with us."

"Oh, I'm very glad," said Ray, wondering if the readers objected to his introduction of hypnotism.
10

"She's a woman of the greatest character," said Mr.
Brandreth, "but she has some old-fashioned notions
about children. I want my boy to be trained as a boy
from the very start. I think there's nothing like a
manly man, unless it's a womanly woman. I hate
anything masculine about a girl; a girl ought to be
yielding and gentle; but I want my boy to be self-
reliant from the word Go. I believe in a man's being
master in his own house; his will ought to be law, and
that's the way I shall bring up my boy. Mrs. Chapley thinks there ought always to be a light in the
nurse's room, but I don't. I want my boy to get used
to the dark, and not be afraid of it, and I shall begin
just as soon as I can, without seeming arbitrary. Mrs.
Chapley is the best soul in the world, and of course I
don't like to differ with her."

"Of course," said Ray. The mention of relation-
ship made him think of the cousin in his story; if he
had not had the cousin killed, he thought it would
have been better; there was too much bloodshed in
the story.

They turned into a cross-street from Lexington Avenue, where they had been walking, and stopped at a
pretty little apartment-house, which had its door painted
black and a wide brass plate enclosing its key-hole, and
wore that air of standing aloof from its neighbors
peculiar to private houses with black doors and brass
plates.

Mr. Brandreth let himself in with a key. "There
are only three families in our house, and it's like

THE WORLD OF CHANCE.

having a house of our own. It's so much easier living
in a flat for your wife, that I put my foot down, and
wouldn't hear of a separate house."

They mounted the carpeted stairs through the twilight that prevails in such entries, and a sound of
flying steps was heard within the door where Mr.
Brandreth applied his latch-key again, and as · he flung
it open a long wail burst upon the ear.

"Hear that?" he asked, with a rapturous smile, as
he turned to Ray for sympathy; and then he called
gayly out in the direction that the wail came from;
"Oh, hello, hello, hello! What's the matter, what's
the matter? You sit down here,"· he said to Ray,
leading the way forward into a pretty drawing-room.
He caught something away from before the fire.
"Confound that nurse! She's always coming in here
in spite of everything. I'll be with you in a moment.
Heigh! What ails the little man?" he called out,
and disappeared down the long narrow corridor, and
he was gone a good while.

At moments Ray caught the sound of voices in
hushed, but vehement dispute; a door slammed vio-
lently; there were murmurs of expostulation. At last
Mr. Brandreth reappeared with his baby in his arms,
and its nurse at his heels, twitching the infant's long
robe into place.

"What do you think of that?" demanded the
father, and Ray got to his feet and came near, so as to
be able to see if he could think anything.

By an inspiration he was able to say, "Well, he *is*

a great fellow!" and this apparently gave Mr. Brandreth perfect satisfaction. His son's downy little oblong skull wagged feebly on his weak neck, his arms waved vaguely before his face.

" Now give him your finger, and see if he won't do the infant Hercules act."

Ray promptly assumed the part of the serpent, but the infant Hercules would not open his tightly-clinched, wandering fist.

" Try the other one," said his father; and Ray tried the other one with no more effect. " Well, he isn't in the humor; he'll do it for you some time. All right, little man!" He gave the baby, which had acquitted itself with so much distinction, back into the arms of its nurse, and it was taken away.

" Sit down, sit down!" he said, cheerily. " Mrs. Chapley will be in directly. It's astonishing," he said, with a twist of his head in the direction the baby had been taken, " but I believe those little things have their moods just like any of us. That fellow knows as well as you do, when he's wanted to show off, and if he isn't quite in the key for it, he won't do it. I wish I had tried him with my hat, and let you see how he notices."

Mr. Brandreth went on with anecdotes, theories, and moral reflections relating to the baby, and Ray answered with praiseful murmurs and perfunctory cries of wonder. He was rescued from a situation which he found more and more difficult by the advent of Mrs. Chapley, and not of Mrs. Chapley alone, but of Mrs. Brandreth. She greeted Ray with a certain severity, which he instinctively divined was not so much for him as for her husband. A like quality imparted itself, but not so authoritatively, from her mother; if Mr. Brandreth was not master in his house, at least his mother-in-law was not. Mrs. Brandreth went about the room and made some housekeeperly rearrangements of its furniture, which had the result of reducing it, as it were, to discipline. Then she sat down, and Ray, whom she waited to have speak first, had a feeling that she was sitting in judgment on him, and the wish, if possible, to justify himself. He began to praise the baby, its beauty, and great size, and the likeness he professed to find in it to its father.

Mrs. Brandreth relented slightly. She said, with magnanimous impartiality, "It's a very *healthy* child."

Her mother made the reservation, "But even healthy children are a great care," and sighed.

The daughter must have found this intrusive. "Oh, I don't know that Percy is any great care as yet, mamma."

"He pays his way," Mr. Brandreth suggested, with a radiant smile. "At least," he corrected himself, "we shouldn't know what to do without him."

His wife said, drily, as if the remark were in bad taste, "It's hardly a question of that, I think. Have you been long in New York, Mr. Ray?" she asked, with an abrupt turn to him.

"Only a few weeks," Ray answered, inwardly wondering how he could render the fact propitiatory.

" Everything is very curious and interesting to me as
a country person," he added, deciding to make this
sacrifice of himself.

It evidently availed somewhat. " But you don't
mean that you are really from the country?" Mrs.
Brandreth asked.

" I'm from Midland; and I suppose that's the
country, compared with New York."

Mrs. Chapley asked him if he knew the Mayquayts
there. He tried to think of some people of that name;
in the meantime she recollected that the Mayquayts
were from Gitchigumee, Michigan. They talked some
irrelevancies, and then she said, " Mr. Brandreth tells
me you have *met* my husband," as if they had been
talking of him.

" Yes; I had that pleasure even before I met Mr.
Brandreth," said Ray.

" And you know Mr. Kane?"

" Oh, yes. He was the first acquaintance I made
in New York."

" Mr. Brandreth told me." Mrs. Chapley made a
show of laughing at the notion of Kane, as a harmless
eccentric, and she had the effect of extending her
kindly derision to Hughes, in saying, " And you've
been taken to sit at the feet of his prophet already,
Mr. Brandreth tells me; that strange Mr. Hughes."

" I shouldn't have said he was Mr. Kane's prophet
exactly," said Ray with a smile of sympathy. " Mr.
Kane doesn't seem to need a prophet; but I've certainly
seen Mr. Hughes. And heard him, for that matter."

He smiled, recollecting his dismay when he heard Hughes calling upon him in meeting. He had a notion to describe his experience, and she gave him the chance.

"Yes?" she said, with veiled anxiety. "Do tell me about him!"

At the end of Ray's willing compliance, she drew a deep breath, and said, "Then he is *not* a follower of Tolstoï?"

"Quite the contrary, I should say."

Mrs. Chapley laughed more easily. "I didn't know but he made shoes that nobody could wear. I couldn't imagine what other attraction he could have for my husband. I believe he would really like to go into the country and work in the fields." Mrs. Chapley laughed away a latent anxiety, apparently, in making this joke about her husband, and seemed to feel much better acquainted with Ray. "How are they living over there? What sort of family has Mr. Hughes? I mean, besides the daughter we know of?"

Ray told, as well as he could, and he said they were living in an apartment.

"Oh!" said Mrs. Chapley, "I fancied a sort of tenement."

"By-the-way," said Mr. Brandreth, "wouldn't you like to see our apartment, Mr. Ray"—his wife quelled him with a glance, and he added,—"some time?"

Ray said he should, very much.

Mrs. Brandreth, like her mother, had been growing

more and more clement, and now she said, "Won't
you stay and take a family dinner with us, Mr. Ray?"

Ray looked at her husband, and saw that he had
not told her of the invitation he had already given.
He did not do so now, and Ray rose and seized his
opportunity.   He thanked Mrs. Brandreth very
earnestly, and said he was so sorry he had an appoint-
ment to keep, and he got himself away at once.

Mrs. Chapley hospitably claimed him for her
Thursdays, at parting; and Mrs. Brandreth said he
must let Mr. Brandreth bring him some other day;
they would always be glad to see him.

Mr. Brandreth went down to the outer door with
him, to make sure that he found the way, and said,
"Then you *will* come some time?" and gratefully
wrung his hand.   "I saw how anxious you were
about those opinions!"

XX.

WITH an impatience whose intensity he began to feel as soon as he permitted himself to indulge it, Ray hurried across to the line of the elevated road. Now he perceived how intolerable it would be to have staid to dinner with the Brandreths. He did not resent the failure of Mr. Brandreth to tell his wife that he had already asked him when she asked him again; he did not even care to know what his reasons or exigencies were; the second invitation had been a chance to get away. From time to time while Mr. Brandreth was showing him the baby, and then while Mrs. Chapley was setting her mind at rest about her husband by her researches into the philosophy and character of Hughes, he had superficially forgotten that the readers' opinions of his story were in, while his nether thought writhed in anguish around the question of what their opinions were. When at moments this fully penetrated his consciousness, it was like a sort of vertigo, and he was light-headed with it now as he walked, or almost ran, away from Mr. Brandreth's door. He meant to see Miss Hughes, and beg for a sight of the criticisms; perhaps she might say something that would save him from the worst, if they were very bad. He imagined a perfect interview, in which he met no one but her.

It was Mrs. Denton who stood at the head of the stairs to receive him when the door promptly opened to his ring; she explained that her husband had put the lock in order since she last admitted him. Ray managed to say that he wished merely to see her sister for a moment, and why, and she said that Peace had gone out, but would be at home again very soon. She said her father would be glad to have him sit down with him till Peace came back.

Ray submitted. He found the old man coughing beside the front window, that looked out on the lines of the railroad, and the ugly avenue beneath.

Hughes knew him at once, and called to him: "Well, young man! I am glad to see you! How do you do?" He held out his hand when he was seated, and when Ray had shaken it, he motioned with it to the vacant chair on the other side of the window.

"I hope you are well, sir?" said Ray.

"I'm getting the better of this nasty cough gradually, and I pick up a little new strength every day. Yes, I'm doing very well. For the present I have to keep housed, and that's tiresome. But it gives me time for a bit of writing that I have in hand; I'm putting together the impressions that this civilization of yours makes on me, in a little book that I call *The World Revisited*."

Ray did not see exactly why Hughes should say *his* civilization, as if he had invented it; but he did not disclaim it; and Hughes went on without interruption from him.

"I hope to get my old friend Chapley to bring it out for me, if I can reconcile him to its radical opinions. He's timid, Chapley is ; and my book's rather bold."

Ray's thought darted almost instantly to his own book, and ran it over in every part, seeking whether there might be something in it that was too bold for a timid publisher, or a timid publisher's professional readers. He was aware of old Hughes monologuing on with the satisfaction of an author who speaks of his work to a listener he has at his mercy.

"My book is a criticism of modern life in all its aspects, though necessarily as the field is so vast, I can touch on some only in the most cursory fashion. For instance, take this whole architectural nightmare that we call a city. I hold that the average tasteless man has no right to realize his ideas of a house in the presence of a great multitude of his fellow-beings. It is an indecent exposure of his mind, and should not be permitted. All these structural forms about us, which with scarcely an exception are ugly and senseless, I regard as so many immoralities, as deliriums, as imbecilities, which a civilized state would not permit, and I say so in my book. The city should build the city, and provide every denizen with a fit and beautiful habitation to work in and rest in."

"I'm afraid," said Ray, tearing his mind from his book to put it on this proposition, "that such an idea might be found rather startling."

"How, startling? Why, startling?" Hughes demanded.

"I don't know. Wouldn't it infringe upon private rights? Wouldn't it be a little tyrannical?"

"What private rights has a man in the outside of his house" Hughes retorted. "The interior might be left to his ignorance and vulgarity. But the outside of my house is not for *me!* It's for others! The public sees it ten times where I see it once. If I make it brutal and stupid, *I* am the tyrant, *I* am the oppressor — I, the individual! Besides, when the sovereign people is really lord of itself, it can and will do no man wrong."

Ray had his misgivings, but he would not urge them, because it was a gnawing misery to think of anything but his story, and he let Hughes break the silence that he let follow.

"And so," the old man said presently, as if speaking of his own book had reminded him of Ray's, "you have written a novel, young man. And what is your justification for writing a novel at a time like this, when we are all trembling on the verge of a social cataclysm?"

"Justification?" Ray faltered.

"Yes. How does it justify itself? How does it serve God and help man? Does it dabble with the passion of love between a girl and boy as if that were the chief concern of men and women? Or does it touch some of the real concerns of life — some of the problems pressing on to their solution, and needing the prayerful attention of every human creature?"

"It isn't merely a love-story," said Ray, glad to get

to it on any terms, "though it is a love-story. But
I've ventured to employ a sort of psychological motive."

"What sort?"

"Well — hypnotism."

"A mere toy, that Poe and Hawthorne played
with in the old mesmerist days, and I don't know how
many others."

"I don't play with it as they did, exactly," said
Ray.

"Oh, I've no doubt you employ it to as new effect
as the scientifics who are playing with it again. But
how can you live in this camp of embattled forces,
where luxury and misery are armed against each
other, and every lover of his kind should give heart
and brain to the solution of the riddle that is madden-
ing brother against brother, — how can you live on
here and be content with the artistic study of
hysteria?"

The strong words of the old man, which fell tingling
with emotion, had no meaning for the soul of youth in
Ray; he valued them æsthetically, but he could not
make personal application of them. He had a kind of
amusement in answering: "Well, I'm not quite so
bad as you think, Mr. Hughes. I wrote my story
several years ago. I don't suppose I could do anything of the kind, now."

Hughes's mouth seemed stopped for the moment by
this excuse. He sat glaring at Ray's bright, handsome
face through his overhanging, shaggy eyebrows, and

seemed waiting to gather strength for another onset, when his daughter Peace came silently into the room behind Ray.

Her father did not give her time to greet their visitor. " Well," he called out with a voice of stormy pathos, " how did you leave that poor woman ? "

" She is dead," answered the girl.

" Good ! " said Hughes. " So far, so good. Who is living ? "

" There are several children. The people in the house are taking care of them."

" Of course ! There, young man," said Hughes, " is a psychological problem better worth your study than the phenomena of hypnotism : the ability of poverty to provide for want out of its very destitution. The miracle of the loaves and fishes is wrought here every day in the great tenement-houses. Those who have nothing for themselves can still find something for others. The direst want may be trusted to share its crust with those who have not a crust ; and still something remains, as if Christ had blessed the bread and broken it among the famishing. Don't you think that an interesting and romantic fact, a mystery meriting the attention of literary art ? "

It did strike Ray as a good notion ; something might be done with it, say in a Christmas story, if you could get hold of a tenement-house incident of that kind, and keep it from becoming allegorical in the working out.

This went through Ray's mind as he stood thinking

also how he should ask the girl for his manuscript and
the criticisms on it without seeming foolishly eager.
Her father's formidable intervention had dispensed
him from the usual greetings, and he could only say,
"Oh! Miss Hughes, Mr. Brandreth told me I might
come and get my story of you — *A Modern Romeo* —
and the readers' opinions. I — I thought I should
like to look them over; and — and " —

"I haven't had time to copy them yet," she answered. "Mr. Brandreth wished you to see them;
but we keep the readers anonymous, and he thought I
had better show them to you all in my handwriting."

"I shouldn't know the writers. He said I could see
them as they are."

"Well, then, I will go and get them for you," she
answered. She left him a moment, and he remained
with her father unmolested. The old man sat staring
out on the avenue, with his head black against its
gathering lights.

She gave him the packet she brought back with her,
and then she followed him out of the apartment upon
the landing, after he had made his acknowledgments
and adieux.

"I thought," she said, timidly, "you would like to
know that I had given your dollar for these poor children. Was that right?"

Ray's head was so full of his story that he answered
vaguely, "My dollar?" Then he remembered. "Oh!
Oh yes! It was right — quite right! I'm glad you
did it. Miss Hughes! Excuse me; but would you

mind telling me whether you have happened to look at
the story yourself?"

She hesitated, and then answered: "Yes, I've read
it."

"Oh, then," he bubbled out, knowing that he was
wrong and foolish, but helpless to refrain, "before I
read those things, won't you tell me — I should care
more — I should like so much to know what *you* — I
suppose I've no right to ask!"

He tried to make some show of decency about the
matter, but in fact he had the heart to ask a dying man
his opinion, in that literary passion which spares nothing, and is as protean as love itself in its disguises.

"I suppose," she answered, "that I had no right to
read it; I wasn't asked to do it."

"Oh, yes, you had.   I'm very glad you did."

"The opinions about it were so different that I
couldn't help looking at it, and then — I kept on," she
said.

"Were they so *very* different?" he asked, trembling
with his author's sensitiveness, while the implication of
praise in her confession worked like a frenzied hope in
his brain.   "And you kept on?   Then it interested
you?"

She did not answer this question, but said: "None
of them thought just alike about it.   But you'll see
them" —

"No, no!   Tell me what you thought of it yourself!   Was there some part that seemed better than
the rest?"

She hesitated. " No, I would rather not say. I oughtn't to have told you I had read it."

" You didn't like it ! "

" Yes ; I did like parts of it. But I musn't say any more."

" But what parts ? " he pleaded.

" You mustn't ask me. The readers' opinions " —

" I don't care for them. I care for your opinion," said Ray, perversely. " What did you mean by their being all different ? Of course, I'm absurd ! But you don't know how much depends upon this book. It isn't that it's the only book I expect ever to write ; but if it should be rejected ! I've had to wait a long while already ; and then to have to go peddling it around among the other publishers ! Do you think that it's hopelessly bad, or could I make it over ? What did you dislike in it ? Didn't you approve of the hypnotism ? That was the only thing I could think of to bring about the climax. And did it seem too melodramatic ? *Romeo and Juliet* is melodramatic ! I hope you won't think I'm usually so nervous about my work," he went on, wondering that he should be giving himself away so freely, when he was really so reserved. " I've been a long time writing the story ; and I've worked over it and worked over it, till I've quite lost the sense of it. I don't believe I can make head or tail of those opinions. That's the reason why I wanted you to tell me what you thought of it yourself."

" But I have no right to do that. It would be inter-
11

fering with other people's work.   It wouldn't be fair towards Mr. Brandreth," she pleaded.

" I see.   I didn't see that before.   And you're quite right, and I beg your pardon.   Good-night ! "

He put his manuscript on the seat in the elevated train, and partly sat upon it, that he might not forget it when he left the car.   But as he read the professional opinions of it he wished the thing could lose him, and never find him again.   No other novel, he thought, could ever have had such a variety of certain faults, together with the vague merit which each of its critics seemed to feel in greater measure or less.   Their work, he had to own, had been faithfully done; he had not even the poor consolation of accusing them of a neglect of duty.   They had each read his story, and they spoke of it with intelligence in a way, if not every way.   Each condemned it on a different ground, but as it stood they all joined in condemning it; and they did not so much contradict one another as dwell on different defects; so that together they covered the whole field with their censure.   One of them reproached it for its crude realism, and the sort of helpless fidelity to provincial conditions which seemed to come from the author's ignorance of anything different. Another blamed the youthful romanticism of its dealings with passion.   A third pointed out the gross improbability of the plot in our modern circumstance. A fourth objected to the employment of hypnotism as a clumsy piece of machinery, and an attempt to reach the public interest through a prevailing fad.   A fifth touched upon the obvious imitation of Hawthorne in the psychical analyses. A sixth accused the author of having adopted Thackeray's manner without Thackeray's material.

Ray resented, with a keen sense of personal affront, these criticisms in severalty, but their combined effect was utter humiliation, though they were less true taken together than they were separately. At the bottom of his sore and angry heart he could not deny their truth, and yet he knew that there was something in his book which none of them had taken account of, and that this was its life, which had come out of his own. He was aware of all those crude and awkward and affected things, but he believed there was something, too, that went with them, and that had not been in fiction before.

It was this something which he hoped that girl had felt in his story, and which he was trying to get her to own to him before he looked at the opinions. They confounded and distracted him beyond his foreboding even, and it was an added anguish to keep wondering, as he did all night, whether she had really found anything more in the novel than his critics had. As he turned from side to side and beat his pillow into this shape and that, he reconstructed the story after one critic's suggestion, and then after another's; but the material only grew more defiant and impossible; if it could not keep the shape it had, it would take no other. That was plain; and the only thing to be done was to throw it away, and write something else; for it

was not reasonable to suppose that Mr. Brandreth
would think of bringing the book out in the teeth of
all these adverse critics.　But now he had no heart to
think of anything else, although he was always thinking of something else, while there was hope of getting
this published.　His career as an author was at an
end; he must look about for some sort of newspaper
work; he ought to be very glad if he could get something to do as a space man.

XXI.

He rose, after a late nap following his night-long vigils, with despair in his soul. He believed it was despair, and so it was to all intents and purposes. But, when he had bathed, he seemed to have washed a little of his despair away; when he had dressed, he felt hungry, and he ate his breakfast with rather more than his usual appetite.

The reaction was merely physical, and his gloom settled round him again when he went back to his attic and saw his manuscript and those deadly opinions. He had not the heart to go out anywhere, and he cowered alone in his room. If he could only get the light of some other mind on the facts he might grapple with them; but without this he was limp and helpless. Now he knew, in spite of all his pretences to the contrary, in spite of the warnings and cautions he had given himself, that he had not only hoped, but had expected, that his story would be found good enough to publish. Yet none of these readers — even those who found some meritorious traits in it — had apparently dreamed of recommending it for publication. It was no wonder that Miss Hughes had been so unwilling to tell him what she thought of it; that she had urged him so strongly to read the opinions first. What a fool she must have thought him!

There was no one else he could appeal to, unless it was old Kane. He did not know where Kane lived, even if he could have gathered the courage to go to him in his extremity; and he bet himself that Kane would not repeat his last Sunday's visit. The time for any reasonable hope of losing passed, and then to his great joy he lost. There came a hesitating step outside his door, as if some one were in doubt where to knock, and then a tap at it.

Ray flung it open, and at sight of Kane the tears came into his eyes, and he could not speak.

"Why, my dear friend!" cried Kane, "what is the matter?"

Ray kept silent till he could say coldly, "Nothing. It's all over."

Kane stepped into the room, and took off his hat. "If you haven't been rejected by the object of your affections, you have had the manuscript of your novel declined. These are the only things that really bring annihilation. I think the second is worse. A man is never so absolutely and solely in love with one woman but he knows some other who is potentially lovable; that is the wise provision of Nature. But while a man has a manuscript at a publisher's, it is the only manuscript in the world. You can readily work out the comparison. I hope you have merely been disappointed in love, my dear boy."

Ray smiled ruefully. "I'm afraid it's worse."

"Then Chapley & Co. have declined your novel definitely?"

"Not in set terms; or not yet. But their readers have all reported against it, and I've passed the night in reading their opinions. I've got them by heart. Would you like to hear me repeat them?" he demanded, with a fierce self-scorn.

Kane looked at him compassionately. "Heaven forbid! I could repeat them, I dare say, as accurately as you; the opinions of readers do not vary much, and I have had many novels declined."

"Have you?" Ray faltered with compunction for his arrogation of all such suffering to himself.

"Yes. That was one reason why I began to write *Hard Sayings*. But if you will let me offer you another leaf from my experience, I will suggest that there are many chances for reprieve and even pardon after the readers have condemned your novel. I once had a novel accepted — the only novel I ever had accepted — after all the publisher's readers had pronounced against it."

"Had you?" Ray came tremulously back at him.

"Yes," sighed Kane. "That is why Chapley is so fond of me; he has forgiven me a deadly injury." He paused to let his words carry Ray down again, and then he asked, with a nod toward the bed where the young fellow had flung his manuscript and the readers' opinions, "Might I?"

"Oh, certainly," said Ray from his depths; and Kane took up the opinions and began to run them over.

"Yes, they have a strangely familiar effect; they are like echoes from my own past." He laid them down again. "Do you think they are right?"

"Yes. Perfectly! That is" —

"Oh! *That is.* There is hope, I see."

"How, hope?" Ray retorted. "Does my differing with them make any difference as to the outcome?"

"For the book, no, perhaps; for you, yes, decidedly. It makes all the difference between being stunned and being killed. It is not pleasant to be stunned, but it is not for such a long time as being killed. What is your story about?"

It astonished Ray himself to find how much this question revived his faith and courage. His undying interest in the thing, by and for itself, as indestructible as a mother's love, revived, and he gave Kane the outline of his novel. Then he filled this in, and he did not stop till he had read some of the best passages. He suddenly tossed his manuscript from him. "What a fool I am!"

Kane gave his soft, thick laugh, shutting his eyes, and showing his small white teeth, still beautifully sound. "Oh, no! Oh, no! I have read worse things than that! I have written worse than that! Come, come! Here is nothing to beat the breast for. I doubt if Chapley's will take it, in defiance of their readers; their experience with me has rendered that very improbable. But they are not the only publishers in New York, or Philadelphia even; I'm told they have very eager ones in Chicago. Why shouldn't the *roman psychologique*, if that's the next thing, as Mr. Brandreth believes, get on its legs at Chicago, and walk East?"

"I wonder," Ray said, rising aimlessly from his chair, "whether it would do to call on Mr. Brandreth to-day? This suspense— Do you know whether he is very religious?"

"How should I know such a thing of my fellow-man in New York? I don't know it even of myself. At times I am very religious, and at times, not. But Mr. Brandreth is rather a formal little man, and a business interview on Sunday, with an agonized author, might not seem exactly decorous to him."

"I got the impression he wasn't very stiff. But it wouldn't do," said Ray, before Kane had rounded his neat period. "What an ass I am!"

"We are all asses," Kane sighed. "It is the great bond of human brotherhood. When did you get these verdicts?"

"Oh, Mr. Brandreth told me Miss Hughes had taken them home with her yesterday, and I couldn't rest till I had his leave to go and get them of her."

"Exactly. If we know there is possible unhappiness in store for us, we don't wait for it; we make haste and look it up, and embrace it. And how did my dear old friend Hughes, if you saw him, impress you this time?"

"I saw him, and I still prefer him to *his* friends," said Ray.

"Naturally. There are not many people, even in a planet so overpeopled as this, who are the peers of David Hughes. He goes far to make me respect my species. Of course he is ridiculous. A man so hopeful as Hughes is the *reductio ad absurdum* of the human proposition. How can there reasonably be hope in a world where poverty and death are? To be sure, Hughes proposes to eliminate poverty and explain death. You know he thinks — he really believes, I suppose — that if he could once get his millenium going, and everybody so blessed in this life that the absolute knowledge of heavenly conditions in another would not tempt us to suicide, then the terror and the mystery of death would be taken away, and the race would be trusted with its benificent meaning. It's rather a pretty notion."

Ray, with his narrow experience, would not have been able to grasp it fully. Now he broke out without the least relevancy to it, "I wonder how it would do to remodel my story so far as to transfer the scene to New York? It might be more popular." The criticism that one of those readers had made on the helplessness of his fidelity to simple rustic conditions had suddenly begun to gall him afresh. "I beg your pardon. I *didn't* notice what you were saying! I can't get my mind off that miserable thing!"

Kane laughed. "Oh, don't apologize. I know how it is. Perhaps a change of scene *would* be good; it's often advised, you know." He laughed again, and Ray with him, ruefully, and now he rose.

"Oh, must you go?" Ray entreated.

"Yes. You are best alone; when we are in pain we *are* alone, anyway. If misery loves company, company certainly does not love misery. I can stand my own troubles, but not other people's. Good-by! We will meet again when you are happier."

XXII.

MR. BRANDRETH tried hard to escape from the logic of his readers' opinions. In the light of his friendly optimism they took almost a favorable cast. He argued that there was nothing absolutely damnatory in those verdicts, that they all more or less tacitly embodied a recommendation to mercy. So far his personal kindliness carried him, but beyond this point business put up her barrier. He did not propose to take the book in spite of his readers; he said he would see; and after having seen for a week longer, he returned the MS. with a letter assuring Ray of his regret, and saying that if he could modify the story according to the suggestions of their readers, Chapley & Co. would be pleased to examine it again.

Ray had really expected some such answer as this, though he hoped against reason for something different. In view of it he had spent the week mentally recasting the story in this form and in that; sometimes it yielded to his efforts in one way or another; when the manuscript came into his hands again, he saw that it was immutably fixed in the terms he had given it, and that it must remain essentially what it was, in spite of any external travesty.

He offered Mr. Brandreth his thanks and his excuses

for not trying to make any change in it until he had first offered it as it was to other publishers. He asked if it would shut him out of Chapley & Co.'s grace if he were refused elsewhere, and received an answer of the most flattering cordiality to the effect that their desire to see the work in another shape was quite unconditioned. Mr. Brandreth seemed to have put a great deal of heart in this answer; it was most affectionately expressed; it closed with the wish that he might soon see Ray at his house again.

Ray could not have believed, but for the experience which came to him, that there could be so many reasons for declining to publish any one book as the different publishers now gave him. For the most part they deprecated the notion of even looking at it. The book-trade had never been so prostrate before; events of the most unexpected nature had conspired to reduce it to a really desperate condition. The unsettled state of Europe had a good deal to do with it; the succession of bad seasons at the West affected it most distinctly. The approach of a Presidential year was unfavorable to this sensitive traffic. Above all, the suspense created by the lingering and doubtful fate of the international copyright bill was playing havoc with it; people did not know what course to take; it was impossible to plan any kind of enterprise, or to risk any sort of project. Men who had been quite buoyant in regard to the bill seemed carried down to the lowest level of doubt as to its fate by the fact that Ray had a novel to offer them; they could see no hope for Amer-

ican fiction, if that English trash was destined to flood
the market indefinitely. They sympathized with him,
but they said they were all in the same boat, and that
the only thing was to bring all the pressure each could
to bear upon Congress. The sum of their counsel and
condolence came to the effect in Ray's mind that his
best hope was to get *A Modern Romeo* printed by Congress as a Public Document and franked by the Sena-
tors and Representatives to their constituents. He
found a melancholy amusement in noting the change
in the mood of those who used to meet him cheerfully and carelessly as the correspondent of a newspaper, and now found themselves confronted with an
author, and felt his manuscript at their throats. Some
tried to joke; some became helplessly serious; some
sought to temporize.

Those whose circumstances and engagements forbade them even to look at his novel were the easiest to
bear with. They did not question the quality or character of his work; they had no doubt of its excellence,
and they had perfect faith in its success; but simply
their hands were so full they could not touch it. The
other sort, when they consented to examine the story,
kept it so long that Ray could not help forming false
hopes of the outcome; or else they returned it with a
precipitation that mortified his pride, and made him
sceptical of their having looked into it at all. He did
not experience unconditional rejection everywhere. In
some cases the readers proposed radical and impossible
changes, as Chapley & Co.'s readers had done. In one

instance they so far recommended it that the publisher
was willing to lend his imprint and manage the book
for the per cent. usually paid to authors, if Ray would
meet all the expenses. There was an enthusiast who
even went so far as to propose that he would publish
it if Ray would pay the cost of the electrotype plates.
He appeared to think this a handsome offer, and Ray
in fact found it so much better than nothing that he
went into some serious estimates upon it. He called
in the help of old Kane, who was an expert in the
matter of electrotyping, aud was able from his sad experience to give him the exact figures. They found
that *A New Romeo* would make some four hundred and thirty or forty pages, and that at the lowest
price the plates would cost more than three hundred
dollars. The figure made Ray gasp ; the mere thought
of it impoverished him. His expenses had already
eaten a hundred dollars into his savings beyond the
five dollars a week he had from the *Midland Echo* for
his letters. If he paid out this sum for his plates, he
should now have some ninety dollars left.

"But then," said Kane, arching his eyebrows, "the
trifling sum of three hundred dollars, risked upon so
safe a venture as *A New Romeo*, will probably result
in riches beyond the dreams of avarice."

"Yes : or it may result in total loss," Ray returned.

"It is a risk. But what was it you have been asking all these other people to do ? One of them turns
and asks you to share the risk with him ; he asks you
to risk less than half on a book that you have written

yourself, and he will risk the other half. What just ground have you for refusing his generous offer?"

"It isn't my business to publish books; it's my business to write them," said Ray, coldly.

"Ah-h-h! Very true! That is a solid position. Then all you have to do to make it quite impregnable is to write such books that other men will be eager to take all the risks of publishing them. It appears that in the present case you omitted to do that." Kane watched Ray's face with whimsical enjoyment. "I was afraid you were putting your reluctance upon the moral ground, and that you were refusing to bet on your book because you thought it wrong to bet."

"I'm afraid," said Ray, dejectedly, "that the moral question didn't enter with me. If people thought it wrong to make bets of that kind, it seems to me that all business would come to a standstill."

"'Sh!" said Kane, putting his finger to his lip, and glancing round with burlesque alarm. "This is open incivism. It is accusing the whole framework of commercial civilization. Go on; it's delightful to hear you; but don't let any one *over*hear you."

"I don't know what you mean," said Ray, with sullen resentment, "about incivism. I'm saying what everybody knows."

"Ah! But what everybody *knows* is just what nobody *says*. If people said what they knew, society would tumble down like a house of cards."

Ray was silent, far withdrawn from these generalities into his personal question.

Kane asked compassionately, "Then you think you can't venture — risk — chance it? Excuse me! I was trying to find a euphemism for the action, but there seems none!"

"No; I daren't do it! The risk is too great."

"That seems to be the consensus of the book trade concerning it. Perhaps you are right. *Would* you mind," asked Kane with all his sweet politeness, "letting me take your manuscript home, and go over it carefully?"

"*Let* you!" Ray began in a rapture of gratitude, but Kane stopped him.

"No, no! Don't expect anything! *Don't* form any hopes. Simply suppose me to be reading it as a lover of high-class fiction, with no ulterior view whatever. I am really the feeblest of conies, and I have not even the poor advantage of having my habitation in the rocks. Good-by! Good-day! Don't try to stop me with civilities! Heaven knows how far my noble purpose will hold if it is weakened by any manner of delay."

Ray lived a day longer in the flimsiest air-castles that ever the vagrant winds blew through. In the evening Kane came back with his story.

"Well, my dear young friend, you have certainly produced the despair of criticism in this extraordinary fiction of yours. I don't wonder all the readers have been of so many minds about it. I only wonder that any one man could be of any one mind about it long enough to get himself down on paper. In some re-

12

spects it is the very worst thing I ever saw, and yet
— and yet — it interested me, it held me to the end.
I will make a confession ; I will tell you the truth.` I
took the thing home, hoping to find justification in it
for approaching a poor friend of mine who is in the
publishing line, and making him believe that his interest lay in publishing it.   But I could not bring myself
to so simple an act of bad faith.   I found I should
have to say to my friend, ' Here is a novel which
might make your everlasting fortune, but most of the
chances are against it.   There are twenty chances
that it will fail to one that it will succeed ; just the
average of failure and success in business life.   You
had better take it.'   Of course he would not take it,
because he could not afford to add a special risk to the
general business risk.   You see ? "

"I see," said Ray, but without the delight that a
case so beautifully reasoned should bring to the logical mind.   At the bottom of his heart, though he
made such an outward show of fairness and imperson-
ality, he was simply and selfishly emotional about his
book.   He could not enter into the humor of Kane's
dramatization of the case ; he tacitly accused him of inconsistency, and possibly of envy and jealousy.   It
began to be as if it were Kane alone who was keeping
his book from its chance with the public.   This conception, which certainly appeared perverse to Ray at
times, was at others entirely in harmony with one of
several theories of the man.   He had chilled Ray
more than once by the cold cynicism of his opinions

concerning mankind at large; and now Ray asked himself why Kane's cynicism should not characterize his behavior towards him, too. Such a man would find a delight in studying him in his defeat, and turning his misery into phrases and aphorisms.

He was confirmed in his notion of Kane's heartlessness by the strange behavior of Mr. Brandreth, who sent for his manuscript one morning, asking if he might keep it a few days, and then returned it the same day, with what Ray thought an insufficient explanation of the transaction. He proudly suffered a week under its inadequacy, and then he went to Mr. Brandreth, and asked him just what the affair meant; it seemed to him that he had a right to know.

Mr. Brandreth laughed in rather a shame-faced way. "I may as well make a clean breast of it. As I told you when we first met, I've been wanting to publish a novel for some time; and although I haven't read yours, the plot attracted me, and I thought I would give it another chance — the best chance I could. I wanted to show it to a friend of yours — I suppose I may say friend, at least it was somebody that I thought would be prejudiced more in favor of it than against it; and I had made up my mind that if the person approved of it I would read it too, and if we agreed about it, I would get Mr. Chapley to risk it. But — I found that the person had read it."

"And didn't like it."

"I can't say that, exactly."

"If it comes to that," said Ray, with a bitter smile,

"it doesn't matter about the precise terms." He could not speak for a moment; then he swallowed the choking lump in his throat, and offered Brandreth his hand. "Thank *you*, Mr. Brandreth! I'm sure *you're* my friend; and I sha'n't forget your kindness."

XXIII.

THE disappointment which Ray had to suffer would have been bad enough simply as the refusal of his book; with the hope raised in him and then crushed after the first great defeat, the trial was doubly bitter. It was a necessity of his suffering and his temperament to translate it into some sort of literary terms, and he now beguiled his enforced leisure by beginning several stories and poems involving his experience. One of the poems he carried so far that he felt the need of another eye on it to admire it and confirm him in his good opinion of it; he pretended that he wanted criticism, but he wanted praise. He would have liked to submit the poem to Kane; but he could not do this now, though the coldness between them was tacit, and they met as friends when they met. He had a vulgar moment when he thought it would be a fine revenge if he could make Kane listen to that passage of his poem which described the poet's betrayal by a false friend, by the man who held his fate in his hand and coolly turned against him. Kane must feel the sting of self-reproach from this through all the disguises of time and place which wrapped it; but the vulgar moment passed, and Ray became disgusted with that part of his poem, and cut it out.

As it remained then, it was the pathetic story of a
poet who comes up to some Oriental court with his
song, but never gains a hearing, and dies neglected
and unknown; he does not even achieve fame after
death. Ray did not know why he chose an Oriental
setting for his story, but perhaps it was because it removed it farther from the fact, and made it less recognizable. It would certainly lend itself more easily to
illustration in that shape, if he could get some magazine to take it.

When he decided that he could not show it to Kane,
and dismissed a fleeting notion of Mr. Brandreth as
impossible, he thought of Miss Hughes. He had in
fact thought of her first of all, but he had to feign that
he had not. There had lingered in his mind a discomfort concerning her which he would have removed
much sooner if it had been the only discomfort there;
mixed with his other troubles, his shame for having
indelicately urged her to speak of his story when he
saw her last, did not persist separately or incessantly.
He had imagined scenes in which he repaired his error,
but he had never really tried to do so. It was now
available as a pretext for showing her his poem; he
could make it lead on to that; but he did not own any
such purpose to himself when he put the poem into his
pocket and went to make his tardy excuses.

The Hughes family were still at table when Denton
let him into their apartment, and old Hughes came
himself into the front room where Ray was provision-
ally shown, and asked him to join them.

"My children thought that I was wanting in the finer hospitalities when you were here before, and I forced my superabundance of reasons upon you. I forget, sometimes, that no man ever directly persuaded me, in my eagerness to have people think as I do. Will you show that you have forgiven me by eating salt with us?"

"There is a little potato to eat it on, Mr. Ray," Mrs. Denton called gayly from the dining-room; and as Ray appeared there, Peace rose and set a plate for him next the old man. In front were the twins in high chairs, one on each side of their father, who from time to time put a knife or fork or cup and saucer beyond their reach, and left them to drub the table with nothing more offensive than their little soft fists.

There were not only potatoes, but some hot biscuits too, and there was tea. Ray had often sat down to no better meal at his father's table, and he thought it good enough, even after several years' sophistication in cities.

"There was to have been steak," Mrs Denton went on, with a teasing look at her husband, "but Ansel saw something on the way home which took away his appetite so completely that he thought we wouldn't want any steak."

Hughes began to fill himself with the tea and biscuit and potatoes, and he asked vaguely, "What did he see?"

"Oh, merely a family that had been put out on the sidewalk for their rent. I think that after this, when

Ansel won't come home by the Elevated, he ought to walk up on the west side, so that he can get some good from the exercise. He won't see families set out on the sidewalk in Fifth Avenue."

Ray laughed with her at her joke, and Peace smiled with a deprecating glance at Denton. Hughes paid no heed to what they were saying, and Denton said: "The more we see and feel the misery around us, the better. If we shut our eyes to it, and live in luxury ourselves " —

"Oh, I don't call salt and potatoes luxury," exactly, said his wife.

Denton remained darkly silent a moment, and then began to laugh with the helplessness of a melancholy man when something breaks through his sadness. "I should like to see a family set out on Fifth Avenue for back rent," he said, and he laughed on ; and then he fell suddenly silent again.

Ray said, for whatever relief it could give the situation, that it was some comfort to realize that the cases of distress which one saw were not always genuine. He told of a man who had begged of him at a certain point that morning, and then met him a few minutes later, and asked alms again on the ground that he had never begged before in his life. "I recalled myself to him, and he apologized handsomely, and gave me his blessing."

"Did he look as if he had got rich begging?" Denton asked.

"No ; he looked as if he could have got a great deal richer working," Ray answered, neatly.

Mrs. Denton laughed, but her laugh did not give him the pleasure it would have done if Peace had not remained looking seriously at him.

"You think so," Denton returned. "How much should you say the average laboring-man with a family could save out of his chances of wages?"

Hughes caught at the word save, and emerged with it from his revery. "Frugality is one of the vices we must hope to abolish. It is one of the lowest forms of selfishness, which can only be defended by reference to the state of Ishmaelitism in which we live."

"Oh, but surely, father," Mrs. Denton mocked, "you want street beggars to save, don't you, so they can have something to retire on?"

"No; let them take their chance with the rest," said the old man, with an imperfect hold of her irony.

"There are so many of them," Ray suggested, "they couldn't all hope to retire on a competency. I never go out without meeting one."

"I wish there were more," said Denton, passionately. I wish they would swarm up from their cellars and garrets into all the comfortable streets of the town, till every rich man's door-step had a beggar on it, to show him what his wealth was based on."

"It wouldn't avail," Hughes replied. "All that is mere sentimentality. The rich man would give to the first two or three, and then he would begin to realize that if he gave continually he would beggar himself. He would harden his heart; he would know, as he does now, that he must not take the chance of suffer-

ing for himself and his family by relieving the suffering of others. He could put it on the highest moral
ground."

"In the Family," said Peace, speaking for the first
time, " there was no chance of suffering."

"No. But the community saved itself from chance
by shutting out the rest of the world. It was selfish,
too. The Family must include the whole world," said
her father. "There is a passage bearing upon that
point in what I have been writing to-day. I will just
read a part of it."

He pushed back his chair, but Peace said, "I'll get
your manuscript, father," and brought it to him.

The passage was a long one, and Hughes read it all
with an author's unsparing zest. At that rate Ray
saw no hope of being able to read his poem, and he
felt it out of taste for Hughes to take up the time.
When he ended at last and left the table, Peace began
to clear it away, while Mrs. Denton sat hearing herself
talk and laugh. The twins had fallen asleep in their
chairs, and she let their father carry them off and be-
stow them in the adjoining room. As he took them
tenderly up from their chairs, he pressed his face close
upon their little slumbering faces, and mumbled their
fingers with his bearded lips. The sight of his affection impressed Ray, even in the preoccupation of following the movements of Peace, as she kept about her
work.

"Is he as homesick as ever?" Ray asked Mrs. Denton, when he was gone.

"Yes; he's worse," she answered lightly. "He hasn't got father's faith in the millennium to keep him up. He would like to go back to-morrow, if there was anything to go back to."

Peace halted a moment in her passing to and fro, and said, as if in deprecation of any slight or censure that her sister's words might seem to imply: "He sees a great many discouraging things. They're doing so much now by process, and unless an engraver has a great deal of talent, and can do the best kind of work, there's very little work for him. Ansel has seen so many of them lose their work by the new inventions. What seems so bad to him is that these processes really make better pictures than the common engravers can, and yet they make life worse. He never did believe that an artist ought to get a living by his art."

"Then I don't see why he objects to the new processes," said Ray, with the heartlessness which so easily passes for wit. Peace looked at him with grave surprise.

Mrs. Denton laughed over the cat which had got up in her lap. "That's what I tell him. But it doesn't satisfy him."

"You know," said the younger sister, with a reproach in her tone, which brought Ray sensibly under condemnation, too, "that he means that art must be free before it can be true, and that there can be no freedom where there is the fear of want."

"Well," said Mrs. Denton, turning her head for a new effect of the sleeping cat, "there was no fear of want in the Family; but there wasn't much art, either."

Ray was tempted to laugh, but he wanted above all to read his poem, and to lead up to it without delay, and he denied himself the pleasure of a giggle with Mrs. Denton. "I suppose," he said, "the experiment of emancipation is tried on too small a scale in a community."

"That is what father thinks," said Peace. "That is why he wants the whole world to be free."

"Yes," said Ray, aware of a relenting in her towards himself; and he added, with apparent inconsequence: "Perhaps it would help forward the time for it if every artist could express his feeling about it, or represent it somehow."

"I don't see exactly how they could in a picture or a statue," said Mrs. Denton.

"No," Ray assented from the blind alley where he had unexpectedly brought up. He broke desperately from it, and said, more toward Peace than toward her sister, "I have been trying to turn my own little disappointment into poetry. You know," he added, "that Chapley & Co. have declined my book?"

"Yes," she admitted, with a kind of shyness.

"I wonder," and here Ray took the manuscript out of his pocket, "whether you would let me read you some passages of my poem."

Mrs. Denton assented eagerly, and Peace less eagerly, but with an interest that was enough for him. Before he began to read, Mrs. Denton said a number of things that seemed suddenly to have accumulated in her mind, mostly irrelevant; she excused herself for leaving the room, and begged Ray to wait till she came back. Several times during the reading she escaped and returned; the poet finished in one of her absences.

XXIV

"You see," Ray said, "it's merely a fragment." He wiped the perspiration from his forehead.

"Of course," the girl answered, with a sigh. "Isn't disappointment always fragmentary?" she asked, sadly.

"How do you mean?"

"Why, happiness is like something complete; and disappointment like something broken off, to me. A story that ends well seems rounded; and one that ends badly leaves you waiting, as you do just after some one dies."

"Is that why you didn't like my story?" Ray asked, imprudently. He added quickly, at an embarrassment which came into her face, "Oh, I didn't mean to add to my offence! I came here partly to excuse it. I was too persistent the other night."

"Oh, no!"

"Yes, I was. I had no right to an opinion from you. I knew it at the time, but I couldn't help it. You were right to refuse. But you can tell me how my poem strikes you. It isn't offered for publication!"

He hoped that she would praise some passages that he thought fine; but she began to speak of the motive, and he saw that she had not missed anything, that she had perfectly seized his intention. She talked to him of it as if it were the work of some one else, and he said impulsively, "If I had you to criticise my actions beforehand, I should not be so apt to make a fool of myself."

Mrs. Denton came back. "I ran off toward the last. I didn't want to be here when Peace began to criticise. She's so severe."

"She hasn't been at all severe this time," said Ray.

"I don't see how she could be," Mrs. Denton returned. "All that I heard was splendid."

"It's merely a fragment," said Ray, with grave satisfaction in her flattery.

"You must finish it, and read us the rest of it."

Ray looked at Peace, and something in her face made him say, "I shall never finish it; it isn't worth it."

"Did Peace say that?"

"No."

Mrs. Denton laughed. "That's just like Peace. She makes other people say the disagreeable things she thinks about them."

"What a mysterious power!" said Ray. "Is it hypnotic suggestion?"

He spoke lightly toward Peace, but her sister answered: "Oh, we're full of mysteries in this house. Did you know that my husband had a Voice?"

"A voice! Is a voice mysterious?"

"This one is. It's an internal Voice. It tells him what to do."

"Oh, like the demon of Socrates."

"I *hope* it isn't a demon!" said Mrs. Denton.

"That depends upon what it tells him to do," said
Ray. In Socrates' day a familiar spirit could be a
demon without being at all bad. How proud you
must be to have a thing like that in the family!"

"I don't know. It has its inconveniences, sometimes. When it tells him to do what we don't want
him to," said Mrs. Denton.

"Oh, but think of the compensations!" Ray urged.
"Why, it's equal to a ghost."

"I suppose it is a kind of ghost," said Mrs. Denton,
and Ray fancied she had the pride we all feel in any
alliance, direct or indirect, with the supernatural.
"Do you believe in dreams?" she asked abruptly.

"Bad ones, I do," said Ray. "We always expect
bad dreams and dark presentiments to come true,
don't we!"

"I don't know. My husband does. He has a
Dream as well as a Voice."

"Oh, indeed!" said Ray; and he added: "I see.
The Voice is the one he talks with in his sleep."

The flippant suggestion amused Mrs. Denton; but
a shadow of pain came over Peace's face, that made
Ray wish to get away from the mystery he had
touched; she might be a believer in it, or ashamed
of it.

"I wonder," he added, "why we never expect our
day-dreams to come true?"

"Perhaps because they're never bad ones — because we know we're just making them," said Mrs. Denton.

"It must be that! But, do we always make them? Sometimes my day-dreams seem to make themselves, and they keep on doing it so long that they tire me to death. They're perfect daymares."

"How awful! The only way would be to go to sleep, if you wanted to get rid of them."

"Yes; and that isn't so easy as waking up. Anybody can wake up; a man can wake up to go to execution; but it takes a very happy man to go to sleep."

The recognition of this fact reminded Ray that he was himself a very unhappy man; he had forgotten it for the time.

"He might go into society and get rid of them that way," Mrs. Denton suggested, with an obliquity which he was too simply masculine to perceive. "I suppose you go into society a good deal, Mr. Ray?"

Peace made a little movement as of remonstrance, but she did not speak, and Ray answered willingly: "*I* go into society? I have been inside of just one house — or flat — besides this, since I came to New York."

"Why!" said Mrs. Denton.

She seemed to be going to say something more, but she stopped at a look from her sister, and left Ray free to go on or not, as he chose. He told them it was Mr. Brandreth's flat he had been in; at some little hints of curiosity from Mrs. Denton, he described it to her.

13

"I have some letters from people in Midland, but I haven't presented them yet," he added at the end. "The Brandreths are all I know of society."

"They're much more than we know. Well, it seems like fairyland," said Mrs. Denton, in amiable self-derision. "I used to think that was the way *we* should live when we left the Family. I suppose there are people in New York that would think it was like fairyland to live like us, and not all in one room. Ansel is always preaching that when I grumble."

The cat sprang up into her lap, and she began to smooth its long flank, and turn her head from side to side, admiring its enjoyment.

"Well," Ray said, "whatever we do, we are pretty sure to be sorry we didn't do something else."

He was going to lead up to his own disappointments by this commonplace, but Mrs. Denton interposed.

"Oh, I'm not sorry we left the Family, if that's what you mean. There's some chance, here, and there everything went by rule; you had your share of the work, and you knew just what you had to expect every day. I used to say I wished something *wrong* would happen, just so as to have *something* happen. I believe it was more than half that that got father out, too," she said, with a look at her sister.

"I thought," said Ray, "but perhaps I didn't understand him, that your father wanted to make the world over on the image of your community."

"I guess he wanted to have the fun of chancing it, too," said Mrs. Denton. "Of course he wants to make the world over, but he has a pretty good time as it is; and I'm glad of all I did and said to get him into it. He had no chance to bring his ideas to bear on it in the Family."

"Then it was you who got him out of the community," said Ray.

"I did my best," said Mrs. Denton. "But I can't say I did it, altogether."

"Did you help?" he asked Peace.

"I wished father to do what he thought was right. He had been doubtful about the life there for a good while—whether it was really doing anything for humanity."

She used the word with no sense of cant in it; Ray could perceive that.

"And do you ever wish you were back in the Family?"

Mrs. Denton called out joyously: "Why, there is no Family to be back in, I'm thankful to say! Didn't you know that?"

"I forgot." Ray smiled, as he pursued, "Well, if there was one to be back in, would you like to be there, Miss Hughes?"

"I can't tell," she answered, with a trouble in her voice. "When I'm not feeling very strong or well, I should. And when I see so many people struggling so hard here, and failing after all they do, I wish they could be where there was no failure, and no danger of it. In the Family we were safe, and we hadn't any care."

"We hadn't any choice, either," said her sister. "What choice has a man who doesn't know where the next day's work is coming from?"

Ray looked round to find that Denton had entered behind them from the room where he had been, and was sitting beside the window apparently listening to their talk. There was something uncanny in the fact of his unknown presence, though neither of the sisters seemed to feel it.

"Oh, you're there," said Mrs. Denton, without turning from her cat. "Well, I suppose that's a question that must come home to you more and more. Did you ever hear of such a dreadful predicament as my husband's in, Mr. Ray? He's just hit on an invention that's going to make us rich, and throw all the few remaining engravers out of work, when he gets it finished." Her husband's face clouded, but she went on: "His only hope is that the invention will turn out a failure. You don't have any such complications in your work, do you, Mr. Ray?"

"No," said Ray, thinking what a good situation the predicament would be, in a story. "If they had taken my novel, and published an edition of fifty thousand, I don't see how it could have reduced a single author to penury. But I don't believe I could resist the advances of a publisher, even if I knew it might throw authors out of work right and left. I could support their families till they got something to do."

"Yes, you might do that, Ansel," his wife suggested, with a slanting smile at him. "I only hope we may have the opportunity. But probably it will be as hard to get a process accepted as a book."

"That hasn't anything to do with the question," Denton broke out. "The question is whether a man ought not to kill his creative thought as he would a snake, if he sees that there is any danger of its taking away work another man lives by. That is what I look at."

"And father," said Mrs. Denton, whimsically, "is so high-principled that he won't let us urge on the millenium by having pandemonium first. If we were allowed to do that, Ansel might quiet his conscience by reflecting that the more men he threw out of work, the sooner the good time would come. I don't see why that isn't a good plan, and it would work in so nicely with what we want to do. Just make everything so bad people cannot bear it, and then they will rise up in their might and make it better for themselves. Don't you think so, Mr. Ray?"

"Oh, I don't know," he said.

All this kind of thinking and feeling, which was a part and parcel of these people's daily life, was alien to his habit of mind. He grasped it feebly and reluctantly, without the power or the wish to follow it to conclusions, whether it was presented ironically by Mrs. Denton, or with a fanatical sincerity by her husband.

"No, no! That won't do," Denton said. "I have tried to see that as a possible thoroughfare; but it isn't possible. If we were dealing with statistics it would do; but it's men we're dealing with: men like

ourselves that have women and children dependent
on them."

"I am glad to hear you say that, Ansel," Peace
said, gently.

"Yes," he returned, bitterly, "whichever way I
turn, the way is barred. My hands are tied, whatever
I try to do. Some one must be responsible. Some
one must atone. Who shall it be?"

"Well," said Mrs. Denton, with a look of comic
resignation, "it seems to be a pretty personal thing,
after all, in spite of father's philosophy. I always
supposed that when we came into the world we should
have an election, and vote down all these difficulties
by an overwhelming majority."

Ray quoted, musingly:

> "The world is out of joint: — O cursed spite!
> That ever I was born to set it right!"

"Yes? Who says that?"

"Hamlet."

"Oh yes. Well, I feel just exactly as Ham does
about it."

Denton laughed wildly out at her saucy drolling,
and she said, as if his mirth somehow vexed her,

"I should think if you're so much troubled by that
hard question of yours, you would get your Voice to
say something."

Her husband rose, and stood looking down, while a
knot gathered between his gloomy eyes. Then he
turned and left the room without answering her.

She sent a laugh after him. "Sometimes," she said to the others, "the Voice doesn't know any better than the rest of us."

Peace remained looking gravely at her a moment, and then she followed Denton out of the room.

Mrs. Denton began to ask Ray about Mrs. Brandreth and Mrs. Chapley, pressing him with questions as to what kind of people they really were, and whether they were proud; she wondered why they had never come to call upon her. It would all have been a little vulgar if it had not been so childlike and simple. Ray was even touched by it when he thought that the chief concern of these ladies was to find out from him just what sort of crank her father was, and to measure his influence for evil on Mr. Chapley.

At the same time he heard Peace talking to Denton in a tone of entreaty and pacification. She staid so long that Ray had risen to go when she came back. He had hoped for a moment alone with her at parting, so that he might renew in better form the excuses that he pretended he had come to make. But the presence of her sister took all the seriousness and delicacy from them; he had to make a kind of joke of them; and he could not tell her at all of the mysterious message from Mr. Brandreth about the friend to whom he wished to submit his book, and of the final pang of disappointment which its immediate return had given him. He had meant that she should say something to comfort him for this, but he had to forego his intended consolation.

XXV.

Ray had no doubt that Kane was the court of final resort which the case against his novel had been appealed to, and he thought it hard that he should have refused to give it a last chance, or even to look at it again. Surely it was not so contemptible as that, so hopelessly bad that a man who seemed his friend could remember nothing in it that would make it valuable in a second reading. If the fault were not in the book, then it must be in the friend, and Ray renounced old Kane by every means he could command. He could not make it an open question ; he could only treat him more and more coldly, and trust to Kane's latent sense of guilt for the justification of his behavior. But Kane was either so hardened, or else regarded his own action as so venial, or perhaps believed it so right, that he did not find Ray's coldness intelligible.

"My dear young friend," he frankly asked, " is there anything between us but our disparity of years ? That existed from the first moment of our acquaintance. I have consoled myself at times with the notion of our continuing together in an exemplary friendship, you growing older and wiser, and I younger and less wise, if possible, like two Swedenborgian spirits in the final state. But evidently something has happened to

tinge our amity with a grudge in your mind. Do you
object to saying just what property in me has imparted
this unpleasant discoloration to it?"

Ray was ashamed to say, or rather unable. He
answered that nothing was the matter, and that he
did not know what Kane meant. He was obliged to
prove this by a show of cordiality, which he began
perhaps to feel when he reasoned away his first resentment. Kane had acted quite within his rights, and if
there was to be any such thing as honest criticism, the
free censure of a friend must be suffered and even desired. He said this to himself quite heroically; he
tried hard to be ruled by a truth so obvious.

In other things his adversity demoralized him, for a
time. He ceased to live in the future, as youth does
and should do; he lived carelessly and wastefully in
the present. With nothing in prospect, it was no
longer important how his time or money went; he did
not try to save either. He never finished his poem,
and he did not attempt anything else.

In the midst of his listlessness and disoccupation
there came a letter from Hanks Brothers asking if he
could not give a little more social gossip in his correspondence for the *Echo;* they reminded him that there
was nothing people liked so much as personalities.
Ray scornfully asked himself, How should he, who
knew only the outsides of houses, supply social gossip,
even if he had been willing? He made a sarcastic
reply to Hanks Brothers, intimating his readiness to
relinquish the correspondence if it were not to their

taste; and they took him at his word, and wrote that they would hereafter make use of a syndicate letter.

It had needed this blow to rouse him from his reckless despair. If he were defeated now, it would be in the face of all the friends who had believed in him and expected success of him. His motive was not high; it was purely egoistic at the best; but he did not know this; he had a sense of virtue in sending his book off to a Boston publisher without undoing the inner wrappings in which the last New York publisher had returned it.

Then he went round to ask Mr. Brandreth if he knew of any literary or clerical or manual work he could get to do. The industrial fury which has subdued a continent, and brought it under the hard American hand, wrought in him, according to his quality, and he was not only willing but eager to sacrifice the scruples of delicacy he had in appealing to a man whom he had sought first on such different terms. His only question was how to get his business quickly, clearly, and fully before him.

Mr. Brandreth received him with a gayety that put this quite out of his mind; and he thought the publisher was going to tell him that he had decided, after all, to accept his novel.

"Ah, Mr. Ray," Mr. Brandreth called out at sight of him, "I was just sending a note to you! Sit down a moment, won't you? The editor of *Every Evening* was in here just now, and he happened to say he wished he knew some one who could make him a synopsis of a rather important book he's had an advanced copy of from the other side. It's likely to be of particular interest in connection with Coquelin's visit; it's a study of French comic acting from Molière down; and I happened to think of you. You know French?"

"Why, yes, thank you — to read. You're very kind, Mr. Brandreth, to think of me."

"Oh, not at all! I didn't know whether you ever did the kind of thing the *Every Evening* wants, or whether you were not too busy; but I thought I'd drop an anchor to windward for you, on the chance that you might like to do it."

"I should like very much to do it; and " —

"I'll tell you why I did it," Mr. Brandreth interrupted, radiantly. "I happened to know they're making a change in the literary department of the *Every Evening*, and I thought that if this bit of work would let you show your hand — See?"

"Yes; and I'm everlastingly " —

"Not at all, not at all!" Mr. Brandreth opened the letter he was holding, and gave Ray a note that it inclosed. "That's an introduction to the editor of the *Every Evening*, and you'll strike him at the office about now, if you'd like to see him."

Ray caught with rapture the hand Mr. Brandreth offered him. "I don't know what to say to you, but I'm extremely obliged. I'll go at once." He started to the door, and turned. "I hope Mrs. Brandreth is well, and—and—the baby?"

"Splendidly. I shall want to have you up there

again as soon as we can manage it. Why haven't you
been at Mrs. Chapley's? Didn't you get her card?"

"Yes; but I haven't been very good company of
late. I didn't want to have it generally known."

"I understand. Well, now you must cheer up.
Good-by, and good luck to you!"

All the means of conveyance were too slow for
Ray's eagerness, and he walked. On his way down
to that roaring and seething maelstrom of business,
whose fierce currents swept all round the *Every Evening* office, he painted his future as critic of the journal
with minute detail; he had died chief owner and had
his statue erected to his memory in Park Square before
he crossed that space and plunged into one of the
streets beyond.

He was used to newspaper offices, and he was not
surprised to find the editorial force of the *Every Evening* housed in a series of dens, opening one beyond the
other till the last, with the chief in it, looked down
on the street from which he climbed. He thought it
all fit enough, for the present; but, while he still dwelt
in the future, and before the office-boy had taken his
letter from him to the chief, he swiftly flung up a
building for the *Every Evening* as lofty and as ugly as
any of the many-storied towers that rose about the
frantic neighborhood. He blundered upon two other
writers before he reached the chief; one of them looked
up from his desk, and roared at him in unintelligible
affliction; the other simply wagged his head, without
lifting it, in the direction of the final room, where Ray

found himself sitting beside the editor-in-chief, without well knowing how he got there. The editor did not seem to know either, or to care that he was there, for some time; he kept on looking at this thing and that thing on the table before him; at everything but the letter Ray had sent in. When he did take that up he did not look at Ray; and while he talked with him he scarcely glanced at him; there were moments when he seemed to forget there was anybody there; and Ray's blood began to burn with a sense of personal indignity. He wished to go away, and leave the editor to find him gone at his leisure; but he felt bound to Mr. Brandreth, and he staid. At last the editor took up a book from the litter of newspapers and manuscripts before him, and said:

"What we want is a rapid and attractive *résumé* of this book, with particular reference to Coquelin and his place on the stage and in art. No one else has the book yet, and we expect to use the article from it in our Saturday edition. See what you can do with it, and bring it here by ten to-morrow. You can run from one to two thousand words — not over two."

He handed Ray the book and turned so definitively to his papers and letters again that Ray had no choice but to go. He left with the editor a self-respectful parting salutation, which the editor evidently had no use for, and no one showed a consciousness of him, not even the office-boy, as he went out.

He ground his teeth in resentment, but he resolved to take his revenge by making literature of that *résumé,* and compelling the attention of the editor to him through his work. He lost no time in setting about it; he began to read the book at once, and he had planned his article from it before he reached his hotel. He finished it before he slept, and he went to bed as the first milkman sent his wail through the street below. His heart had worked itself free of its bitterness, and seemed to have imparted its lightness to the little paper, which he was not ashamed of even when he read it after he woke from the short rest he suffered himself. He was sure that the editor of *Every Evening* must feel the touch which he knew he had imparted to it, and he made his way to him with none of the perturbation, if none of the romantic interest of the day before.

The editor took the long slips which Ray had written his copy on, and struck them open with his right hand while he held them with his left.

"Why the devil," he demanded, "don't you write a better hand?" Before Ray could formulate an answer, he shouted again, "Why the devil don't you begin with a *fact?*"

He paid no heed to the defence which the hurt author-pride of the young fellow spurred him to make, but went on reading the article through. When he had finished he threw it down and drew toward him a narrow book like a check-book, and wrote in it, and then tore out the page, and gave it to Ray. It was an order on the counting-room for fifteen dollars.

Ray had a weak moment of rage in which he wished

to tear it up and fling it in the editor's face. But he overcame himself and put the order in his pocket. He vowed never to use it, even to save himself from starving, but he kept it because he was ashamed to do otherwise. Even when the editor at the sound of his withdrawal called out, without looking round, "What is your address?" he told him; but this time he wasted no parting salutations upon him.

The hardest part was now to make his acknowledgments to Mr. Brandreth, without letting him know how little his personal interest in the matter had availed. He succeeded in keeping everything from him but the fact that his work had been accepted, and Mr. Brandreth was delighted.

"Well, that's first-rate, as far as it goes, and I believe it's going to lead to something permanent. You'll be the literary man of *Every Evening* yet; and I understand the paper's making its way. It's a good thing to be connected with; thoroughly clean and decent, and yet lively."

Though Ray hid his wrath from Mr. Brandreth, because it seemed due to his kindness, he let it break out before Kane, whom he found dining alone at his hotel that evening when he came down from his room.

"I don't know whether I ought to sit down with you," he began, when Kane begged him to share his table. "I've just been through the greatest humiliation I've had yet. It's so thick on me that I'm afraid some of it will come off. And it wasn't my fault, either; it was my misfortune."

"We can bear to suffer for our misfortunes," said Kane, dreamily. "To suffer for our faults would be intolerable, because then we couldn't preserve our self-respect. Don't you see? But the consciousness that our anguish is undeserved is consoling; it's even flattering."

"I'm sorry to deprive you of a *Hard Saying*, if that's one, but my facts are against you."

"Ah, but facts must always yield to reasons," Kane began.

Ray would not be stopped. But he suddenly caught the humorous aspect of his adventure with the editor of *Every Evening*, and gave it with artistic zest. He did not spare his ridiculous hopes or his ridiculous pangs.

From time to time Kane said, at some neat touch: "Oh, good!" "Very good!" "Capital!" "Charming, charming!" When Ray stopped, he drew a long breath, and sighed out: "Yes, I know the man. He's not a bad fellow. He's a very good fellow."

"A good fellow?" Ray demanded. "Why did he behave like a brute, then? He's the only man who's been rude to me in New York. Why couldn't he have shown me the same courtesy that all the publishers have? Every one of them has behaved decently, though none of them, confound them! wanted my book."

"Ah," said Kane, "his conditions were different. They had all some little grace of leisure, and according to your report he had none. I don't know a more

pathetic picture than you've drawn of him, trying to
grasp all those details of his work, and yet seize a
new one. It's frightful. Don't you feel the pathos
of it?"

"No man ought to place himself in conditions where
he has to deny himself the amenities of life," Ray persisted, and he felt that he had made a point, and
languaged it well. "He's to blame if he does."

"Oh, no man willingly places himself in hateful or
injurious conditions," said Kane. "He is pushed into
them, or they grow up about him through the social
action. He's what they shape him to, and when he's
taken his shape from circumstances, he knows instinctively that he won't fit into others. So he stays
put. You would say that the editor of *Every Evening*
ought to forsake his conditions at any cost, and go
somewhere else and be a civilized man; but he
couldn't do that without breaking himself in pieces and
putting himself together again. Why did I never go
back to my own past? I look over my life in New
York, and it is chiefly tiresome and futile in the
retrospect; I couldn't really say why I've staid here.
I don't expect anything of it, and yet I can't leave it.
The *Every Evening* man does expect a great deal of
his conditions; he expects success, and I understand
he's getting it. But he didn't place himself in his
conditions in any dramatic way, and he couldn't dra-
matically break with them. They may be gradually
detached from him and then he may slowly change.
Of course there *are* signal cases of renunciation.
14

People have abdicated thrones and turned monks ; but they've not been common, and I dare say, if the whole truth could be known, they have never been half the men they were before, or become just the saints they intended to be. ' If you'll take the most extraordinary instance of modern times, or of all times — if you'll take Tolstoï himself, you'll see how impossible it is for a man to rid himself of his environment. Tolstoï believes unquestionably in a life of poverty and toil and trust ; but he has not been able to give up his money; he is defended against want by the usual gentlemanly sources of income; and he lives a ghastly travesty of his unfulfilled design. He's a monumental warning of the futility of any individual attempt to escape from conditions. That's what I tell my dear old friend Chapley, who's quite Tolstoï mad, and wants to go into the country and simplify himself."

" Does he, really ? " Ray asked, with a smile.

Why not? Tolstoï convinces your reason and touches your heart. There's no flaw in his logic and no falsity in his sentiment. I think that if Tolstoï had not become a leader, he would have had a multitude of followers."

The perfection of his paradox afforded Kane the highest pleasure. He laughed out his joy in it, and clapped Ray on the shoulder, and provoked him to praise it, and was so frankly glad of having made it that all Ray's love of him came back.

XXVI.

FROM one phase of his experience with his story, Ray took a hint, and made bold to ask Mr. Brandreth if he could not give him some manuscripts to read ; he had rather a fancy for playing the part of some other man's destiny since he could have so little to do with deciding his own. Chapley & Co. had not much work of that kind to give, but they turned over a number of novels to him, and he read them with a jealous interest; he wished first of all to find whether other people were writing better novels than his, and he hoped to find that they were not. Mostly, they really were not, and they cumulatively strengthened him against an impulse which he had more than once had to burn his manuscript. From certain of the novels he read he got instruction both of a positive and negative kind ; for it was part of his business to look at their construction, and he never did this without mentally revising the weak points of his story, and considering how he could repair them.

There was not a great deal of money in this work ; but Ray got ten or fifteen dollars for reading a manuscript and rendering an opinion of it, and kept himself from the depravation of waiting for the turn of the cards. He waited for nothing ; he worked contin-

ually, and he filled up the intervals of the work that
was given to him with work that he made for himself.
He wrote all sorts of things, — essays, stories, sketches,
poems, — and sent them about to the magazines and
the weekly newspapers and the syndicates. When
the editors were long in reporting upon them he went
and asked for a decision ; and in audacious moments
he carried his manuscript to them, and tried to surprise an instant judgment from them. This, if it were
in the case of a poem, or a very short sketch, he could
sometimes get ; and it was usually adverse, as it usually was in the case of the things he sent them by
mail. They were nowhere unkindly ; they were often
sympathetic, and suggested that what was not exactly
adapted to their publications might be adapted to the
publication of a fellow-editor ; they were willing to
sacrifice one another in his behalf. They did not
always refuse his contributions. Kane, who witnessed
his struggles at this period with an interest which he
declared truly paternal, was much struck by the fact
that Ray's failures and successes exactly corresponded
to those of business men ; that is, he failed ninety-five
times out of a hundred to get his material printed.
His effort was not of the vast range suggested by these
numbers ; he had a few manuscripts that were refused
many times over, and made up the large sum of his
rejections by the peculiar disfavor that followed them.

Besides these regular attacks on the literary periodi-
cals, Ray carried on guerilla operations of several
sorts. He sold jokes at two dollars apiece to the

comic papers ; it sometimes seemed low for jokes, but the papers paid as much for a poor joke as a good one, and the market was steady. He got rather more for jokes that were ordered of him, as when an editor found himself in possession of an extremely amusing illustration without obvious meaning. He developed a facility wholly unexpected to himself in supplying the meaning for a picture of this kind ; if it were a cartoon, he had the courage to ask as much as five dollars for his point.

A mere accident opened up another field of industry to him, when one day a gentleman halted him at the foot of the stairway to an elevated station, and after begging his pardon for first mistaking him for a Grand Army man, professed himself a journalist in momentary difficulty.

"I usually sell my things to the *Sunday Planet,* but my last poem was too serious for their F. S., and I'm down on my luck. Of course, I see *now,*" said the journalist in difficulty, "that you *couldn't* have been in the war ; at first glance I took you for an old comrade of mine ; but if you'll leave your address with me — Thank you, sir ! Thank you ! "

Ray had put a quarter in his hand, and he thought he had bought the right to ask him a question.

"I know that I may look twice my age when people happen to see double " —

"Capital ! " said the veteran. "First-rate ! " and he clapped Ray on the shoulder, and then clung to him long enough to recover his balance.

" But *would* you be good enough to tell me what the
F. S. of the *Sunday Planet* is ? "

" Why, the Funny Side — the page where they put
the jokes and the comic poetry. F. S. for short.
Brevity is the soul of wit, you know."

Ray hurried home and put together some of the
verses that had come back to him from the comic
papers, and mailed them to the *Sunday Planet.* He
had learned not to respect his work the less for being
rejected, but the *Planet* did not wane in his esteem
because the editor of the F. S. accepted all his outcast
verses. The pay was deplorably little, however, and
for the first time he was tempted to consider an offer
of partnership with a gentleman who wrote advertisements for a living, and who, in the falterings of his
genius from overwork, had professed himself willing to
share his honors and profits with a younger man ; the
profits, at any rate, were enormous.

But this temptation endured only for a moment of
disheartenment. In all his straits Ray not only did
his best, but he kept true to a certain ideal of himself
as an artist. There were some things he could not do
even to make a living. He might sell anything he
wrote, and he might write anything within the bounds
of honesty that would sell, but he could not sell his
pen, or let it for hire, to be used as the lessee wished.
It was not the loftiest grade of æsthetics or ethics, and
perhaps the distinctions he made were largely imagi-
nary. But he refused the partnership offered him,
though it came with a flattering recognition of his

literary abilities, and of his peculiar fitness for the work proposed.

He got to know a good many young fellows who were struggling forward on the same lines with himself, and chancing it high and low with the great monthlies, where they offered their poems and short stories, and with the one-cent dailies, where they turned in their space-work. They had a courage in their risks which he came to share in its gayety, if not its irreverence, and he enjoyed the cheerful cynicism with which they philosophized the facts of the newspaper side of their trade: they had studied its average of successes and failures, and each of them had his secret for surprising the favor of the managing editor, as infallible as the gambler's plan for breaking the bank at Monaco.

"You don't want to be serious," one blithe spirit volunteered for Ray's instruction in a moment of defeat; "you want to give a light and cheerful cast to things. For instance, if a fireman loses his life in a burning building, you mustn't go straight for the reader's pity; you must appeal to his sense of the picturesque. You must call it, 'Knocked out in a Fight with Fire,' or something like that, and treat the incident with mingled pathos and humor. If you've got a case of suicide by drowning, all you've got to do is to call it 'Launch of one more Unfortunate,' and the editor is yours. Go round and make studies of our metropolitan civilization; write up the 'Leisure Moments of Surface-Car Conductors,' or 'Talks with the

Ticket-Choppers.' Do the amateur scavenger, and describe the 'Mysteries of the Average Ash-Barrel.' "

As the time wore on, the circle of Ray's acquaintance widened so much that he no longer felt those pangs of homesickness which used to seize him whenever he got letters from Midland. He rather neglected his correspondence with Sanderson; the news of parties and sleigh-rides and engagements and marriages which his friend wrote, affected him like echoes from some former life. He was beginning to experience the fascination of the mere city, where once he had a glimpse of the situation fleeting and impalpable as those dream-thoughts that haunt the consciousness on the brink of sleep. Then it was as if all were driving on together; no one knew why or whither; but some had embarked on the weird voyage to waste, and some to amass; their encounter formed the opportunity of both, and a sort of bewildered kindliness existed between them. Their common ignorance of what it was all for was like a bond, and they clung involuntarily together in their unwieldy multitude because of the want of meaning, and prospered on, suffered on, through vast cyclones of excitement that whirled them round and round, and made a kind of pleasant drunkenness in their brains, and consoled them for never resting and never arriving.

The fantastic vision passed, and Ray again saw himself and those around him full of distinctly intended effort, each in his sort, and of relentless energy, which were self-sufficing and self-satisfying. Most of the people he knew were, like himself, bent upon getting a story, or a poem, or an essay, or an article, printed in some magazine or newspaper, or some book into the hands of a publisher. They were all, like himself, making their ninety-five failures out of a hundred en-deavors; but they were all courageous, if they were not all gay, and if they thought the proportion of their failures disastrous, they said nothing to show it. They did not try to blink them, but they preferred to celebrate their successes; perhaps the rarity of these merited it more.

XXVII.

As soon as Ray had pulled himself out of his slough of despond, and began to struggle forward on such footing as he found firm, he felt the rise of the social instinct in him. He went about and delivered his letters ; he appeared at one of Mrs. Chapley's Thursdays, and began to be passed from one afternoon tea to another. He met the Mayquaits at Mrs. Chapley's, those Gitchigumee people she had asked him about, and at their house he met a lady so securely his senior that she could let him see at once she had taken a great fancy to him. The Mayquaits have since bought a right of way into the heart of society, but they were then in the peripheral circles, and this lady seemed anxious to be accounted for in that strange company of rich outcasts. Something in Ray's intelligent young good looks must have appealed to her as a possible solvent. As soon as he was presented to her she began to ply him with subtle questions concerning their hostess and their fellow-guests, with whom she professed to find herself by a species of accident springing from their common interest in a certain charity : that particular tea was to promote it. Perhaps it was the steadfast good faith of the pretty boy in refusing to share in her light satire, while he could

not help showing that he enjoyed it, which commended
Ray more and more to her. He told her how he came
to be there, not because she asked, for she did not ask,
but because he perceived that she wished to know, and
because it is always pleasant to speak about one's self
upon any pretext, and he evinced a delicate sympathy
with her misgiving. It flattered him that she should
single him out for her appeal as if he were of her sort,
and he eagerly accepted an invitation she made him.
Through her favor and patronage he began to go to
lunches and dinners; he went to balls, and danced
sometimes when his pockets were so empty that he
walked one way to save his car fares. But his poverty was without care; it did not eat into his heart,
for no one else shared it; and those spectres of want
and shame which haunt the city's night, and will not
always away at dawn, but remain present to eyes that
have watched and wept, vanished in the joyous light
that his youth shed about him, as he hurried home
with the waltz music beating in his blood. A remote
sense, very remote and dim, of something all wrong
attended him at moments in his pleasure; at moments
it seemed even he who was wrong. But this fled
before his analysis; he could not see what harm he
was doing. To pass his leisure in the company of
well-bred, well-dressed, prosperous, and handsome
people was so obviously right and fit that it seemed
absurd to suffer any question of it. He met mainly
very refined persons, whose interests were all elevated,
and whose tastes were often altruistic. He found

himself in a set of young people, who loved art and literature and music, and he talked to his heart's content with agreeable girls about pictures and books and theatres.

It surprised him that with all this opportunity and contiguity he did not fall in love; after the freest give and take of æsthetic sympathies he came away with a kindled fancy and a cold heart. There was one girl he thought would have let him be in love with her if he wished, but when he questioned his soul he found that he did not wish, or could not. He said to himself that it was her money, for she was rich as well as beautiful and wise; and he feigned that if it had not been for her money he might have been in love with her. Her people, an aunt and uncle, whom she lived with, made much of him, and the way seemed clear. They began to tell each other about themselves, and once he interested her very much by the story of his adventures in first coming to New York.

"And did you never meet the two young women afterwards?" she asked.

"Yes. That was the curious part of it," he said, and piqued that she called them "two young women," he went on to tell her of the Hugheses, whom he set forth in all the picturesqueness he could command. She listened intensely, and even provoked him with some questions to go on; but at the end she said nothing; and after that she was the same and not the same to him. At first he thought it might be her objection to his knowing such queer people; she was very proud; but he was still made much of by her family, and there was nothing but this difference in her that marked with its delicate distinctness the loss of a chance.

He was not touched except in his vanity. Without the subtle willingness which she had subtly withdrawn, his life was still surpassingly rich on the side where it had been hopelessly poor; and in spite of his personal poverty he was in the enjoyment of a social affluence beyond the magic of mere money. Sometimes he regarded it all as his due, and at all times he took it with simple ingratitude; but he had moments of passionate humility when he realized that he owed his good fortune to the caprice of a worldly old woman, whom he did not respect very much.

; When he began to go into society, he did not forget his earlier friends; he rather prided himself on his constancy; he thought it was uncommon, and he found it a consolation when other things failed him. It was even an amusement full of literary suggestion for him to turn from his own dream of what the world was to Hughes's dream of what the world should be; and it flattered him that the old man should have taken the sort of fancy to him that he had. Hughes consulted him as a person with a different outlook on life, and valued him as a practical mind, akin to his own in quality, if not in direction. First and last, he read him his whole book; he stormily disputed with him about the passages which Ray criticised as to their basal facts; but he adopted some changes Ray suggested.

The young fellow was a whole gay world to Mrs. Denton, in his reproduction of his society career for her. She pursued him to the smallest details of dress and table and manner; he lived his society events over again for her with greater consciousness than he had known in their actual experience; and he suffered patiently the little splenetic resentment in which her satiety was apt finally to express itself. He decided that he must not take Mrs. Denton in any wise seriously; and he could see that Peace was grateful to him for his complaisance and forbearance. She used to listen, too, when he described the dinners and dances for her sister, and their interest gave the material a fascination for Ray himself: it emphasized the curious duality of his life, and lent the glamor of unreality to the regions where they could no more have hoped to follow him than to tread the realms of air. Sometimes their father hung about him — getting points for his morals, as Ray once accused him of doing.

"No, no!" Hughes protested. "I am interested to find how much better than their conditions men and women always are. The competitive conditions of our economic life characterize society as well as business. Yet business men and society women are all better and kinder than you would believe they could be. The system implies that the weak must always go to the wall, but in actual operation it isn't so."

"From Mr. Ray's account there seem to be a good many wall-flowers," Mrs. Denton suggested.

Hughes ignored her frivolity. "It shows what glorious beings men and women would be if they were rightly conditioned. There is a whole heaven of mercy and loving-kindness in human nature waiting to open itself: we know a little of what it may be when a man or woman rises superior to circumstance and risks a generous word or deed in a selfish world. Then for a moment we have a glimpse of the true life of the race."

"Well, I wish I had a glimpse of the untrue life of the race, myself," said Mrs. Denton, as her father turned away. "I would give a whole year of the millennium for a week in society."

"You don't know what you're talking about," said her husband. He had been listening in gloomy silence to Ray's talk, and he now turned on his wife. "I would rather see you dead than in such 'good society' as that."

"Oh, well," she answered, "you're much likelier to see me dead. If I understand Mr. Ray, it's a great deal easier to get into heaven than to get into good society." She went up to her husband and pushed his hair back from his eyes. "If you wore it that way, people could see what a nice forehead you've got. You look twice as 'brainy,' now, Ansel."

He caught her hand and flung it furiously away. "Ansel," she said, "is beginning to feel the wear and tear of the job of setting the world right as much as I do. He never had as much faith in the millennium as father has; he thinks there's got to be some sort of sacrifice first; he hasn't made up his mind quite what it's to be, yet."

Denton left them abruptly, and after a while Ray heard him talking in the next room; he thought he must be talking to some one there, till his wife said, "Ansel doesn't say much in company, but he's pretty sociable when he gets by himself."

XXVIII.

THE next time Ray came, he found Denton dreamily picking at the strings of a violin which lay in his lap; the twins were clinging to his knees, and moving themselves in time to the music.

" You didn't know Ansel was a musician ? " his wife said. " He's just got a new violin — or rather it's a second-hand one; but it's splendid, and he got it so cheap."

" I profited by another man's misfortune," said Denton. " That's the way we get things cheap."

" Oh, well, never mind about that, now. Play the ' Darky's Dream,' won't you, Ansel? I wish we had our old ferry-boat darky here to whistle ! "

After a moment in which he seemed not to have noticed her, he put the violin to his chin, and began the wild, tender strain of the piece. It seemed to make the little ones drunk with delight. They swayed themselves to and fro, holding by their father's knees, and he looked down softly into their uplifted faces. When he stopped playing, their mother put out her hand toward one of them, but it clung the faster to its father.

" Let me take your violin a moment," said Ray. He knew the banjo a little, and now he picked out on
15

the violin an air which one of the girls in Midland had taught him.

The twins watched him with impatient rejection; and they were not easy till their father had the violin back. Denton took them up one on each knee, and let them claw at it between them; they looked into his face for the effect on him as they lifted themselves and beat the strings. After a while Peace rose and tried to take it from them, for their father seemed to have forgotton what they were doing; but they stormed at her, in their baby way, by the impulse that seemed common to them, and screamed out their shrill protest against her interference.

" Let them alone," said their father, gently, and she desisted.

" You'll spoil those children, Ansel," said his wife, " letting them have their own way so. The first thing you know, they'll grow up capitalists."

He had been looking down at them with dreamy melancholy, but he began to laugh helplessly, and he kept on till she said :

"I think it's getting to be rather out of proportion to the joke ; don't you, Mr. Ray ? Not that Ansel laughs too much, as a rule."

Denton rose, when the children let the violin slip to the floor at last, and improvised the figure of a dance with them on his shoulders, and let himself go in fantastic capers, while he kept a visage of perfect seriousness.

Hughes was drawn by the noise, and put his head into the room.

"We've got the old original Ansel back, father!" cried Mrs. Denton, and she clapped her hands and tried to sing to the dance, but broke down, and mocked at her own failure.

When Denton stopped breathless, Peace took the children from him, and carried them away. His wife remained.

"Ansel was brought up among the Shakers; that's the reason he dances so nicely."

"Oh, was that a Shaker dance?" Ray asked, carelessly.

"No. The Shaker dance is a rite," said Denton, angrily. "You might as well expect me to burlesque a prayer."

"Oh, I beg your pardon," said Ray. "I'm afraid I don't know much about it."

But Denton left the room without visible acceptance of his excuse.

"You must be careful how you say anything about the Shakers before Ansel," his wife explained. "I believe he would be willing to go back to them now, if he knew what to do with the children and me."

"If it were not for their unpractical doctrine of celibacy," said Hughes, "the Shakers, as a religious sect, could perform a most useful office in the transition from the status to better conditions. They are unselfish, and most communities are not."

"We might all go back with Ansel," said Mrs. Denton, "and they could distribute us round in the different Families. I wonder if Ansel's bull is hanging up in the South Family barn yet? You know," she said, "he painted a red bull on a piece of shingle when they were painting the barn one day, and nailed it up in a stall; when the elders found it they labored with him, and then Ansel left the community, and went out into the world. But they say, once a Shaker always a Shaker, and I believe he's had a bad conscience ever since he's left them."

Not long after this Ray came in one night dressed for a little dance that he was going to later, and Mrs. Denton had some moments alone with him before Peace joined them. She made him tell where he was going, and who the people were that were giving the dance, and what it would all be like — the rooms and decorations, the dresses, the supper.

"And don't you feel very strange and lost, in such places?" she asked.

"I don't know," said Ray. "I can't always remember that I'm a poor Bohemian with two cents in my pocket. Sometimes I imagine myself really rich and fashionable. But to-night I shan't, thank you, Mrs. Denton."

She laughed at the look he gave her in acknowledgment of her little scratch. "Then you wouldn't refuse to come to a little dance here, if we were rich enough to give one?" she asked.

"I would come instantly."

"And get your fashionable friends to come?"

"That might take more time. When are you going to give your little dance?"

"As soon as Ansel's invention is finished."

"Oh! Is he going on with that?"

"Yes. He has seen how he can do more good than harm with it — at last."

"Ah! We can nearly always coax conscience along the path of self-interest."

This pleased Mrs. Denton too. "That sounds like Mr. Kane."

Peace came in while Mrs. Denton was speaking, and gave Ray her hand, with a glance at his splendor, enhanced by his stylish manner of holding his silk hat against his thigh.

"Who was it told you that Mr. Kane was sick?" Mrs. Denton asked.

Peace answered, "Mr. Chapley."

"Kane? Is Mr. Kane sick?" said Ray. "I must go and see him."

He asked Peace some questions about Kane, but she knew nothing more than that Mr. Chapley said he was not very well, and he was going to step round and see him on his way home. Ray thought of the grudge he had borne for a while against Kane, and he was very glad now that there was none left in his heart.

"It's too late to-night; but I'll go in the morning. He usually drops in on me Sundays; he didn't come last Sunday; but I never thought of his being sick." He went on to praise Kane, and he said, as if it were one of Kane's merits, "He's been a good friend of mine. He read my novel all over after Chapley declined it, and tried to find enough good in it to justify

him in recommending it to some other publisher. I
don't blame him for failing, but I did feel hard about
his refusing to look at it afterwards; I couldn't help
it for a while." He was speaking to Peace, and he
said, as if it were something she would be cognizant
of, "I mean when Mr. Brandreth sent for it again
after he first rejected it."

"Yes," she admitted, briefly, and he was subtly
aware of the withdrawal which he noticed in her
whenever the interest of the moment became personal.

But there was never any shrinking from the personal interest in Mrs. Denton; her eagerness to ex-
plore all his experiences and sentiments was vivid and
untiring.

"Why did he send for it?" she asked. "What in
the world for?"

Ray was willing to tell, for he thought the whole
affair rather creditable to himself. "He wanted to
submit it to a friend of mine; and if my friend's judgment was favorable he might want to reconsider his
decision. He returned the manuscript the same day,
with a queer note which left me to infer that my mysterious friend had already seen it, and had seen enough
of it. I knew it was Mr. Kane, and for a while I
wanted to destroy him. But I forgave him, when I
thought it all over."

"It was pretty mean of him," said Mrs. Denton.

"No, no! He had a perfect right to do it, and I
had no right to complain. But it took me a little
time to own it."

Mrs. Denton turned to Peace. "Did you know about it?"

Denton burst suddenly into the room, and stared distractedly about as if he were searching for something.

"What is it, Ansel?" Peace asked.

"That zinc plate."

"It's on the bureau," said his wife.

He was rushing out, when she recalled him.

"Here's Mr. Ray."

He turned, and glanced at Ray impatiently, as if he were eager to get back to his work; but the gloomy face which he usually wore was gone; his eyes expressed only an intense preoccupation through which gleamed a sudden gayety, as if it flashed into them from some happier time in the past. "Oh, yes," he said to his wife, while he took hold of Ray's arm and turned him about; "this is the way you want me to look."

"As soon as your process succeeds, I expect you to look that way all the time. And I'm going to go round and do my work in a low-neck dress; and we are going to have champagne at every meal. I am going to have a day, on my card, and I am going to have afternoon teas and give dinners. We are going into the best society."

Denton slid his hand down Ray's arm, and kept Ray's hand in his hot clasp while he rapidly asked him about the side of his life which that costume represented, as though now for the first time he had a reason for caring to know anything of the world and its pleasures.

"And those people don't do anything else?" he asked, finally.

"Isn't it enough?" Ray retorted. "They think they do a great deal."

Denton laughed in a strange nervous note, catching his breath, and keeping on involuntarily. "Yes; too much. I pity them."

"Well," said his wife, "I want to be an object of pity as soon as possible. Don't lose any more time, now, Ansel, from that precious process." The light went out of his face again, and he jerked his head erect sharply, like one listening, while he stood staring at her. "Oh, now, don't be ridiculous, Ansel!" she said.

XXIX.

THE next day after a little dance does not dawn very early. Ray woke late, with a vague trouble in his mind, which he thought at first was the sum of the usual regrets for awkward things done and foolish things said the night before. Presently it shaped itself as an anxiety which had nothing to do with the little dance, and which he was helpless to deal with when he recognized it. Still, as a definite anxiety, it was more than half a question, and his experience did not afford him the means of measuring its importance or ascertaining its gravity. He carried it loosely in his mind when he went to see Kane, as something he might or might not think of.

Kane was in bed, convalescent from a sharp gastric attack, and he reached Ray a soft moist hand across the counterpane and cheerily welcomed him. His coat and hat hung against a closet door, and looked so like him that they seemed as much part of him as his hair and beard, which were smoothly brushed, and gave their silver delicately against the pillow. A fire of soft coal purred in the grate, faded to a fainter flicker by the sunlight that poured in at the long south windows, and lit up the walls book-lined from floor to ceiling.

"Yes," he said, in acceptance of the praises of its comfort that Ray burst out with, "I have lived in this room so long that I begin to cherish the expectation of dying in it. But, really, is this the first time you've been here?"

"The first," said Ray. "I had to wait till you were helpless before I got in."

"Ah, no; ah, no! Not so bad as that. I've often meant to ask you, when there was some occasion; but there never seemed any occasion; and I've lived here so much alone that I'm rather selfish about my solitude; I like to keep it to myself. But I'm very glad to see you; it was kind of you to think of coming." He bent a look of affection on the young fellow's handsome face. "Well, how wags the gay world?" he asked.

"Does the gay world do anything so light-minded as to wag?" Ray asked in his turn, with an intellectual coxcombry that he had found was not offensive to Kane. "It always seems to me very serious as a whole, the gay world, though it has its reliefs, when it tries to enjoy itself." He leaned back in his chair, and handled his stick a moment, and then he told Kane about the little dance which he had been at the night before. He sketched some of the people and made it amusing.

"And which of your butterfly friends told you I was ill?" asked Kane.

"The butterflyest of all: Mrs. Denton."

"Oh! Did *she* give the little dance?"

"No. I dropped in at the Hugheses' on the way to

the dance. But I don't know how soon she may be doing something of the kind. They're on the verge of immense prosperity. Her husband has invented a new art process, and it's going to make them rich. He doesn't seem very happy about it, but she does. He's a dreary creature. At first I used to judge her rather severely, as we do with frivolous people. But I don't know that frivolity is so bad; I doubt if it's as bad as austerity; they're both merely the effect of temperament, it strikes me. I like Mrs. Denton, though she does appear to care more for the cat than the twins. Perhaps she thinks she can safely leave them to him. He's very devoted to them; it's quite touching. It's another quality of paternal devotion from Mr. Brandreth's; it isn't half so voluble. But it's funny, all the same, to see how much more care of them he takes than their mother does. He looks after them at table, and he carries them off and puts them to bed with his own hands apparently," said Ray, in celibate contempt of the paternal tenderness.

"I believe that in David's community," Kane suggested, "the male assisted the female in the care of their offspring. We still see the like in some of the feathered tribes. In the process of social evolution the father bird will probably leave the baby bird entirely to the mother bird; and the mother bird, as soon as she begins to have mind and money, will hire in some poor bird to look after them. Mrs. Denton seems to have evolved in the direction of leaving them entirely to the father bird."

"Well, she has to do most of the talking. Have you ever heard," Ray asked from the necessary association of ideas, "about her husband's Voice?"

"What do you mean?"

"Why, it seems that Mr. Denton has an inward monitor of some kind, like the demon of Socrates, that they call a Voice, and that directs his course in life, as I understand. I suppose it's authorized him to go on with his process, which he was doubtful about for a good while, because if it succeeded it would throw a lot of people out of work. Then you've never heard of his Voice?"

"No," said Kane. He added: "I suppose it's part of the psychical nonsense that they go into in all sorts of communities. And Hughes," he asked after a moment — "how is Hughes now?"

"He's generally busy with his writing, and I don't always see him. He's a fine old fellow, if he does prefer to call me out of my name; he still addresses me generally as Young Man. Mrs. Denton has tried to teach him better; but he says that names are the most external of all things, and that I am no more essentially Ray than I am Hughes. There's something in it; I think one might get a kind of story out of the notion."

Kane lay silent in a pensive muse, which he broke to ask with a smile: "And how is Peace these days? Do you see her?"

"Yes; she's very well, I believe," said Ray, briefly, and he rose.

"Oh!" said Kane, "must you go?"

He kept Ray's hand affectionately, and seemed loath to part with him. "I'm glad you don't forget the Hugheses in the good time you're having. It shows character in you not to mind their queerness; I'm sure you won't regret it. Your visits are a great comfort to them, I know. I was afraid that you would not get over the disagreeable impression of that first Sunday, and I've never been sure that you'd quite forgiven me for taking you."

"Oh yes, I had," said Ray, and he smiled with the pleasure we all feel when we have a benefaction attributed to us. "I've forgiven you much worse things than that!"

"Indeed! You console me! But for example?"

"Refusing to look at my novel a second time," answered Ray, by a sudden impulse.

"I don't understand you," said Kane, letting his hand go.

"When Mr. Brandreth offered to submit it to you in the forlorn hope that you might like it and commend it."

"Brandreth never asked me to look at it at all; the only time I saw it was when you let me take it home with me. What do you mean?"

"Mr. Brandreth wrote me saying he wanted to try it on a friend of mine, and it came back the same day with word that my friend had already seen it," said Ray, in an astonishment which Kane openly shared.

"And was that the reason you were so cold with

me for a time? Well, I don't wonder! You had a right to expect that I would say anything in your behalf under the circumstances. And I'm afraid I should. But I never was tempted. Perhaps Brandreth got frightened and returned the manuscript with that message because he knew he couldn't trust me."

"Perhaps," said Ray, blankly.

"Who else could it have been? Have you any surmise?"

"What is the use of surmising?" Ray retorted. "It's all over. The story is dead, and I wish it was buried. Don't bother about it! And try to forgive me for suspecting *you*."

"It was very natural. But you ought to have known that I loved you too much not to sacrifice a publisher to you if I had him fairly in my hand."

"Oh, thank you! And — good-by. Don't think anything more about it. I sha'n't."

XXX.

THERE could be only one answer to the riddle, if Kane's suggestion that Mr. Brandreth had returned the manuscript without showing it to any one were rejected. The publisher could speak of no one besides Kane as a friend except Miss Hughes, and it was clearly she who had refused to look again at Ray's book. She had played a double part with him; she had let him make a fool of himself; she had suffered him to keep coming to her, and reading his things to her, and making her his literary confidante. He ground his teeth with shame to think how he had sought her advice and exulted in her praise; but the question was not merely, it was not primarily, a question of truth or untruth, kindness or unkindness toward himself, but of justice toward Kane. He had told her of the resentment he had felt toward Kane; he had left her to the belief that he still suspected Kane of what she had done. If she were willing that he should remain in this suspicion, it was worse than anything he now accused her of.

He kept away from Chapley's all day, because of the embarrassment of seeing her with that in his mind. He decided that he must never see her again till she showed some wish to be relieved from the false position she had suffered herself to be placed in. At the end of the afternoon there came a knock at his door, and he set the door open and confronted Mr. Brandreth, who stood smiling at the joke of his being there, with his lustrous silk hat and gloves and light overcoat on. Ray passed some young banter with him in humorous recognition of the situation, before they came to business, as Mr. Brandreth called it.

"Look here!" said the publisher, with a quizzical glance at him from Ray's easy-chair, while Ray himself lounged on the edge of his bed. "Did you think I wanted to show your novel to old Kane, that time when I sent back for it?"

"Yes," said Ray; and he could not say any more for his prescience of what was coming.

"Well, I didn't," Mr. Brandreth returned. "And if I'd ever thought you suspected him, I should have told you so long ago. The person that I did want it for is anxious you should know it wasn't Kane, and I thought I'd better come and tell you so by word of mouth; I rather made a mess of it before, in writing. If you've any feeling about the matter, it's only fair to Kane to assure you that he wasn't at all the person."

"Kane told me so himself to-day," said Ray; "and all the grudge I felt was gone long ago."

"Well, of course! It's a matter of business." In turning it off in this common-sense way Mr. Brandreth added lightly, "I'm authorized to tell you who it really was, if you care to know."

Ray shook his head. "I don't care to know. What's the use?"

"There isn't any. I'm glad you take it the way you do, and it will be a great relief to — the real one."

"It's all right."

Ray had been strengthening his defences against any confidential approach from the moment Mr. Brandreth began to speak; he could not help it. Now they began to talk of other things. At the end the publisher returned to the book with a kind of desperate sigh : " You haven't done anything with your story yet, I suppose ? "

"No," said Ray.

Mr. Brandreth, after a moment's hesitation, went away without saying anything more. Even that tentative inquiry about the fate of his book could not swerve Ray now from his search for the motives which had governed Peace in causing this message to be sent him. It could only be that she had acted in Kane's behalf, who had a right to justice from her, and she did not care what Ray thought of her way of doing justice. In the complex perversity of his mood the affair was so humiliating to him, as it stood, that he could not rest in it. That evening he went determined to make an opportunity to speak with her alone, if none offered.

It was she who let him in, and then she stood looking at him in a kind of daze, which he might well have taken for trepidation. It did not give him courage, and he could think of no better way to begin than to say, "I have come to thank you, Miss Hughes, for your consideration for Mr. Kane. I couldn't have
16

expected less of you, when you found out that I had been suspecting him of that friendly refusal to look at my manuscript the second time."

His hard tone, tense with suppressed anger, had all the effect he could have wished. He could see her wince, and she said, confusedly, "I told Mr. Brandreth, and he said he would tell you it wasn't Mr. Kane."

"Yes," said Ray, stiffly, "he came to tell me."

She hesitated, and then she asked, " Did he tell you who it was ? "

" No. But I knew."

If she meant him to say something more, he would not; he left to her the strain and burden that in another mood he would have shared so willingly, or wholly assumed.

At a little noise she started, and looked about, and then, as if returning to him by a painful compliance with his will, she said, " When he told me what he had done to get the manuscript back, I couldn't let him give it to me."

She stopped, and Ray perceived that, for whatever reason, she could say nothing more, at least of her own motion. But it was not possible for him to leave it so.

"Of course," he said, angrily, " I need'nt ask you why."

"It was too much for me to decide," she answered, faintly.

"Yes," he assented, "it's a good deal to take another's fate in one's hands. But you knew," he added, with a short laugh, "you had my fortune in your hands, anyway."

"I didn't see that then," she answered, and she let her eyes wander, and lapsed into a kind of absence, which vexed him as a slight to the importance of the affair.

"But it doesn't really matter whether you decided it by refusing or consenting to look at the book again," he said. "The result would have been the same, in any case."

She lifted her eyes to his with a scared look, and began, "I didn't say that"—and then she stopped again, and looked away from him as before.

"But if I can't thank you for sparing me an explicit verdict," he pushed on, "I can appreciate your consideration for Kane, and I will carry him any message you will trust me with." He rose as he said this, and he found himself adding, "And I admire your strength in keeping your own counsel when I've been talking my book over with you. It must have been amusing for you."

When he once began to revenge himself he did not stop till he said all he had thought he thought. She did not try to make any answer or protest. She sat passive under his irony; at times he thought her hardly conscious of it, and that angered him the more, and he resented the preoccupation, and then the distraction with which she heard him to the end.

"Only I don't understand exactly," he went on, "how you could let me do it, in spite of the temptation. I can imagine that the loss of my acquaintance will be a deprivation to you; you'll miss the pleasure of leading me on to make a fool of myself; but you know you can still laugh at me, and that ought to keep you in spirits for a long time. I won't ask your motive in sending word to me by a third person. I dare say you didn't wish to tell me to my face; and it couldn't have been an easy thing to write."

"I ought to have written," she said, meekly. "I see that now. But to-day, I couldn't. There is something — He offered to go to you — he wished to; and — I let him. I was wrong. I didn't think how it might seem."

"Oh, there was no reason why you should have thought of me in the matter. I'm glad you thought of Mr. Kane; I don't ask anything more than that."

"Oh, you don't understand," she began. "You don't know?" —

"Yes, I understand perfectly, and I know all that I wish to know. There was no reason why you should have protected me against my own folly. I have got my deserts, and you are not to blame if I don't like them. Good-by." -

As he turned to go, she lifted her eyes, and he could see that they were blind with tears.

He went out and walked up and down the long, unlovely avenue, conscious of being the ugliest thing in it, and unconsciously hammered by its brutal noises, while he tried to keep himself from thinking how, in spite of all he had said, he knew her to be the soul of truth and goodness. He knew that all he had said was from the need of somehow venting his wounded vanity. As far as any belief in wrong done him was concerned, the affair was purely histrionic on his part; but he had seen that the pain he gave was real; the image of her gentle sufferance of his upbraiding went visibly before him. The wish to go back and own everything to her became an intolerable stress, and then he found himself again at her door.

He rang, and after waiting a long time to hear the click of the withdrawing latch, he rang again. After a further delay the door opened, and he saw Hughes standing at the top of the stairs with a lamp held above his head.

"Who is there?" the old man called down, with his hoarse voice.

"It's I, Mr. Hughes," Ray answered, a new trouble blending with his sense of the old man's picturesque pose, and the leonine grandeur of his shaggy head. "Mr. Ray," he explained.

"Oh!" said Hughes. "I'm glad to see you. Will you come up?" He added, as Ray mounted to him, and they entered his room together, "I am alone here for the time. My daughters have both gone out. Will you sit down?" Ray obeyed, with blank disappointment. Hughes could not have known of his earlier visit, or had forgotten it. "They will be in presently. Peace was here till a little while ago; when Ansel and Jenny came in, they all went out together." He lapsed into a kind of muse, staring absently at Ray from his habitual place beside the window. He came back to a sense of him with words that had no evident bearing upon the situation.

"The thing which renders so many reformers nuga-
tory and ridiculous, and has brought contempt and
disaster on so many good causes, is the attempt to
realize the altruistic man in competitive conditions.
That must always be a failure or worse." He went
on at length to establish this position. Then, "Here
is my son-in-law "— and the old man had the effect of
stating the fact merely in illustration of the general
principle he had laid down—"who has been giving
all his spare time this winter to an invention in the
line of his art, and had brought it to completion within
a few days. He has all along had misgivings as to the
moral bearing of his invention, since every process of
the kind must throw a number of people out of work,
and he has shown a morbid scruple in the matter which
I have tried to overcome with every argument in my
power."

"I thought," Ray made out to say, in the pause
Hughes let follow, "he had come to see all that in another light."

"Yes," the old man resumed, "he has commonly
yielded to reason, but there is an unpractical element
in the man's nature. In fact, here, this morning,
while we supposed he was giving the finishing touches
to his work, he was busy in destroying every vestige
of result which could commend it to the people interested in it. Absolutely nothing remains to show that
he ever had anything of the kind successfully in hand."

"Is it possible?" said Ray, deeply shocked. "I
am so sorry to hear it "—

The old man had not heard him or did not heed him. "He has been ln a very exalted state through the day, and my daughters have gone out to walk with him; it may quiet his nerves. He believes that he has acted in obedience to an inner Voice which governs his conduct. I know nothing about such things; but all such suggestions from beyond are to my thinking mischievous. Have you ever been interested in the phenomena of spiritualism, so-called?"

Ray shook his head decidedly. "Oh, no!" he said, with abhorrence.

"Ah! The Family were at one time disposed to dabble in those shabby mysteries. But I discouraged it; I do not deny the assumptions of the spiritualists; but I can see no practical outcome to the business; and I have used all my influence with Ansel to put him on his guard against this Voice, which seems to be a survival of some supernatural experiences of his among the Shakers. It had lately been silent, and had become a sort of joke with us. But he is of a very morbid temperament, and along with this improvement, there have been less favorable tendencies. He has got a notion of expiation, of sacrifice, which is perhaps a survival of his ancestral Puritanism. I suppose the hard experiences of the city have not been good for him. They prey upon his fancy. It would be well if he could be got into the country somewhere; though I don't see just how it could be managed."

Hughes fell into another muse, and Ray asked, "What does he mean by expiation?"

The old man started impatiently. "Mere nonsense; the rags and tatters of man's infancy, outworn and outgrown. The notion that sin is to be atoned for by some sort of offering. It makes me sick; and of late I haven't paid much attention to his talk. I supposed he was going happily forward with his work; I was necessarily much preoccupied with my own; I have many interruptions from irregular health, and I must devote every available moment to my writing. There is a passage, by-the-way, which I had just completed when you rang, and which I should like to have your opinion of, if you will allow me to read it to you. It is peculiarly apposite to the very matter we have been speaking of; in fact, I may say it is an amplification of the truth that I am always trying to impress upon Ansel, namely, that when you are in the midst of a battle, as we all are here, you must fight, and fight for yourself, always, of course, keeping your will fixed on the establishment of a lasting peace." Hughes began to fumble among the papers on the table beside him for his spectacles, and then for the scattered sheets of his manuscript. "Yes, there is a special obligation upon the friends of social reform to a life of common-sense. I have regarded the matter from rather a novel standpoint, and I think you will be interested."

The old man read on and on. At last Ray heard the latch of the street door click, and the sound of the opening and then the shutting of the door. A confused noise of feet and voices arrested the reading which Hughes seemed still disposed to continue, and light steps ascended the stairs, while as if in the dark below a parley ensued. Ray knew the high, gentle tones of Peace in the pleading words, "But try, try to believe that if it says that, it can't be the Voice you used to hear, and that always told you to do what was right. It is a wicked Voice, now, and you must keep saying to yourself that it is wicked and you mustn't mind it."

"But the words, the words! Whose words were they? Without the shedding of blood : what does that mean? If it was a sin for me to invent my process, how shall the sin be remitted?"

"There is that abject nonsense of his again!" said old Hughes, in a hoarse undertone which drowned for Ray some further words from Denton. "It's impossible to get him away from that idea. Men have nothing to do with the remission of sins; it is their business to cease to do evil! But you might as well talk to a beetle!"

Ray listened with poignant eagerness for the next words of Peace, which came brokenly to his ear. He heard — ". . . justice and not sacrifice. If you try to do what is right — and — and to be good, then " —

"I will try, Peace, I will try. O Lord, help me!" came in Denton's deep tones. "Say the words again. The Voice keeps saying those — But I will say yours after you!"

"I will have justice." The girl's voice was lifted with a note in it that thrilled to Ray's heart, and made him start to his feet; Hughes laid a detaining hand upon his arm.

"I will have justice." Denton repeated.

"And not sacrifice," came in the girl's tremulous accents.

"And not sacrifice," followed devoutly from the man. "I will have justice, without the shedding of blood — it gets mixed; I can't keep the Voice out! — and not sacrifice. What is justice? What is justice but sacrifice?"

"Yes, it is self-sacrifice! All our selfish wishes "—

"I have burnt them in a fire, and scattered their ashes!"

"And all gloomy and morbid thoughts that distress other people."

"Oh, you know I wouldn't distress any one! You know how my heart is breaking for the misery of the world."

"Let her alone!" said old Hughes to Ray, in his thick murmur, as if he read Ray's impulse in the muscle of his arm. "She will manage him."

"But say those words over again!" Denton implored. "The Voice keeps putting them out of my mind!"

She said the text, and let him repeat it after her word by word, as a child follows its mother in prayer.

"And try hard, Ansel! Remember the children and poor Jenny!"

"Yes, yes. I will, Peace! Poor Jenny! I'm sorry for her. And the children— You know I wouldn't harm any one for the whole world, don't you, Peace?"

"Yes, I do know, Ansel, how good and kind you

are ; and I know you'll see all this in the true light
soon. But now you're excited."

" Well, say it just once more, and then I shall have
it."

Once more she said the words, and he after her.
He got them straight this time, without admixture
from the other text. There came a rush of his feet on
the stairs, and a wild laugh.

" Jenny! Jenny! It's all right now, Jenny!" he
shouted, as he plunged into the apartment, and was
heard beating as if on a door closed against him. It
must have opened, for there was a sound like its
shutting, and then everything was still except a little
pathetic, almost inaudible murmur as of suppressed
sobbing in the dark of the entry below. Presently
soft steps ascended the stairs and lost themselves in
the rear of the apartment.

" Now, young man," said Hughes, " I think you
had better go. Peace will be in here directly to look
after me, and it will distress her to find any one else.
It is all right now."

" But hadn't I better stay, Mr. Hughes? Can't I
be of use?"

" No. I will defer reading that passage to another
time. You will be looking in on us soon again. We
shall get on very well. We are used to these hypo-
chrondriacal moods of Ansel's."

XXXI.

THERE was nothing for Ray to do but to accept his dismissal. He got himself stealthily down stairs and out of the house, but he could not leave it. He walked up and down before it, doubting whether he ought not to ring and try to get in again. When he made up his mind to this he saw that the front windows were dark. That decided him to go home.

He did not sleep, and the next morning he made an early errand to the publishers'. He saw Peace bent over her work in Mr. Chapley's room. He longed to go and speak to her, and assure himself from her own words that all was well; but he had no right to do that, and with the first stress of his anxiety abated, he went to lay the cause of it before Kane.

"It was all a mere chance that I should know of this; but I thought you ought to know," he explained.

"Yes, certainly," said Kane; but he was less moved than Ray had expected, or else he showed his emotion less. "Hughes is not a fool, whatever Denton is; this sort of thing must have been going on a good while, and he's got the measure of it. I'll speak to Chapley about it. They mustn't be left altogether to themselves with it."

As the days began to go by, and Ray saw Peace

constantly in her place at the publishers', his unselfish anxiety yielded to the question of his own relation to her, and how he should make confession and reparation. He went to Kane in this trouble, as in the other, after he had fought off the necessity as long as he could, but they spoke of the other trouble first.

Then Ray said, with the effort to say it casually, " I don't think I told you that the great mystery about my manuscript had been solved." Kane could not remember at once what the mystery was, and Ray was forced to add, " It seems that the unknown friend who wouldn't look twice at my book was — Miss Hughes."

Kane said, after a moment, " Oh !" and then, as if it should be a very natural thing, he asked, " How did you find that out ?"

" She got Mr. Brandreth to tell me it wasn't you, as soon as she knew that I had suspected you."

" Of course. Did he tell you who it was ? "

" He was to tell me if I wished. But I knew it couldn't be anybody but she, if it were not you, and I went to see her about it."

" Well ? " said Kane, with a kind of expectation in his look and voice that made it hard for Ray to go on.

" Well, I played the fool. I pretended that I thought she had used me badly. I don't know. I tried to make her think so."

" Did you succeed ? "

" I succeeded in making her very unhappy."

" That was success — of a kind," said Kane, and he lay back in his chair looking into the fire, while Ray sat uncomfortably waiting at the other corner of the hearth.

" Did she say why she wouldn't look at your manuscript a second time? " Kane asked finally.

" Not directly."

" Did you ask? "

" Hardly ! "

" You knew? "

" It was very simple," said Ray. " She wouldn't look at it because it wasn't worth looking at. I knew that. That was what hurt me, and made me wish to hurt her."

Kane offered no comment. After a moment he asked: " Has all this just happened? Have you just found it out? "

" Oh, it's bad enough, but isn't so bad as that," said Ray, forcing a laugh. " Still, it's as bad as I could make it. I happened to go to see her that evening when I overheard her talk with Denton."

" Oh! And you spoke to her after that? "

There was a provisional condemnation in Kane's tone which kindled Ray's temper and gave him strength to retort: " No, Mr. Kane! I spoke to her before that; and it was when I came back — to tell her I was all wrong, and to beg her pardon — that I saw her father, and heard what I've told you."

" Oh, I didn't understand; I might have known that the other thing was impossible," said Kane.

They were both silent, and Ray's anger had died down into the shame that it had flamed up from, when Kane thoughtfully asked, "And you want my advice?"

"Yes."

"Concretely?"

"As concretely as possible."

"Then, if you don't really know the reason why a girl so conscientious as Peace Hughes wouldn't look at your manuscript again when she was practically left to decide its fate, I think you'd better not go there any more."

Kane spoke with a seriousness the more impressive because he was so rarely serious, and Ray felt himself reddening under his eye.

"Aren't you rather enigmatical?" he began.

"No, I don't think so," said Kane, and then neither spoke.

Some one knocked at the door. Kane called out, "Come in!" and Mr. Chapley entered.

After he had shaken hands with Kane and made Ray out, and had shaken hands with him, he said, with not more than his usual dejection, "I'm afraid poor David is in fresh trouble, Kane."

"Yes?" said Kane, and Ray waited breathlessly to hear what the trouble was.

"That wretched son-in-law of his — though I don't know why I should condemn him — seems to have been somewhere with his children and exposed them to scarlet fever; and he's down with diphtheritic sore throat himself. Peace has been at home since the trouble declared itself, helping take care of them."

"Is it going badly with them?" Kane asked.

"I don't know.   It's rather difficult to communicate with the family under the circumstances."

"You might have said impossible, without too great violence, Henry," said Kane.

"I had thought of seeing their doctor," suggested Mr. Chapley, with his mild sadness. "Ah, I wish David had stayed where he was."

"We are apt to think these things are accidents," said Kane. "Heaven knows. But scarlet fever and diphtheria are everywhere, and they take better care of them in town than they do in the country. Who did you say their doctor was?"

"Dear me! I'm sure I don't know who he is. I promised Mr. Brandreth to look the matter up," said Mr. Chapley. "He's very anxious to guard against any spread of the infection to his own child, and my whole family are so apprehensive that's it's difficult. I should like to go and see poor David, myself, but they won't hear of it. They're quite in a panic as it is."

"They're quite right to guard against the danger," said Kane, and he added, "I should like to hear David philosophize the situation. I can imagine how he would view the effort of each one of us to escape the consequences that we are all responsible for."

"It is civilization which is in the wrong," said Mr. Chapley.

"True," Kane assented. "And yet our Indians suffered terribly from the toothache and rheumatism.

You can carry your return to nature too far, Henry; Nature must meet Man half-way." Kane's eye kindled with pleasure in his phrase, and Ray could perceive that the literary interest was superseding the personal interest in his mind. "The earth is a dangerous planet; the great question is how to get away from it alive," and the light in Kane's eyes overspread his face in a smile of deep satisfaction with his paradox.

The cold-blooded talk of the two elderly men sent a chill to Ray's heart. For him, at least, there was but one thing to do; and half an hour later he stood at the open street door of the Hughes apartment, looking up at Mrs. Denton silhouetted against the light on the landing as he had first seen her there.

"Oh, Mrs. Denton," he called up, "how are the children?"

"I—I don't know. They are very sick. The doctor is afraid"—

"Oh!" Ray groaned, at the stop she made. "Can I help—can't I do something? May I come up?"

"Oh, yes," she answered mechanically, and Ray was stooping forward to mount the stairs when he saw her caught aside, and Peace standing in her place.

"Don't come up, Mr. Ray! You can't do any good. It's dangerous."

"I don't care for the danger," he began. "Some one—some one must help you! Your father"—

"My father doesn't need any help, and we don't. Every moment you stay makes the danger worse!"

"But you, *you* are in danger! You"—
17

"It's my *right* to be. But it's wrong for you. Oh, do go away!" She wrung her hands, and he knew that she was weeping. "I do thank you for coming. I was afraid you would come."

"Oh, were you?" he exulted. "I am glad of that! You know how I must have felt, when I came to think what I had said."

"Yes — but, go, now!"

"How can I do that? I should be ashamed" —

"But you mustn't," she entreated. "It would put others in danger, too. You would carry the infection. You must go," she repeated.

"Well, I shall come again. I must know how it is with you. When may I come again!"

"I don't know. You mustn't come inside again." She thought a moment. "If you come I will speak to you from that window over the door. You must keep outside. If you will ring the bell twice, I shall know it is you."

She shut the door, and left him no choice but to obey. It was not heroic; it seemed cowardly; and he turned ruefully away. But he submitted, and twice a day, early in the morning and late at night, he came and rang for her. The neighbors, such as cared, understood that he was the friend of the family who connected its exile with the world; sometimes the passers mistook these sad trysts for the happy lovers' meetings which they resembled, and lingered to listen, and then passed on.

They caught only anxious questions and hopeless

answers; the third morning that Ray came, Peace told him that the little ones were dead.

They had passed out of the world together, as they had entered it, and Ray stood with their mother beside the grave where they were both laid, and let her cling to his hand as if he were her brother. Her husband was too sick to be with them, and there had been apparently no question of Hughes's coming, but Peace was there. The weather was that of a day in late March, bitter with a disappointed hope of spring. Ray went back to their door with the mourners. The mother kept on about the little ones, as if the incidents of their death were facts of a life that was still continuing.

"Oh, I know well enough," she broke off from this illusion, "that they are gone, and I shall never see them again; perhaps their father will. Well, I don't think I was so much to blame. I didn't make myself, and I never asked to come here, any more than they did."

She had the woe-begone hopeless face which she wore the first day that Ray saw her, after the twins had thrown her porte-monnaie out of the car window; she looked stunned and stupefied.

They let her talk on, mostly without interruption. Only, at this point Peace said, "That will be thought of, Jenny," and the other asked, wistfully, "Do you think so, Peace? Well!"

XXXII.

PEACE did not come back to her work at the publishers' for several weeks. The arrears began to accumulate, and Mr. Brandreth asked Ray to help look after it; Ray was now so often with him that their friendly acquaintance had become a confidential intimacy.

Men's advance in these relations is rapid, even in later life; in youth it is by bounds. Before a week of their daily contact was out, Ray knew that Mrs. Chapley, though the best soul in the world, and the most devoted of mothers and grandmothers, had, in Mr. Brandreth's opinion, a bad influence on his wife, and through her on his son. She excited Mrs. Brandreth by the long visits she paid her; and she had given the baby medicine on one occasion at least that distinctly had not agreed with it. "That boy has taken so much belladonna, as a preventive of scarlet fever, that I believe it's beginning to affect his eyes. The pupils are tremendously enlarged, and he doesn't notice half as much as he did a month ago. I don't know when Mrs. Chapley will let us have Miss Hughes back again. Of course, I believe in taking precautions too, and I never could forgive myself if anything really happened. But I don't want to be a perfect slave to my fears, or my mother-in-law's, either — should you ? "

He asked Ray whether, under the circumstances, he did not think he ought to get some little place near New York for the summer, rather than go to his country home in Massachusetts, where the Chapleys had a house, and where his own mother lived the year round. When Ray shrank from the question as too personal for him to deal with, Mr. Brandreth invited him to consider the more abstract proposition that if the two grandmothers had the baby there to quarrel over all summer, they would leave nothing of the baby, and yet would not part friends.

"I'll tell you another reason why I want to be near my business so as to keep my finger on it all the time, this year," said Mr. Brandreth, and he went into a long and very frank study of the firm's affairs with Ray, who listened with the discreet intelligence which made everybody trust him. "With Mr. Chapley in the state he's got into about business, when he doesn't care two cents whether school keeps or not, I see that I've got to take the reins more and more into my own hands." Mr. Brandreth branched off into an examination of his own character, and indirectly paid himself some handsome tributes as a business man. "I don't mean to say," he concluded, "that I've got the experience of some of the older men, but I do mean to say that experience doesn't count for half of what they claim, in the book business, and I can prove it out of their own mouths. They all admit

that nobody can forecast the fate of a book. Of course
if you've got a book by a known author, you've got
something to count on, but not so much as people
think, and some unknown man may happen along
with a thing that hits the popular mood and outsell
him ten times over. It's a perfect lottery."

Chance

"I wonder they let you send your lists of new publications through the mails," said Ray, dryly.

"Oh, it isn't quite as bad as that," said Mr. Brandreth. "Though there are a good many blanks too.
I suppose the moral difference between business and
gambling is that in business you do work for a living,
and you don't propose to give nothing for something,
even when you're buying as cheap as you can to sell
as dear as you can. With a book it's even better. It's
something you've put value into, and you have a right
to expect to get value out of it. That's what I tell
Mr. Chapley when he gets into one of his Tolstoi
moods, and wants to give his money to the poor and
eat his bread in the sweat of his brow."

The two young men laughed at these grotesque con-
ceptions of duty, and Mr. Brandreth went on :

"Yes, sir, if I could get hold of a good, strong,
lively novel " —

"Well, there is always *A Modern Romeo*," Ray
suggested.

Mr. Brandreth winced. "I know." He added,
with the effect of hurrying to get away from the subject, "I've had it over and over again with Mr. Chapley till I'm tired of it. Well, I suppose it's his age,

somewhat, too. Every man, when he gets to Mr. Chapley's time of life, wants to go into the country and live on the land. I'd like to see him living on the land in Hatboro', Massachusetts! You can stand up in your buggy and count half-a-dozen abandoned farms wherever you've a mind to stop on the road. By-the-way," said Mr. Brandreth, from an association of ideas that Ray easily followed, "have you seen anything of the book that Mr. Hughes is writing? He's got a good title for it. 'The World Revisited' ought to sell the first edition of it at a go."

"Before people found out what strong meat it was? It condemns the whole structure of society; he's read me parts of it."

"Well, well," said Mr. Brandreth, in a certain perplexity, "that might make it go too. People like strong meat. They like to have the structure of society condemned. There's a good deal of sympathy with the underpinning; there's no use trying to deny it Confound it! I should like to try such a book as that in the market. But it would be regarded by everybody who knew him as an outcome of Mr. Chapley's Tolstoï twist."

"I understand that Mr. Hughes's views are entirely opposed to Tolstoï's. He regards him as unpractical," said Ray, with a smile for Hughes's practicality.

"It wouldn't make any difference. They would call it Tolstoïan on Mr. Chapley's account. People don't know. There was *Looking Backward;* they took that at a gulp, and didn't know that it was the

rankest sort of socialism. My! If I could get hold
of a book like *Looking Backward!*"

"I might have it come out that the wicked cousin
in *A Modern Romeo* was a secret Anarchist. That
ought to make the book's fortune."

Ray could deal lightly with his rejected novel, but
even while he made an open jest of it, the book was
still inwardly dear to him. He still had his moments
of thinking it a great book, in places. He was
always mentally comparing it with other novels that
came out, and finding it better. He could not see
why they should have got publishers, and his book
not; he had to fall back upon that theory of mere
luck which first so emboldens and then so embitters
the heart; and the hope that lingered in him was mixed
with cynicism.

XXXIII.

WHEN Peace came back to her work, Mr. Brandreth, in admiration of her spirit, confided to Ray that she had refused to take pay for the time she had been away, and that no arguments availed with her.

"They must have been at unusual expense on account of this sickness, and I understand that the son-in-law hasn't earned anything for a month. But what can you do?"

"You can't do anything," said Ray. Their poverty might be finally reached from without, and it was not this which made him chiefly anxious in his futile sympathy for Peace. He saw her isolated in the presence of troubles from which he was held as far aloof as her father lived in his dream of a practicable golden age. Their common sorrow, which ought to have drawn the mother and father of the dead children nearer together, seemed to have alienated them. After the first transports of her grief Mrs. Denton appeared scarcely to miss the little ones; the cat, which they had displaced so rarely, was now always in her lap, and her idle, bantering talk went on, about anything, about everything, as before, but with something more of mockery for her husband's depressions and exaltations. It might have been from a mistaken wish to rouse him to some sort of renewed endeavor that she let her reckless tongue run upon what he had done with his process; it might have been from her perception that he was most vulnerable there; Ray could not decide. For the most part Denton remained withdrawn from the rest, a shadow and a silence which they ignored. Sometimes he broke in with an irrelevant question or comment, but oftener he evaded answering when they spoke to him. If his wife pressed him at such times he left them; and then they heard him talking to himself in his room, after an old habit of his; now and then Ray thought he was praying. If he did not come back, Peace followed him, and then her voice could be heard in entreaty with him.

"She's the only one that can do anything with Ansel," her sister lightly explained one evening. "She has so much patience with him; father hasn't any more than I have; but Peace can persuade him out of almost anything except his great idea of sacrifice."

"Sacrifice?" Ray repeated.

"Yes. I don't know what he means. But he thinks he's been very wicked, trying to invent that process, and he can't get forgiveness without some kind of sacrifice. He's found it in the Old Testament somewhere. *I* tell him it's a great pity he didn't live in the days of the prophets; he might have passed for one. I don't know what he's going to do. He says we must make some sacrifice; but I can't see what

we've got left to sacrifice. We might make a burnt
offering of the chairs in father's stove; the coal's
about gone."

She stopped, and looked up at Denton, who had
come in with a book in his hand; Peace glided in behind him.

"Oh, are you going to read us something, Ansel?"
his wife asked with her smile of thoughtless taunting.
"I don't see why you don't give public readings. You
could read better than the elocutionists that used to
read to us in the Family. And it wouldn't be taking
the bread out of any one else's mouth." She turned
to Ray: "You know Ansel's given up his place so as
to let another man have his chance. It was the least
he could do after he had tried to take away the liveli-
hood of so many by inventing that wicked process of
his."

Denton gave no sign of having heard her. He
fixed his troubled eyes on Ray. "Do you know that
poem?" he asked, handing him the open book.

"Oh, yes," said Ray.

"It's a mistake," said Denton, "all a mistake. I
should like to write to Tennyson and tell him so. I've
thought it out. The true sacrifice would have been
the best, not the dearest; the best."

The next day was Sunday, and it broke, with that
swift, capricious heat of our climate, after several days
of cloudy menace. The sun shone, and the streets
were thronged with people. They were going to
church in different directions, but there was every-

where a heavy trend toward the stations of the elevated road, and the trains were crammed with men, women and children going to the Park. When Ray arrived there with one of the throngs he had joined, he saw the roads full of carriages, and in the paths black files of foot-passengers pushing on past the seats packed with those who had come earlier, and sat sweltering under the leafless trees. The grass was already green; some of the forwarder shrubs were olive-gray with buds.

Ray walked deep into the Park. He came in sight of a bench near a shelf of rock in a by-path, with a man sitting alone on it. There was room for two, and Ray made for the place.

The man sat leaning forward with his heavy blonde head hanging down as if he might have been drunk. He suddenly lifted himself, and Ray saw that it was Denton. His face was red from the blood that had run into it, but as it grew paler it showed pathetically thin. He stared at Ray confusedly, and did not know him till he spoke.

Then he said, "Oh!" and put out his hand. A sudden kindness in Ray, more than he commonly felt for the man whom he sometimes pitied, but never liked, responded to the overture.

"May I have part of your bench?" he asked.

"Yes," said Denton. "Sit down," and he made way for him. "It isn't mine; it's one of the few things in this cursed town that belongs to every one."

"Well," said Ray, cheerfully, "I suppose we're all

proprietors of the Park, even if we're not allowed to walk on our own grass."

"Yes; but don't get me thinking about that. There's been too much of that in my life. I want to get away — away from it all. We are going into the country. Do you know about those abandoned farms in New England? Could we go and take up one of them?"

"I'm sure I don't know. But what could you do with it, if you did? The owners left those farms because they couldn't live on them. You would have to fight a battle you're not strong enough for. Better wait till you get fairly on your feet."

"Yes, I'm sick; I'm no good. But it would be expiation."

Ray did not speak at once. Then, partly because he thought he might be of use to the man by helping him to an objective vision of what was haunting him, and partly from an æsthetic desire to pry into the confusion of his turbid soul, he asked: "Do you mean for that invention of yours?"

"No; that's nothing; that was a common crime."

"Well, I have no right to ask you anything further. But in any given case of expiation, the trouble is that a man can't expiate alone; he makes a lot of other people expiate with him."

"Yes; you can't even sin alone. That is the curse of it, and then the innocent have to suffer with the sinners. But I meant — the children."

"The children?"

"Yes; I let them die."

Ray understood now that it was remorse for his exposure of the little ones to contagion which was preying on him. "I don't think you were to blame for that. It was something that might have happened to any one. For the sake of your family you ought to look at it in the true light. You are no more responsible for your children's death than I am." Ray stopped, and Denton stared as if listening.

"What? What? What?" he said, in the tone of a man who tries to catch something partly heard. "Did you hear?" he asked. "They are both talking at once — with the same voice; it's the twin nature." He shook his head vehemently, and said, with an air of relief: "Well, now it's stopped. What did you say?"

"I didn't say anything," Ray answered.

"Oh! It was the Voice, then. You see it was a mistake not to do it sooner; I ought to have *given* them; not waited for them to be *taken*. I couldn't understand, because in the flesh they couldn't speak. They had to speak in the spirit. That was it — why they died. I thought that if I took some rich man who had made his millions selfishly, cruelly — you see? — it would satisfy justice; then the reign of peace and plenty could begin. But that was wrong. That would have made the guilty suffer for the innocent; and the innocent must suffer for the guilty. Always! There is no other atonement. Now I see that. Oh, my soul, my soul! What? No! Yes,

yes! The best, the purest, the meekest! Always
that! Without the shedding of blood, there is no
remission — Who do you think is the best person in
New York — the purest, the meekest?"

"Who?" Ray echoed.

"Yes," said Denton. Then he broke off. "She
said, No! No! No!" He started up from the seat.
"For their life, their life, their life! That was where
the wrong was. I knew it was all wrong, always.
Oh, my soul, my soul! What shall the atonement
be?" He moved away, and at a few paces' distance
he began to run.

Ray watched him running, running, till he was out
of sight.

He passed a restless, anxious day, and in the evening he could not keep from going to the Hugheses'.
He found them all together, and gayer than he had
seen them since the children's death. He tried to join
in the light-hearted fun that Mrs. Denton was making
with her husband; she was unusually fond, and she
flattered him with praises of his talent and good looks ;
she said his pallor became him.

"Do you know," she asked Ray, "that we're all
going to New Hampshire to live on an abandoned
farm?"

She made Denton get his violin, and he played a
long time. Suddenly he stopped, and waited in the
attitude of listening. He called out, "Yes!" and
struck the instrument over a chair-top, breaking it to
splinters. He jumped up as if in amaze at what had

happened; then he said to Peace, "I've made you some kindling."

His wife said with a smile, "A man must do *something* for a living."

Denton merely looked at her with a kind of vague surprise. After a moment's suspense he wheeled about and caught his hat from the wall, and rushed down the stairs into the street.

Hughes came in from the front room, with his pen in his hand, and hoarsely gasping. "What is the matter?" he weakly whispered. No one spoke, but the ruin of the violin answered for itself. "Some more of that fool's work, I suppose. It is getting past all endurance. He was always the most unpractical creature, and of late, he's become utterly worthless." He kept on moving his lips as if he were speaking, but no sound came from them.

Mrs. Denton burst into a crowing laugh: "It's too bad Ansel should have *two* voices and father none at all!"

The old man's lips still moved, and now there came from them, "A fool, a perfect fool!"

"Oh, no, father," said Peace, and she went up to the old man. "You know Ansel isn't a fool. You know he has been tried; and he is good, you know he is! He has worked hard for us all; and I can't bear to have you call him names."

"Let him show some common-sense, then," said her father. "I have no wish to censure him. But his continual folly wears me out. He owes it to the cause, if not to his family, to be sensible and — and — practical. Tell him I wish to see him when he comes in," he added, with an air of authority, like the relic of former headship. " It's high time I had a talk with him. These disturbances in the family are becoming very harassing. I cannot fix my mind on anything."

He went back into his own room, where they heard him coughing. It was a moment of pain without that dignity which we like to associate with the thought of suffering, but which is seldom present in it; Ray did not dare to go ; he sat keenly sensible of the squalor of it, unable to stir. He glanced toward Peace for strength ; she had her face hidden in her hands. He would not look at Mrs. Denton, who was saying : " I think father is right, and if Ansel can't control himself any better than he has of late, he'd better leave us. It's wearing father out. Don't you think he looks worse, Mr. Ray ? "

He did no answer, but remained wondering what he had better do.

Peace took down her hands and looked at him, and he saw that she wished him to go. He went, but in the dark below he lingered, trying to think whom he should turn to for help. He ran over Mr. Chapley, Brandreth, Kane in his mind with successive rejection, and then he thought of Kane's doctor ; he had never really seen him, but he feigned him the wisest and most efficient of the doctors known to fiction. Of course it must be a doctor whom Ray should speak to ; but he must put the affair hypothetically, so that if the doctor

18

thought it nothing, no one would be compromised. It must be a physician of the greatest judgment, a man of sympathy as well as sagacity ; no, it could be any sort of doctor, and he ought to go to him at once.

He was fumbling in the dark for the wire that pulled the bolt of the street door when a night-latch was thrust into the key-hole outside, and the door was burst open with a violence that flung him back against the wall behind it. Before it could swing to again he saw Denton's figure bent in its upward rush on the stairs ; he leaped after him.

" Now, then ! " Denton shouted, as they burst into the apartment together. " The time has come ! The time has come ! They are calling you, Peace ! You wouldn't let me give them, and the Lord had to take them, but they have reconciled Him to you ; He will accept you for their sake ! "

Old Hughes had entered from his room, and stood looking on with a frowning brows, but with more vexation than apprehension. " Be done with that arrant nonsense ! " he commanded. " What stuff are you talking ? "

Denton's wife shrank into the farthest corner, with the cat still in her arms. Peace stood in the middle of the room staring at him. He did not heed Hughes except to thrust him aside as he launched himself towards the girl.

Ray slipped between them, and Denton regarded him with dull wavering eyes like a drunken man's. " Oh, you're here still, are you ? " he said ; a cunning gleam came into his eyes, and he dropped his voice from its impassioned pitch. He kept his right hand in his coat pocket, and Ray watched that hand too solely. Denton flashed past him, and with his left swept away the hands which Peace mechanically lifted to her face, and held them in his grip. Ray sprang upon him, and pinioned his right wrist.

"Hold him fast!" Hughes added his grip to Ray's. "He's got something in his pocket, there! Run to the window, Jenny, and call for help!"

"No, no, Jenny, don't!" Peace entreated. "Don't call out. Ansel won't hurt me! I know he'll listen to me; won't you Ansel? Oh, what is it you want to do?"

"Here!" cried Denton. "Take it! In an instant you will be with them! The sin will be remitted." He struggled to reach her lips with the hand which he had got out of his pocket. Old Hughes panted out:

"Open his fist! Tear it open. If I had a knife"—

"Oh, don't hurt him!" Peace implored. "He isn't hurting me."

Denton suddenly released her wrists, and she sank senseless. Ray threw himself on his knees beside her, and stretched his arms out over her.

Denton did not look at them; he stood a moment listening; then with a formless cry he whirled into the next room. The door shut crashing behind him, and then there came the noise of a heavy fall within. The rush of a train made itself loudly heard in the silence.

A keen bitter odor in the air rapt Ray far away to

an hour of childhood when a storm had stripped the
blossoms from a peach-tree by the house, and he noted
with a child's accidental observance the acrid scent
which rose from them.

"That is prussic acid," Hughes whispered, and he
moved feebly towards the door and pushed it open.
Denton lay on the floor with his head toward the
threshold, and the old man stood looking down into his
dead face.

"It must have been that which he had in his hand."

XXXIV

"WELL, old fellow, I've got some good news for you," said Mr. Brandreth, when Ray showed himself at the door of the publisher's little den the next morning. Ray thought that he carried the record of the event he had witnessed in every lineament, but Mr. Brandreth could have seen nothing unusual in his face. "The editor of *Every Evening* has just been here, and he wants to see you about taking hold of his literary department." Ray stared blankly. Mr. Brandreth went on with generous pleasure: "He's had some trouble with the man who's been doing it, and it's come to a complete break at last, and now he wants you to try. He's got some new ideas about it. He wants to make something specially literary of the Saturday issue; he has a notion of restoring the old-fashioned serial. If you take charge, you could work in the *Modern Romeo* on him; and then, if it succeeds as a serial, we can republish it in book form! Better see him at once! Isn't it funny how things turn out? He said he was coming down town in a Broadway car, and happened to catch sight of Coquelin's name on a poster at the theatre, and it made him think of you. He'd always liked that thing you did for him, and when he got down here, he jumped out and came in to ask about you. I talked you into him good and strong, and he wants to see you."

Ray listened in nerveless passivity to news that would have transported him with hope a few hours before. Mr. Brandreth might well have mistaken his absent stare for the effect of such a rapture. He said, as a man does when tempted a little beyond prudence by the pleasure he is giving:

"The fact is, I've been thinking about that work of yours, myself. I want to try *some* novel for the summer trade; and I want you to let me see it again. I want to read it myself this time. They say a publisher oughtn't to know anything about the inside of a book, but I think we might make an exception of yours." Ray's face remained unchanged, and Mr. Brandreth now asked, with a sudden perception of its strangeness: "Hello! What's the matter? Anything gone wrong with you?"

"No, no," Ray struggled out, "not with me. But"—

"Nothing new with the Hugheses, I hope?" said Mr. Brandreth, with mounting alarm. "Miss Hughes was to have come back to work this morning, but she hasn't yet. No more diphtheria, I hope? By Jove, my dear fellow, I don't think you ought to come here if there is! I don't think it's quite fair to me."

"It isn't diphtheria," Ray gasped. "But they're in great trouble. I hardly know how to tell you. That wretched creature, Denton, has killed himself. He's been off his base for some time, and I've been dreading — I've been there all night with them. He took prussic acid and died instantly. Mr. Hughes and I had a struggle with him to prevent — prevent him; and the old man got a wrench, and then he had a hemorrhage. He is very weak from it, but the doctor's brought him round for the present. Miss Hughes wanted me to come and tell you."

"Has it got out yet?" Mr. Brandreth asked. "Are the reporters on to it?"

"The fact has to come out officially through the doctor, but it isn't known yet."

"I wish it hadn't happened," said Mr. Brandreth. "It will be an awful scandal."

There had been a moment with Ray too when the scandal of the fact was all he felt. "Yes," he said, mechanically.

"You see," Mr. Brandreth explained, "those fellows will rummage round in every direction, for every bit of collateral information, relevant and irrelevant, and they will make as much as they can of the fact that Miss Hughes was employed here."

"I see," said Ray.

Mr. Brandreth fell into a rueful muse, but he plucked himself out of it with self-reproachful decency. "It's awful for them, poor things!"

"It's the best thing that could have happened, under the circumstances," said Ray, with a coldness that surprised himself, and a lingering resentment toward Denton that the physical struggle had left in his nerves. "It was a question whether he should kill himself, or kill some one else. He had a mania of sacrifice, of atonement. Somebody had to be offered up. He was a crank." Ray pronounced the word with a strong disgust, as if there were nothing worse to be said of a man. He paused, and then he went on. " I shall have to tell you all about it, Brandreth ; " and he went over the event again, and spared nothing.

Mr. Brandreth listened with starting eyes. As if the additional details greatly discouraged him, he said, " I don't think those things can be kept from coming out. It will be a terrible scandal. Of course, I pity the family ; and Miss Hughes. It's strange that they could keep living on with such a danger hanging over them for weeks and months, and not try to do anything about it — not have him shut up."

" The doctor says we've no idea what sort of things people keep living on with," said Ray, gloomily. " The danger isn't always there, and the hope is. The trouble keeps on, and in most cases nothing happens. The doctor says nothing would have happened in this case, probably, if the man had staid quietly in the country, in the routine he was used to. But when he had the stress of new circumstances put on him, with the anxieties and the chances, and all the miseries around him, his mind gave way; I don't suppose it was ever a very strong one."

" Oh, I don't see how the strongest stands it, in this infernal hurly-burly," said Mr. Brandreth, with an introspective air. He added, with no effect of relief

from his reflection, " I don't know what I'm going to
say to my wife when all this comes out. I've got to
prepare her, somehow — her and her mother. Look
here! Why couldn't you go up to Mr. Chapley's with
me, and see him? He wasn't very well, yesterday,
and said he wouldn't be down till this afternoon. My
wife's going there to lunch, and we can get them all
together before the evening papers are out. Then I
think we could make them see it in the right light.
What do you say?"

"I don't see why I shouldn't go with you. If I
can be of any use," said Ray, with an inward regret
that he could think of no excuse for not going.

"I think you can be of the greatest use," said Mr.
Brandreth. He called a clerk, and left word with
him that he should not be in again till after lunch.
"You see," he explained, as they walked out together, "if we can get the story to Mrs. Brandreth
and her mother before it comes to them in print it
won't seem half as bad. Some fellow is going to get
hold of the case and work it for all it is worth. He
is going to unearth Mr. Hughes's whole history, and
exploit him as a reformer and a philosopher. He's
going to find out everybody who knows him, or has
ever had anything to do with him, and interview
people right and left."

Ray had to acknowledge that this was but too prob-
able. He quailed to think of the publicity which he
must achieve in the newspapers, and how he must
figure before the people of Midland, who had expected
such a different celebrity for him.

"You must look out for yourself. I'm going to put Mr. Chapley on his guard, and warn the ladies not to see any reporters or answer any questions. By-the-way, does Mr. Kane know about this yet?"

" I've just come from his place ; he wasn't at home; I left a note for him."

"I wonder if we hadn't better go round that way and tell him?" Mr. Brandreth faltered a moment, and then pushed on. "Or, no! He's a wary old bird, and I don't think he'll say anything that will commit anybody." They walked on in silence for awhile before Mr. Brandreth said, with an air of relevance, "Of course, I shouldn't want you to count too much upon our being able to do anything with your book this year, after all."

"Of course," said Ray. "If I'm mixed up with this business in the papers, my name won't be a very good one for a respectable house to conjure with for some years to come. Perhaps never."

At that moment he was mere egoïst, feeling nothing but the mockery and the malice of fortune; all his compassion for the hapless creatures whose misery had involved him died within him.

"Oh, I don't mean that, exactly," said Mr. Brandreth. "But isn't it curious how we're all bound together here? It's enough to make one forswear all intercourse with his fellow-beings. Here we are in same boat with people whom I didn't know the existence of six months ago; and because Mr. Chapley has stood by his old friend and tried to help him along, he will probably be pilloried with him before the public as a fellow-Tolstoïan, and people all over the country that used to order their books through us will think we're in sympathy with the anarchists, and won't have any more to do with us than if we had published the *Kreuzer Sonata*."

Ray thought how he had never asked to know the Hugheses at all, and was not justly responsible for them, even through a tie of ancient friendship. But in the presence of Mr. Brandreth's shameless anxieties, he was ashamed to air his own. He only said, cynically : "Yes, it appears that a homicidal lunatic can't take himself harmlessly out of the world. His fate reaches out in every direction, and covers everybody that knew him with confusion. And they talk of a moral government of the universe!"

"Yes!" said Mr. Brandreth, with as much satisfaction in Ray's scorn of the order of things as his mild nature could probably feel.

At Mr. Chapley's house they learned that Mrs. Brandreth had brought the baby to spend the day with her mother. Her sister, whom Ray knew, met the two men at the door on her way out to a young ladies' lunch, and told them they would find her father in his library. She said Mr. Kane was there with him; and Mr. Brandreth, with a glance at Ray, said, " Well, that's first-rate!" and explained, as they pushed on upstairs, " He may be able to suggest something."

Kane did not suggest anything at once. He lis-

tened in silence and without apparent feeling to Ray's
story.

"Dear me!" Mr. Chapley lamented. "Dreadful,
dreadful! Poor David must be in a sad state about
it! And I'm not fit to go to him!"

"He wouldn't expect you, sir," Mr. Brandreth began.

"I don't know; he would certainly come to me if I
were in trouble. Dear, dear! Was the hemorrhage
very exhausting, Mr. — er — Ray?"

Ray gave the doctor's word that there was no immediate danger from it, and Mr. Brandreth made haste to
say that he had come to tell the ladies about the affair
before they saw it in the papers, and to caution them
against saying anything if reporters called.

"Yes, that's very well," said Mr. Chapley. "But I
see nothing detrimental to us in the facts."

"No, sir. Not unless they're distorted, and — in
connection with your peculiar views, sir. When those
fellows get on to your old friendship with Mr. Hughes,
and *his* peculiar views, there's no telling what they
won't make of them." Kane glanced round at Ray
with arched eyes and pursed mouth. Mr. Brandreth
turned toward Ray, and asked sweetly, "Should you
mind my lighting one of those after-dinner pastilles?"
He indicated the slender stem in the little silver-holder
on the mantel. "Of course there's no danger of infection now; but it would be a little more reassuring to
my wife, especially as she's got the boy here with her."

"By all means," said Ray, and the pastille began

sending up a delicate thread of pungent blue smoke, while Mr. Brandreth went for his wife and mother-in-law.

"It seems to me you're in a parlous state, Henry," said Kane. "I don't see but you'll have to renounce Tolstoï and all his works if you ever get out of this trouble. I'm sorry for you. It takes away half the satisfaction I feel at the lifting of that incubus from poor David's life. I think I'd better go." He rose, and went over to give his hand to Mr. Chapley, where he sat in a reclining-chair.

Mr. Chapley clung to him, and said feebly : "No, no! Don't go, Kane. We shall need your advice, and — and — counsel," and while Kane hesitated, Mr. Brandreth came in with the ladies, who wore a look of mystified impatience.

"I thought they had better hear it from you, Mr. Ray," he said, and for the third time Ray detailed the tragical incidents. He felt as if he had been inculpating himself.

Then Mrs. Chapley said : "It is what we might have expected from the beginning. But if it will be a warning to Mr. Chapley "—

Mrs. Brandreth turned upon her mother with a tone that startled Mr. Chapley from the attitude of gentle sufferance in which he sat resting his chin upon his hand. "I don't see what warning there can be for papa in such a dreadful thing. Do you think he's likely to take prussic acid?"

"I don't say that, you know well enough, child.

But I shall be quite satisfied if it is the last of Tol-
stoïsm in *this* family."

"It has nothing to do with Tolstoï," Mrs. Brandreth
returned, with surprising energy. "If we'd all been
living simply in the country, that wretched creature's
mind wouldn't have been preyed upon by the misery of
the city."

"There's more insanity in proportion to the popula-
tion in the country than there is in the city," Mrs.
Chapley began.

Mrs. Brandreth ignored her statistical contribution.
"There's no more danger of father's going out to live
on a farm, or in a community, than there is of his taking poison; and at any rate he hasn't got anything to
do with what's happened. He's just been faithful to
his old friend, and he's given his daughter work. I
don't care how much the newspapers bring that in. We
haven't done anything wrong."

Mr. Brandreth looked at his wife in evident surprise;
her mother said, "Well, my dear!"

Her father gently urged: "I don't think you've
quite understood your mother. She doesn't look at life
from my point of view."

"No, Henry, I'm thankful to say I don't," Mrs.
Chapley broke in; "and I don't know anybody who
does. If I had followed you and your prophet, we
shouldn't have had a roof over our heads."

"A good many people have no roofs over their
heads," Mr. Chapley meekly suggested.

"That's no reason why we shouldn't," said his wife.

"No; you're right there, my dear. That's the hopeless part of it. Perhaps poor David is right, and the man who attempts to solve the problem of altruism singly and in his own life"—

Mrs. Brandreth would not let him finish. "The question is, what are we going to do for these poor things in their trouble?" She looked at Ray, who had sat by trying in his sense of intrusion and superfluity to shrink into as small a space as possible. He now blushed to find himself appealed to. He had not seen Mrs. Brandreth often, and he had not reversed his first impression of a narrow, anxious, housewifely spirit in her, sufficient to the demands of young motherhood, but of few and scanty general sympathies. "When did you see them last?" she asked.

He told her, and she said, "Well, I am going right up there with Percy."

"And bring back the scarlet fever to your child!" cried her mother. "You shall neither of you go, as long as I have anything to say about it. Or, if you do, you shall not come back to this house, and I shall keep the baby here till there isn't the least fear of danger; and I don't know how long that will be." All the grandmother rose in Mrs. Chapley; she lifted her voice, and in the transport of her alarm and indignation she suddenly appealed to Mr. Kane from the wilfulness she evidently feared in her daughter: "What do you think, Mr. Kane?"

"I wouldn't presume to decide such a question finally; it's too important," Kane said, in his mellow murmur. "But I wish that for the moment Mrs. Brandreth would let me be the bearer of her kind messages and inquiries. If you haven't been in the habit of calling there " —

"I have never been there at all, I'm sorry to say," Mrs. Brandreth frankly declared.

"Ah! Well, I don't see what good could come of it, just at present; and there might be some lingering infection."

"It has been carried in clothes across the ocean months afterwards, and in letters," Mrs. Chapley triumphed.

Kane abandoned the point to her. "The situation might be very much worse for the Hugheses, as I was saying to Henry before you came in. The Powers are not commonly so considerate. It seems to me distinctly the best thing that could have happened, at least as far as Denton is concerned."

"Surely," said Mrs. Chapley, "you don't approve of suicide ? "

"Not in the case of sane and happy people," Kane blandly replied. "The suicide of such persons should be punished with the utmost rigor of the law. But there seem to be extenuating circumstances in the present instance; I hope the coroner's jury will deal leniently with the culprit. I must go and see if I can do anything for David. Probably I can't. It's always a question in these cases whether you are not adding to the sufferings of the mourners by your efforts to alleviate them; but you can only solve it at their expense by trying."

"And you will let us know," said Mrs. Chapley, "whether *we* can do anything, Mr. Kane."

Mrs. Brandreth did not openly persist in her determination to go to the Hugheses. She said, "Yes, be sure you let us know," and when Kane had gone on an errand of mercy which he owned was distasteful to him, her husband followed Ray down to the door.

"You see what splendid courage she has," he whispered, with a backward glance up the stairs. "I must confess that it surprised me, after all I've seen her go through, that stand she took with her mother. But I don't altogether wonder at it; they were disagreeing about keeping up the belladonna when I found them, upstairs, and I guess Mrs. Brandreth's opposition naturally carried over into this question about the Hugheses. Of course Mrs. Chapley means well, but if Mrs. Brandreth could once be got from under her influence she would be twice the woman she is. I think she's right about the effect of our connection with the family before the public. They can't make anything wrong out of it, no matter how they twist it or turn it. I'm not afraid. After all, it isn't as if Mr. Hughes was one of those howling socialists. An old-time Brook Farmer — it's a kind of literary tradition; it's like being an original abolitionist. I'm going to see if I can't get a glimpse of that book of his without committing myself. Well, let me know how you get on. I wouldn't let that chance on *Every Evening* slip. Better see the man. Confound the papers! I hope they won't drag us in!"

19

XXXV.

A FEW lines, with some misspelling of names, told the story of the suicide and inquest in the afternoon papers, and it dwindled into still smaller space and finer print the next morning. The publicity which those least concerned had most dreaded was spared them. Ray himself appeared in print as a witness named Bray; there was no search into the past of Hughes and his family, or their present relations; none of the rich sensations of the case were exploited; it was treated as one of those every-day tragedies without significance or importance, which abound in the history of great cities, and are forgotten as rapidly as they occur. The earth closed over the hapless wretch for whom the dream of duty tormenting us all, more or less, had turned to such a hideous nightmare, and those whom his death threatened even more than his life drew consciously or unconsciously a long breath of freedom.

Mr. Brandreth's courage rose with his escape; there came a moment when he was ready to face the worst; the moment did not come till the danger of the worst was past. Then he showed himself even eager to retrieve the effect of anxieties not compatible with a scrupulous self-respect.

"Why should we laugh at him?" Kane philosophized, in talking the matter over with Ray. "The ideals of generosity and self-devotion are preposterous in our circumstances. He was quite right to be cautious, to be prudent, to protect his business and his bosom from the invasion of others' misfortunes, and to look anxiously out for the main chance. Who would do it for him, if he neglected this first and most obvious duty? He has behaved most thoughtfully and kindly toward Peace through it all, and I can't blame him for not thrusting himself forward to offer help when nothing could really be done."

Kane had himself remained discreetly in the background, and had not cumbered his old acquaintance with offers of service. He kept away from the funeral, but he afterwards visited Hughes frequently, though he recognized nothing more than the obligation of the early kindness between them. This had been affected by many years of separation and wide divergence of opinion, and it was doubtful whether his visits were altogether a pleasure to the invalid. They disputed a good deal, and sometimes when Hughes lost his voice from excitement and exhaustion, Kane's deep pipe kept on in a cool smooth assumption of positions which Hughes was physically unable to assail.

Mr. Chapley went out of town to his country place in Massachusetts, to try and get back his strength after a touch of the grippe. The Sunday conventicles had to be given up because Hughes could no longer lead them, and could not suffer the leadership of others. He

was left mainly for society and consolation to the young
fellow who did not let him feel that he differed from
him, and was always gently patient with him.

Ray had outlived the grudge he felt at Kane for
delivering him over to bonds which he shirked so
lightly himself; but this was perhaps because they were
no longer a burden. It was not possible for him to
refuse his presence to the old man when he saw that
it was his sole pleasure; he had come to share the
pleasure of these meetings himself. As the days which
must be fewer and fewer went by he tried to come
every day, and Peace usually found him sitting with
her father when she reached home at the end of the
afternoon. Ray could get there first because his work
on the newspaper was of a more flexible and desultory
sort; and he often brought a bundle of books for review with him, and talked them over with Hughes, for
whom he was a perspective of the literary world, with
its affairs and events. Hughes took a vivid interest
in the management of Ray's department of *Every
Evening,* and gave him advice about it, charging him
not to allow it to be merely æsthetic, but to imbue it
with an ethical quality; he maintained that literature
should be the handmaid of reform; he regretted that
he had not cast the material of *The World Revisited* in
the form of fiction, which would have given it a charm
impossible to a merely polemical treatise.

"I'm convinced that if I had it in that shape it
would readily find a publisher, and I'm going to see
what I can do to work it over as soon as I'm about
again."

"I hope you'll be luckier than I've been with fiction," said Ray. "I don't know but it might be a good plan to turn *A Modern Romeo* into a polemical treatise. We might change about, Mr. Hughes."

Hughes said, "Why don't you bring your story up here and read it to me?'

"Wouldn't that be taking an unfair advantage of you?" Ray asked. "Just at present my chief's looking over it, to see if it won't do for the *feuilleton* we're going to try. He won't want it; but it affords a little respite for you, Mr. Hughes, as long as he thinks he may.'

He knew that Peace must share his constraint in speaking of his book. When they were alone for a little while before he went away that evening he said to her, "You have never told me yet that you forgave me for my bad behavior about my book the last time we talked about it."

"Did you wish me to tell you?" she asked, gently. "I thought I needn't."

"Yes, do," he urged. "You thought I was wrong?"

"Yes," she assented.

"Then you ought to say, in so many words, 'I forgive you.'"

He waited, but she would not speak.

"Why can't you say that?"

She did not answer, but after a while she said, "I think what I did was a good reason for" —

"My being in the wrong? Then why did you do it? Can't you tell me that?"

"Not — now."

"Some time?"

"Perhaps," she murmured.

"Then I may ask you again?"

She was silent, sitting by the window in the little back room, where her head was dimly outlined against the late twilight. Between the rushing trains at the front they could hear Mrs. Denton talking to her father, joking and laughing. Our common notion of tragedy is that it alters the nature of those involved, as if it were some spiritual chemistry combining the elements of character anew. But it is merely an incident of our being, and, for all we can perceive, is of no more vital effect than many storms in the material world. What it does not destroy, it leaves essentially unchanged. The light creature whom its forces had beaten to the earth, rose again with the elasticity of light things, when it had passed. She was meant to be what she was made, and even Ray, with the severity of his young morality, and the paucity of his experience, perceived that the frivolity which shocked him was comfort and cheer to the sick old man. She sat with him, and babbled and jested; and Ray saw with a generous resentment that she must always have been his favorite. There was probably a responsive lightness in Hughes's own soul to which hers brought the balm of kinship and of perfect sympathy. There was no apparent consciousness of his preference in the sisters; each in her way accepted it as something just and fit. Peace looked after the small housekeeping, and her sister had more and more the care of their father.

Mrs. Denton's buoyant temperament served a better purpose in the economy of sorrow than a farther-sighted seriousness. In virtue of all that Ray had ever read or fancied of such experiences, the deaths that had bereaved her ought to have chastened and sobered her, and he could not forgive her because she could not wear the black of a hushed and spiritless behavior. It even shocked him that Peace did nothing to restrain her, but took her from moment to moment as she showed herself, and encouraged her cheerful talk, and smiled at her jokes. He could not yet understand how the girl's love was a solvent of all questions that harass the helpless reason, and embitter us with the faults of others ; but from time to time he had a sense of quality in her that awed him from all other sense of her. There is something in the heart of man that puts a woman's charm before all else, and that enables evil and foolish women to find husbands, while good and wise women die unwed. But in the soul of incontaminate youth there is often a passionate refusal to accept this instinct as the highest. The ideal of womanhood is then something too pure and hallowed even for the dreams of love. It was something like this, a mystical reverence or a fantastic exaltation, which removed Ray further from Peace, in what might have joined their lives, than he was the first day they met, when he began to weave about her the reveries which she had no more part in than if they had been the dreams of his sleep. They were of the stuff of his literature, and like the innumerably trooping, insubstantial fancies

that followed each other through his brain from nothing
in his experience. When they ceased to play, as they
must after the little romance of that first meeting had
yielded to acquaintance, what had taken their place?
At the end of the half-year which had united them in
the intimacy of those strange events and experiences,
he could not have made sure of anything but a sort of
indignant compassion that drew him near her, and the
fantastic sentiment that held him aloof. The resentment in his pity was toward himself as much as her
father; when he saw her in the isolation where the old
man's preference for her sister left her, he blamed himself as much as them.

Peace blamed no one by word or look. He doubted
if she saw it, till he ventured one day to speak of her
father's fondness for her sister, and then she answered
that he would always rather have Jenny with him than
any one else. Ray returned some commonplaces, not
too sincere, about the compensation the care of her
father must be to Mrs. Denton in her bereavement,
and Peace answered as frankly as before that they had
got each other back again. "Father didn't want her
to marry Ansel, and he didn't care for the children.
He couldn't help that; he was too old; and after we
were all shut up here together they fretted him."

She sighed gently, in the way she had, and Ray said,
with the fatuity of comforters, "I suppose they are
better off out of this world."

"They were born into this world," she answered.

"Yes," he had to own.

He saw how truly and deeply she grieved for the little ones, and he realized without umbrage that she mourned their wretched father too, with an affection as simple and pure. There were times when he thought how tragical it would be for her to have cared for Denton, in the way his wife cared so little ; and then his fancy created a situation in whose unreality it ran riot. But all the time he knew that he was feigning these things, and that there was no more truth in them than in the supposition which he indulged at other times that he was himself in love with Mrs. Denton, and always had been, and this was the reason why he could not care for Peace. It was the effect in both cases of the æsthetic temperament, which is as often the slave as the master of its reveries.

It was in Mrs. Denton's favor that she did not let the drift of their father's affections away from Peace carry her with them. The earthward bodily decline of the invalid implied a lapse from the higher sympathies to the lower, and she seemed to have some vague perception of this, which she formulated in her own way, once, when she wished to account for the sick man's refusal of some service from Peace which he accepted from herself.

"He has more use for me here, Peace, because I'm of the earth, earthy, but he'll want you somewhere else."

The old man clung to the world with a hope that admitted at least no open question of his living. He said that as soon as the spring fairly opened, and the weather would allow him to go out without taking more cold, he should carry his manuscript about to the different publishers, and offer it personally. He thought his plan carefully out, and talked it over with Ray, whom he showed that his own failure with his novel was from a want of address in these interviews. He proposed to do something for Ray's novel as soon as he secured a publisher for himself, and again he bade him bring it and read it to him. Ray afterwards realized with shame that he would have consented to this if Hughes had persisted. But the invitation was probably a mere grace of civility with him, an effect of the exuberant faith he had in his own success.

As the season advanced, and the heat within-doors increased, they had to open the windows, and then the infernal uproar of the avenue filled the room, so that they could not hear one another speak till the windows were closed again. But the rush and clank of the elevated trains, the perpetual passage of the surface cars, with the clatter of their horses' hoofs, and the clash of the air-slitting bells, the grind and jolt of the heavy trucks, the wild clatter of express carts across the rails or up and down the tracks, the sound of feet and voices, the cries of the fruit-venders, and the whiffs of laughter and blasphemy that floated up from the turmoil below like filthy odors, seemed not so keenly to afflict the sick man, or to rend his nerves with the anguish that forced the others to shut it all out, and rather stifle in the heat. Yet, in some sort, he felt it too, for once when Ray spoke of it, he said yes, it was atrocious. "But," he added, "I am glad I came and placed myself where I could fully realize the hideousness of a competitive metropolis. All these abominations of sight and sound, these horrible discords, that offend every sense, physically express the spiritual principle underlying the whole social framework. It has been immensely instructive to me, and I have got some color of it into my book : not enough, of course, but infinitely more than I could possibly have imagined. No one can imagine the horror, the squalor, the cruel and senseless turpitude which these things typify, except in their presence. I have merely represented the facts in regard to them, and have left the imagination free to deal with the ideal city as a contrast, with its peaceful streets, cleanly and quiet, its stately ranks of beautiful dwellings, its noble piles of civic and religious architecture, its shaded and colonnaded avenues, its parks and gardens, and all planned and built, not from the greed and the fraud of competition, but from the generous and unselfish spirit of emulation, wherein men join to achieve the best instead of separating to get the most. Think of a city operated by science, as every city might be now, without one of the wretched animals tamed by the savage man, and still perpetuated by the savage man for the awkward and imperfect uses of a barbarous society ! A city without a horse, where electricity brought every man and everything silently to the door. Jenny ! Get me that manuscript, will you ? The part I was writing on to-day — in the desk — the middle drawer — I should like to read " —

Mrs. Denton dropped her cat from her lap and ran to get the manuscript. But when she brought it to her father, and he arranged the leaves with fluttering fingers, he could not read. He gasped out a few syllables, and in the paroxysm of coughing which began, he thrust the manuscript toward Ray.

"He wants you to take it," said Peace. "You can take it home with you. You can give it to me in the morning."

Ray took it, and stood by, looking on, not knowing how to come to their help for the sick man's relief, and anxious not to cumber them. When they had got him quiet again, and Ray had once more thrown up the window, and let in the mild night air which came laden with that delirium of the frenzied city, Peace followed him into the little back room, where they stood a moment.

"For Heaven's sake," he said, "why don't you get him away from here, where he could be a little more out of the noise? It's enough to drive a well man mad."

"He doesn't feel it as if he were well," she answered. "We have tried to get him to let us bring his bed out here. But he won't. I think," she added, "that he believes it would be a bad omen to change."

"Surely," said Ray, "a man like your father couldn't care for that ridiculous superstition. What possible connection could his changing to a quieter place have with his living or " —

"It isn't a matter of reason with him. I can see

how he's gone back to his early life in a great many things in these few days. He hasn't been so much like himself for a long time as he has to-night."

"What does the doctor say?"

"He says to let him have his own way about it. He says that — the noise can't make any difference — now."

They were in the dark; but he knew from her voice that tears were in her eyes. He felt for her hand to say good-night. When he had found it, he held it a moment, and then he kissed it. But no thrill or glow of the heart justified him in what he had done. At the best he could excuse it as an impulse of pity.

XXXVI.

THE editor of *Every Evening* gave Ray his manuscript back. He had evidently no expectation that Ray could have any personal feeling about it, or could view it apart from the interests of the paper. He himself betrayed no personal feeling where the paper was concerned, and he probably could have conceived of none in Ray.

"I don't think it will do for us," he said. "It is a good story, and I read it all through, but I don't believe it would succeed as a serial. What do you think, yourself?"

"I?" said Ray. "How could I have an unprejudiced opinion?"

"I don't see why you shouldn't. You know what we want; we've talked it over enough; and you ought to know whether this is the kind of thing. Anyhow, it's within your province to decide. I don't think it will do, but if you think it will, I'm satisfied. You must take the responsibility. I leave it to you, and I mean business."

Ray thought how old Kane would be amused if he could know of the situation, how he would inspect and comment it from every side, and try to get novel phrases for it. He believed himself that no author had ever' been quite in his place before; it was like something in Gilbert's operas; it was as if a prisoner were invited to try himself and pronounce his own penalty. His chief seemed to see no joke in the affair; he remained soberly and somewhat severely waiting for Ray's decision.

"I'm afraid you're right," said Ray. "I don't think it would do for *Every Evening*. Even if it would, I should doubt the taste of working in something of my own on the reader at the beginning."

"I shouldn't care for that," said the chief, "if it were the thing."

Ray winced, but the chief did not see it. Now, as always, it was merely and simply a question of the paper. He added carelessly:

"I should think such a story as that would succeed as a book."

"I wish you would get some publisher to think so."

The chief had nothing to say to that. He opened his desk and began to write.

In spite of the rejected manuscript lying on the table before him, Ray made out a very fair day's work himself, and then he took it up town with him. He did not go at once to his hotel, but pushed on as far as Chapley's, where he hoped to see Peace before she went home, and ask how her father was getting on; he had not visited Hughes for several weeks; he made himself this excuse. What he really wished was to confront the girl and divine her thoughts concerning himself. He must do that, now; but if it were not

for the cruelty of forsaking the old man, it might be
the kindest and best thing never to go near any of
them again.

He had the temporary relief of finding her gone
home when he reached Chapley's. Mr. Brandreth was
there, and he welcomed Ray with something more than
his usual cordiality.

"Look here," he said, shutting the door of his little
room. "Have you got that story of yours where you
could put your hand on it easily?"

"I can put my hand on it instantly," said Ray, and
he touched it.

"Oh!" Mr. Brandreth returned, a little daunted.
"I didn't know you carried it around with you."

"I don't usually — or only when I've got it from
some publisher who doesn't want it."

"I thought it had been the rounds," said Mr. Brandreth, still uneasily.

"Oh, it's an editor, this time. It's just been offered
to me for serial use in *Every Evening*, and I've declined it."

"What do you mean?" Mr. Brandreth smiled in
mystification.

"Exactly what I say." Ray explained the affair as
it had occurred. "It makes me feel like Brutus and
the son of Brutus rolled into one. I'm going round to
old Kane, to give the facts away to him. I think he'll
enjoy them."

"Well! Hold on! What did the chief say about
it?"

"Oh, he liked it. Everybody likes it, but nobody wants it. He said he thought it would succeed as a book. The editors all think that. The publishers think it would succeed as a serial."

Ray carried it off buoyantly, and enjoyed the sort of daze Mr. Brandreth was in.

"See here," said the publisher, "I want you to leave that manuscript with me."

"Again?"

"Yes. I've never read it myself yet, you know."

"Take it and be happy!" Ray bestowed it upon him with dramatic effusion.

"No, seriously!" said Mr. Brandreth. "I want to talk with you. Sit down, won't you? You know the first time you were in here, I told you I was anxious to get Chapley & Co. in line as a publishing house again; I didn't like the way we were dropping out and turning into mere jobbers. You remember."

Ray nodded.

"Well, sir, I've never lost sight of that idea, and I've been keeping one eye out for a good novel, to start with, ever since. I haven't found it, I don't mind telling you. You see, all the established reputations are in the hands of other publishers, and you can't get them away without paying ridiculous money, and violating the comity of the trade at the same time. If we are to start new, we must start with a new man."

"I don't know whether I'm a new man or not," said Ray, "if you're working up to me. Sometimes I
20

feel like a pretty old one. I think I came to New
York about the beginning of the Christian era. But
A Modern Romeo is as fresh as ever. It has the dew
of the morning on it still — rubbed off in spots by the
nose of the professional smeller."

"Well," said Mr. Brandreth, "it's new enough for
all practical purposes. I want you to let me take it
home with me."

"Which of the leading orchestras would you like to
have accompany you to your door?" asked Ray.

"No, no! Don't expect too much!" Mr. Brandreth entreated.

"I don't expect anything," Ray protested.

"Well, that's right — that's the only business basis.
But if it *should* happen to be the thing, I don't believe
you'd be personally any happier about it than I
should."

"Oh, thank you!"

"I'm not a fatalist" —

"But it would look a good deal like fatalism."

"Yes, it would. It would look as if it were really
intended to be, if it came back to us now, after it had
been round to everybody else."

"Yes; but if it was fated from the beginning, I
don't see why you didn't take it in the beginning.
I should rather wonder what all the bother had been
for."

"You might say that," Mr. Brandreth admitted.

Ray went off on the wave of potential prosperity,
and got Kane to come out and dine with him. They

decided upon Martin's, where the dinner cost twice as much as at Ray's hotel, and had more the air of being a fine dinner ; and they got a table in the corner, and Ray ordered a bottle of champagne.

"Yes," said Kane, "that is the right drink for a man who wishes to spend his money before he has got it. It's the true gambler's beverage."

"You needn't drink it," said Ray. "You shall have the *vin ordinaire* that's included in the price of the dinner."

"Oh, I don't mind a glass of champagne now and then, after I've brought my host under condemnation for ordering it," said Kane.

"And I want to let my heart out to-night," Ray pursued. "I may not have the chance to-morrow. Besides, as to the gambling, it isn't I betting on my book; it's Brandreth. I don't understand yet why he wants to do it. To be sure, it isn't a great risk he's taking."

"I rather think he *has* to take some risks just now," said Kane, significantly. He lowered his soft voice an octave as he went on. "I'm afraid that poor Henry, in his pursuit of personal perfectability, has let things get rather behindhand in his business. I don't blame him — you know I never blame people — for there is always a question as to which is the cause and which is the effect in such matters. My dear old friend may have begun to let his business go to the bad because he had got interested in his soul, or he may have turned to his soul for refuge because he knew his business had begun to go to the bad. At any rate, he seems to have found the usual difficulty in serving God and Mammon; only, in this case Mammon has got the worst of it, for once: I suppose one ought to be glad of that. But the fact is that Henry has lost heart in business; he doesn't respect business; he has a bad conscience; he wants to be out of it. I had a long talk with him before he went into the country, and I couldn't help pitying him. I don't think his wife and daughter even will ever get him back to New York. He knows it's rather selfish to condemn them to the dulness of a country life, and that it's rather selfish to leave young Brandreth to take the brunt of affairs here alone. But what are you to do in a world like this, where a man can't get rid of one bad conscience without laying in another?"

In his pleasure with his paradox Kane suffered Ray to fill up his glass a second time. Then he looked dissatisfied, and Ray divined the cause. "Did you word that quite to your mind?"

"No, I didn't. It's too diffuse. Suppose we say that in our conditions no man can do right without doing harm?"

"That's more succinct," said Ray. "Is it known at all that they're in difficulties?"

Kane smoothly ignored the question. "I fancy that the wrong is in Henry's desire to cut himself loose from the ties that bind us all together here. Poor David has the right of that. We must stand or fall together in the pass we've come to; and we cannot

helpfully eschew the world except by remaining in it."
He took up Ray's question after a moment's pause.
"No, it isn't known that they're in difficulties, and I
don't say that it's so. Their affairs have simply been
allowed to run down, and Henry has left Brandreth to
gather them up single-handed. I don't know that
Brandreth will complain. It leaves him unhampered,
even if he can do nothing with his hands but clutch at
straws."

"Such straws as the *Modern Romeo?*" Ray asked.
"It seems to me that *I* have a case of conscience here.
Is it right for me to let Mr. Brandreth bet his money
on my book when there are so many chances of his
losing?"

"Let us hope he won't finally bet," Kane suggested,
and he smiled at the refusal which instantly came into
Ray's eyes. "But if he does, we must leave the end
with God. People," he mused on, "used to leave the
end with God a great deal oftener than they do now.
I remember that I did, myself, once. It was easier. I
think I will go back to it. There is something very
curious in our relation to the divine. God is where
we believe He is, and He is a daily Providence or not,
as we choose. People used to see His hand in a corner, or a deal, which prospered them, though it ruined
others. They may be ashamed to do that now. But
we might get back to faith by taking a wider sweep
and seeing God in our personal disadvantages — finding
Him not only in luck but in bad luck. Chance may
be a larger law, with an orbit far transcending the

range of the little statutes by which fire always burns, and water always finds its level."

"That is a better Hard Saying than the other," Ray mocked. "'I' faith an excellent song.' Have some more champagne. Now go on; but let us talk of *A Modern Romeo*."

"We will drink to it," said Kane, with an air of piety.

XXXVII.

"Well, sir," said Mr. Brandreth when he found Ray waiting for him in his little room the next morning, "I haven't slept a wink all night."

Ray had not slept a wink himself, and he had not been able to keep away from Chapley's in his fear and his hope concerning his book. He hoped Mr. Brandreth might have looked at it; he feared he had not. His heart began to go down, but he paused in his despair at the smiles that Mr. Brandreth broke into.

"It was that book of yours. I thought I would just dip into it after dinner, and try a chapter or two on Mrs. Brandreth; but I read on till eleven o'clock, and then she went to bed, and I kept at it till I finished it, about three this morning. Then the baby took up the strain for about half an hour and finished *me*."

Ray did not know what to say. He gasped out, "I'm proud to have been associated with young Mr. Brandreth in destroying his father's rest."

The publisher did not heed this poor attempt at nonchalance. "I left the manuscript for Mrs. Brandreth — she called me back to make sure, before I got out of doors — and if she likes it as well to the end — But I know she will! She likes you, Ray."

"Does she?" Ray faintly questioned back.

"Yes; she thinks you're all kinds of a nice fellow, and that you've been rather sacrificed in some ways. She thinks you behaved splendidly in that Denton business."

Ray remained mutely astonished at the flattering opinions of Mrs. Brandreth; he had suspected them so little. Her husband went on, smiling:

"She wasn't long making out the original of your hero." Ray blushed consciously, but made no attempt to disown the self-portraiture. "Of course," said Mr. Brandreth, "we're all in the dark about the heroine. But Mrs. Brandreth doesn't care so much for her."

Now that he was launched upon the characters of the story, Mr. Brandreth discussed them all, and went over the incidents with the author, whose brain reeled with the ecstacy of beholding them objectively in the flattering light of another's appreciation.

"Well," said Mr. Brandreth, at last, when Ray found strength to rise from this debauch of praise, "you'll hear from me, now, very soon. I've made up my mind about the story, and unless Mrs. Brandreth should hate it very much before she gets through with it — Curious about women, isn't it, how they always take the personal view? —I believe the main reason why my wife dislikes your heroine is because she got her mixed up with the girl that took the part of Juliet away from her in our out-door theatricals. I tell her that you and I are not only the two Percys, we're the two Romeos, too. She thinks your heroine is rather weak; of course you meant her to be so."

Ray had not, but he said that he had, and he made a noisy pretence of thinking the two Romeos a prodigious joke. His complaisance brought its punishment.

"Oh!" said Mr. Brandreth, "I must tell you a singular thing that happened. Just as I got to that place where he shoots himself, you know, and she starts up out of her hypnotic trance, our baby gave a frightful scream, and Mrs. Brandreth woke and thought the house was on fire. I suppose the little fellow had a bad dream; it's strange what dreams babies *do* have! But wasn't it odd, happening when I was wrought up so? Looks like telepathy, doesn't it? Of course my mind's always on the child. By-the-way, if this thing goes, you must try a telepathic story. It hasn't been done yet."

"Magnificent!" said Ray. "I'll do it!"

They got away from each other, and Ray went down to his work at the *Every Evening* office. He enslaved himself to it by an effort twice as costly as that of writing when he was in the deepest and darkest of his despair; his hope danced before him, and there was a tumult in his pulses which he could quiet a little only by convincing himself that as yet he had no promise from Mr. Brandreth, and that if the baby had given Mrs. Brandreth a bad day, it was quite within the range of possibility that the publisher might, after all, have perfectly good reasons for rejecting his book. He insisted with himself upon this

view of the case ; it was the only one that he could
steady his nerves with ; and besides, he somehow felt
that if he could feign it strenuously enough, the fates
would be propitiated, and the reverse would happen.

It is uncertain whether it was his pretence that produced the result intended, but in the evening Mr.
Brandreth came down to Ray's hotel to say that he
had made up his mind to take the book.

" We talked it over at dinner, and my wife made me
come right down and tell you. She said you had been
kept in suspense long enough, and she wasn't going to
let you go overnight. It's the first book *we've* ever
taken, and I guess she feels a little romantic about the
new departure. By-the-way, we found out what ailed
the baby. It was a pin that had got loose, and stuck
up through the sheet in his crib. You can't trust
those nurses a moment. But I believe that telepathic
idea is a good one."

" Yes, yes ; it is," said Ray. Now that the certainty
of acceptance had come, he was sobered by it, and he
could not rejoice openly, though he was afraid he was
disappointing Mr. Brandreth. He could only say,
" It's awfully kind of Mrs. Brandreth to think of me."

" That's her way," said Mr. Brandreth, and he
added briskly, " Well, now, let's come down to busi
ness. How do you want to publish ? Want to make
your own plates ? "

" No," Ray faltered ; " I can't afford to do that ; I
had one such offer " —

" I supposed you wouldn't," Mr. Brandreth cut in,

but I thought I'd ask. Well, then, we'll make the plates ourselves, and we'll pay you ten per cent. on the retail price of the book. That is the classic arrangement with authors, and I think it's fair." When he said this he swallowed, as if there were something in his throat, and added, " Up to a certain point. And as we take all the risk, I think we ought to have — You see, on one side it's a perfect lottery, and on the other side it's a dead certainty. You can't count on the public, but you can count on the landlord, the salesman, the bookkeeper, the printer, and the paper-maker. We're at all the expense — rent, clerk-hire, plates, printing, binding, and advertising, and the author takes no risk whatever."

It occurred to Ray afterwards that an author took the risk of losing his labor if his book failed; but the public estimates the artist's time at the same pecuniary value as the sitting hen's, and the artist insensibly accepts the estimate. Ray did not think of his point in season to urge it, but it would hardly have availed if he had. He was tremulously eager to close with Mr. Brandreth on any terms, and after they had agreed, he was afraid he had taken advantage of him.

When the thing was done it was like everything else. He had dwelt so long and intensely upon it in a thousand reveries that he had perhaps exhausted his possibilities of emotion concerning it. At any rate he found himself curiously cold ; he wrote to his father about it, and he wrote to Sanderson, who would be sure to make a paragraph for the *Echo*, and unless

Hanks Brothers killed his paragraph, would electrify Midland with the news. Ray forecast the matter and the manner of the paragraph, but it did not excite him.

"What is the trouble with me?" he asked Kane, whom he hastened to tell his news. "I ought to be in a transport; I'm not in anything of the kind."

"Ah! That is very interesting. No doubt you'll come to it. I had a friend once who was accepted in marriage by the object of his affections. His first state was apathy, mixed, as nearly as I could understand, with dismay. He became more enthusiastic later on, and lived ever after in the belief that he was one of the most fortunate of men. But I think we are the victims of conventional acceptations in regard to most of the great affairs of life. We are taught that we shall feel so and so about such and such things: about success in love or in literature; about the birth of our first-born; about death. But probably no man feels as he expected to feel about these things. He finds them of exactly the same quality as all other experiences; there may be a little more or a little less about them, but there isn't any essential difference. Perhaps when we come to die ourselves, it will be as simply and naturally as — as " —

"As having a book accepted by a publisher," Ray suggested.

"Exactly!" said Kane, and he breathed out his deep, soft laugh.

"Well, you needn't go on. I'm sufficiently accounted

for." Ray rose, and Kane asked him what his hurry was, and where he was going.

"I'm going up to tell the Hugheses."

"Ah! then I won't offer to go with you," said Kane. "I approve of your constancy, but I have my own philosophy of such things. I think David would have done much better to stay where he was; I do not wish to punish him for coming to meet the world, and reform it on its own ground; but I could have told him he would get beaten. He is a thinker, or a dreamer, if you please, and in his community he had just the right sort of distance. He could pose the world just as he wished, and turn it in this light and in that. But here he sees the exceptions to his rules, and when I am with him I find myself the prey of a desire to dwell on the exceptions, and I know that I afflict him. I always did, and I feel it the part of humanity to keep away from him. I am glad that I do, for I dislike very much being with sick people. Of course I shall go as often as decency requires. For Decency," Kane concluded, with the effect of producing a Hard Saying, "transcends Humanity. So many reformers forget that," he added.

The days were now getting so long that they had just lighted the lamps in Hughes's room when Ray came in, a little after seven. He had a few words with Peace in the family room first, and she told him that her father had passed a bad day, and she did not know whether he was asleep or not.

"Then I'll go away again," said Ray.

"No, no; if he is awake, he will like to see you. He always does. And now he can't see you much oftener,"

"Oh, Peace! Do you really think so?"

"The doctor says so. There is no hope any more." There was no faltering in her voice, and its steadiness strengthened Ray, standing so close to one who stood so close to death.

"Does he — your father — know?"

"I can't tell. He is always so hopeful. And Jenny won't hear of giving up. She is with him more than I am, and she says he has a great deal of strength yet. He can still work at his book a little. He has every part of it in mind so clearly that he can tell her what to do when he has the strength to speak. The worst is, when his voice fails him — he gets impatient. That was what brought on his hemorrhage to-day."

"Peace! I am ashamed to think why I came to-night. But I hoped it might interest him."

"About your book? Oh yes. Mr. Brandreth spoke to me about it. I thought you would like to tell him."

"Thank you," said Ray. He was silent for a moment. She stood against the pale light of one of the windows, a shadowy outline, and he felt as if they were two translated spirits meeting there exterior to the world and all its interests; he made a mental note of his impression for use some time. But now he said: "I thought I should like to tell him, too. But after all, I'm not so sure. I'm not like you, Peace.

And I suppose I'm punished for my egotism in the very hour of my triumph. It isn't like a triumph; it's like — nothing. I've looked forward to this so long — I've counted on it so much — I've expected it to be like having the world in my hand. But if I shut my hand, it's empty."

He knew that he was appealing to her for comfort, and he expected her to respond as she did.

"That's because you don't realize it yet. When you do, it will seem the great thing that it is."

"Do you think it's a great thing?"

"As great as any success can be."

"Do you think it will succeed?"

"Mr. Brandreth thinks it will. He's very hopeful about it."

"Sometimes I wish it would fail. I don't believe it deserves to succeed. I'm ashamed of it in places. Have I any right to let him foist it on the public if I don't perfectly respect it? You wouldn't if it were yours."

He wished her to deny that it was bad in any part, but she did not. She merely said: "I suppose that's the way our work always seems to us when it's done. There must be a time when we ought to leave what we've done to others; it's for them, not for ourselves; why shouldn't they judge it?"

"Yes; that is true! How generous you are! How can you endure to talk to me of my book? But I suppose you think that if I can stand it, you can."

"I will go in, now," said Peace, ignoring the drift

of his words, "and see if father is awake." She returned in a moment, and murmured softly, "Come!"

"Here is Mr. Ray, father," said Mrs. Denton. She
had to lift her voice to make the sick man hear, for
the window was open, and the maniacal clamor of the
street flooded the chamber. Hughes lay at his thin
full-length in his bed, like one already dead.

He stirred a little at the sound of his daughter's
voice, and when he had taken in the fact of Ray's
presence, he signed to her to shut the window. The
smells of the street, and the sick, hot whiffs from the
passing trains were excluded; the powerful odors of
the useless drugs burdened the air; by the light of the
lamp shaded from Hughes's eyes Ray could see the
red blotches on his sheet and pillow.

He no longer spoke, but he could write with a pencil
on the little memorandum-block which lay on the
stand by his bed. When Peace said, "Father, Mr.
Ray has come to tell you that his book has been accepted; Chapley & Co. are going to publish it," the
old man's face lighted up. He waved his hand
toward the stand, and Mrs. Denton put the block and
pencil in it, and held the lamp for him to see.

Ray took the block, and read, faintly scribbled on
it: "Good! You must get them to take my *World
Revisited*."

The sick man smiled as Ray turned his eyes toward
him from the paper.

"What is it?" demanded Mrs. Denton, after a
moment. "Some secret? What is it, father?" she

pursued, with the lightness that evidently pleased him, for he smiled again, and an inner light shone through his glassy eyes. "Tell us, Mr. Ray!"

Hughes shook his head weakly, still smiling, and Ray put the leaf in his pocket. Then he took up the old man's long hand where it lay inert on the bed.

"I will do my very best, Mr. Hughes. I will do everything that I possibly can."

21

XXXVIII.

A purpose had instantly formed itself in Ray's mind which he instantly set himself to carry out. It was none the less a burden because he tried to think it heroic and knew it to be fantastic; and it was in a mood of equally blended devotion and resentment that he disciplined himself to fulfil it. It was shocking to criticise the dying man's prayer from any such point of view, but he could not help doing so, and censuring it for a want of taste, for a want of consideration. He did not account for the hope of good to the world which Hughes must have had in urging him to befriend his book; he could only regard it as a piece of literature, and judge the author's motives by his own, which he was fully aware were primarily selfish.

But he went direct to Mr. Brandreth and laid the matter before him.

"Now I'm going to suggest something," he hurried on, "which may strike you as ridiculous, but I'm thoroughly in earnest about it. I've read Mr. Hughes's book, first and last, all through, and it's good literature, I can assure you of that. I don't know about the principles in it, but I know it's very original and from a perfectly new stand-point, and I believe it would make a great hit."

Mr. Brandreth listened, evidently shaken. "I couldn't do it, now. I'm making a venture with your book."

"That's just what I'm coming to. Don't make your venture with my book; make it with his! I solemnly believe that his would be the safest venture of the two; I believe it would stand two chances to one of mine."

"Well, I'll look at it for the fall."

"It will be too late, then, as far as Hughes is concerned. It's now or never, with him! You want to come out with a book that will draw attention to your house, as well as succeed. I believe that Hughes's book will be an immense success. It has a taking name, and it's a novel and taking conception. It'll make no end of talk."

"It's too late," said Mr. Brandreth. "I couldn't take such a book as that without passing it round among all our readers, and you know what that means. Besides, I've begun to make my plans for getting out your book at once. There isn't any time to lose. I've sent out a lot of literary notes, and you'll see them in every leading paper to-morrow morning. I'll have Mr. Hughes's book faithfully examined, and if I can see my way to it — I tell you, I believe I shall make a success of the *Modern Romeo*. I like the title better and better. I think you'll be pleased with the way I've primed the press. I've tried to avoid all vulgar claptrap, and yet I believe I've contrived to pique the public curiosity."

He went on to tell Ray some of the things he had
said in his paragraphs, and Ray listened with that
mingled shame and pleasure which the artist must feel
whenever the commercial side of his life presents itself.
"I kept Miss Hughes pretty late this afternoon,
working the things into shape, so as to get them to the
papers at once. I just give her the main points, and
she has such a neat touch."

Ray left his publisher with a light heart, and a
pious sense of the divine favor. He had conceived of
a difficult duty, and he had discharged it with un-
flinching courage. He had kept his word to Hughes ;
he had done all that he could for him, even to offering
his own chance of fame and fortune a sacrifice to him.
Now he could do no more, and if he could not help
being glad that the sacrifice had not been accepted of
him, he was not to be blamed. He was very much to
be praised, and he rewarded himself with a full recognition of his virtue; he imagined some words, few but
rare, from Peace, expressing her sense of his mag-
nanimity, when she came to know of it. He hoped
that a fact so creditable to him, and so characteristic,
would not escape the notice of his biographer. He
wished that Hughes could know what he had done,
and in his revery he contrived that his generous endeavor should be brought to the old man's knowledge ;
he had Hughes say that such an action was more to
him than the publication of his book.

Throughout his transport of self-satisfaction there
ran a nether torment of question whether Peace Hughes

could possibly suppose that he was privy to that paragraphing about his book, and this finally worked to the surface, and become his whole mood. After his joyful riot it was this that kept him awake till morning, that poisoned all his pleasure in his escape from self-sacrifice. He could only pacify himself and get some sleep at last by promising to stop at the publisher's on his way down to the *Every Evening* office in the morning, and beseech her to believe that he had nothing to do with priming the press, and that he wished Mr. Brandreth had not told him of it. Nothing less than this was due him in the character that he desired to appear in hereafter.

He reached the publisher's office before Mr. Brandreth came down, and when he said he would like to see Miss Hughes, the clerk answered that Miss Hughes had sent word that her father was not so well, and she would not be down that day.

"He's pretty low, I believe," the clerk volunteered.

"I'm afraid so," said Ray.

He asked if the clerk would call a messenger to take a note from him to his office, and when he had despatched it he went up to see Hughes.

"Did you get our message?" Peace asked him the first thing.

"No," said Ray. "What message?"

"That we sent to your office. He has been wanting to see you ever since he woke this morning. I knew you would come!"

"O yes. I went to inquire of you about him at

Chapley's, and when I heard that he was worse, of
course I came. Is he much worse?"

"He can't live at all. The doctor says it's no use.
He wants to see you. Will you come in?"   .

"Peace!" Ray hesitated. "Tell me! Is it about
his book?"

"Yes, something about that. He wishes to speak
with you."

"Oh, Peace! I've done all I could about that. I
went straight to Mr. Brandreth and tried to get him
to take it. But I couldn't. What shall I tell your
father, if he asks me?"

"You must tell him the truth," said the girl, sadly.

"Is that Mr. Ray?" Mrs. Denton called from the
sick-room. "Come in, Mr. Ray. Father wants you."

"In a moment. Come here, Mrs. Denton," Ray
called back.

She came out, and he told her what he had told
Peace. She did not seem to see its bearing at once.
When she realized it all, and had spent her quick
wrath in denunciation of Mr. Brandreth's heartlessness,
she said desperately: "Well, you must come now.
Perhaps it isn't his book; perhaps it's something else.
But he wants you."

She had to rouse her father from the kind of torpor
in which he lay like one dead. She made him understand who was there, and then he smiled, and turned
his eyes appealingly toward Ray. "Put your ear as
close to his lips as you can. He can't write any more.
He wants to say something to you."

Ray stooped over and put his ear to the drawn lips. A few whiffs of inarticulate breath mocked the dying man's endeavor to speak. "I'm sorry; I can't catch a syllable," said Ray.

A mute despair showed itself in the old man's eyes.

"Look at me father!" cried Mrs. Denton. "Is it about your book?"

The faintest smile came over his face.

"Did you wish to ask Mr. Ray if he would speak to Mr. Brandreth about it?"

The smile dimly dawned again.

"Well, he has spoken to him. He went to see him last night, and he's come to tell you "—Ray shuddered and held his breath—" to tell you that Mr. Brandreth will take your book, and he's going to publish it right away!"

A beatific joy lit up Hughes's face; and Ray drew a long breath.

Peace looked at her sister.

"I don't care!" said Mrs. Denton, passionately, dropping her voice. "You have your light, and I have mine."

XXXIX

RAY followed Hughes to his grave in the place where Denton and his children were already laid. It did not seem as if the old man were more related to them in death than he had been in life by their propinquity; but it satisfied a belated maternal and conjugal sentiment in Mrs. Denton. She did not relinquish the leading place in the family affairs which she had taken in her father's last days. She decided against staying in their present apartment after their month was out, and found a tiny flat of three rooms in a better neighborhood down-town, where she had their scanty possessions established, including the cat.

Kane did not go to the funeral because of a prejudice which he said he had against such events; David Hughes, he said, would have been the first to applaud his sincerity in staying away. But he divined that there might be need of help of another kind in the emergency, and he gave it generously and delicately. He would not suffer Mr. Brandreth to render any part of this relief; he insisted that it was his exclusive privilege as Hughes's old friend. Now that David was gone, he professed a singularly vivid sense of his presence; and he owned that he had something like the pleasure of carrying a point against him in defraying his funeral expenses.

Hughes's daughters accepted his help frankly, each after her kind : Mrs. Denton as a gift which it must long continue to be ; Peace as a loan which must some day be repaid. The girl went back to her work in due time, and whenever Ray visited his publisher he saw her at her desk.

He did not always go to speak to her, for he had a shamefaced fear that she was more or less always engaged in working up hints from Mr. Brandreth into paragraphs about a *A Modern Romeo.* His consciousness exaggerated the publisher's activity in this sort; and at first he shunned all these specious evidences of public interest in the forthcoming novel. Then he began jealously to look for them, and in his mind he arraigned the journals where they did not appear for envy and personal spite. It would have been difficult for him to prove why there should have been either in his case, unless it was because their literary notes were controlled by people whose books had been ignored or censured by *Every Evening*, and this theory could not hold with all. Most of the papers, however, published the paragraphs, with that munificence which journalism shows towards literature. The author found the inspired announcements everywhere ; sometimes they were varied by the office touch, but generally they were printed exactly as Mr. Brandreth framed them ; however he found them, they gave Ray an insensate joy. Even the paragraphs in the trade journals, purely perfunctory as they were, had a flavor of sincere appreciation; the very advertisements which accompanied them there affected him like favorable expressions of opinion. His hunger for them was inappeasable; in his heart he accused Mr. Brandreth of a stinted proclamation.

The publisher was hurrying the book forward for the summer trade, and was aiming it especially at the reader going into the country, or already there. He had an idea that the summer resorts had never been fully worked in behalf of the better sort of light literature, and he intended to make any sacrifice to get the book pushed by the news companies. He offered them rates ruinously special, and he persuaded Ray to take five per cent. on such sales if they could be made. He pressed forward the printing, and the author got his proofs in huge batches, with a demand for their prompt return. The nice revision which he had fancied himself giving the work in type was impossible; it went from his hand with crudities that glared in his tormented sense, till a new instalment eclipsed the last. He balanced the merits and defects against one another, and tried to believe that the merits would distract the attention of criticism from the defects. He always knew that the story was very weak in places; he conceived how it could be attacked in these; he attacked it himself with pitiless ridicule in a helpless impersonation of different reviewers; and he gasped in his self-inflicted anguish. When the last proof left his hands the feeblest links were the strength of the whole chain, which fell to pieces from his grasp like a rope of sand.

There was some question at different times whether the book had not better be published under a pseudonym, and Ray faithfully submitted it to the editor of *Every Evening*, as something he was concerned in. It was to be considered whether it was advisable for a critic to appear as an author, and whether the possible failure of the book would not react unfavorably upon the criticisms of the journal. The chief decided that it would make no difference to him, and at the worst it could do no more than range Ray with the other critics who had failed as authors. With the publisher it was a more serious matter, and he debated much whether the book, as a stroke of business, had not better go to the public anonymously. They agreed that P. B. S. Ray on the title-page would be rather formidable from the number of the initials which the reader would have to master in speaking of the author. Shelley Ray, on the other hand, would be taken for a sentimental pseudonym. They decided that anonymity was the only thing for it.

" But then, it will be losing the interest of your money, if the book goes," Mr. Brandreth mused. " You have a right to the cumulative reputation from it, so that if you should write another " —

" Oh, don't be afraid of there ever being another ! " said Ray, with his distracted head between his hands. He suddenly lifted it. " What is the matter with the Spartan severity of S. Ray ? "

"S. Ray might do," Mr. Brandreth assented, thoughtfully. "Should you mind my asking Mrs. Brandreth how it strikes her?"

"Not at all. Very glad to have you. It's short, and unpretentious, and non-committal. I think it might do."

Mrs. Brandreth thought so too, and in that form the author's name appeared on the title-page. Even in that form it did not escape question and censure. One reviewer devoted his criticism of the story to inquiry into the meaning of the author's initial; another surmised it a mask. But, upon the whole, its simplicity piqued curiosity, and probably promoted the fortune of the book, as far as that went.

There was no immediate clamor over it. In fact, it was received so passively by the public and the press that the author might well have doubted whether there was any sort of expectation of it, in spite of the publisher's careful preparation of the critic's or the reader's mind. There came back at once from obscure quarters a few echoes, more or less imperfect, of the synopsis of the book's attractions sent out with the editorial copies, but the influential journals remained heart-sickeningly silent concerning *A Modern Romeo*. There was a boisterous and fatuous eulogy of the book in the Midland *Echo*, which Ray knew for the expression of Sanderson's friendship; but eager as he was for recognition, he could not let this count; and it was followed by some brief depreciatory paragraphs in which he perceived the willingness of Hanks Brothers to compensate themselves for having so handsomely let Sanderson have his swing. He got some letters of acknowledgment from people whom he had sent the book ; he read them with hungry zest, but he could not make himself believe that they constituted impartial opinion ; not even the letter of the young lady who had detected him in the panoply of his hero, and who now wrote to congratulate him on a success which she too readily took for granted. One of his sisters replied on behalf of his father and mother, and said they had all been sitting up reading the story aloud together, and that their father liked it as much as any of them ; now they were anxious to see what the papers would say ; had he read the long review in the *Echo,* and did not he think it rather cool and grudging for a paper that he had been connected with ? He hardly knew whether this outburst of family pride gave him more or less pain than an anonymous letter which he got from his native village, and which betrayed the touch of the local apothecary ; his correspondent, who also dealt in books, and was a man of literary opinions, heaped the novel with ridicule and abuse, and promised the author a coat of tar and feathers on the part of his betters whom he had caricatured, if ever he should return to the place. Ray ventured to offer a copy to the lady who had made herself his social sponsor in New York, and he hoped for some intelligent praise from her. She asked him where in the world he had got together such a lot of queer people, like nothing on earth but those one used to meet in the old days when one took country board; she mocked at the sufferings of his hero, and said what a vulgar little piece his heroine was; but she supposed he meant them to be what they were, and she complimented him on his success in handling them. She confessed, though, that she never read American novels, or indeed any but French ones, and that she did not know exactly where to rank his work; she burlesqued a profound impression of the honor she ought to feel in knowing a distinguished novelist. "You'll be putting us all into your next book, I suppose. Mind you give me golden hair, not yet streaked with silver."

In the absence of any other tokens of public accept-ance, Ray kept an eager eye out for such signs of it as might be detected in the booksellers' windows and on their sign-boards. The placards of other novels flamed from their door-jambs, but they seemed to know nothing of *A Modern Romeo*. He sought his book in vain among those which formed the attractions of their casements; he found it with difficulty on their counters, two or three rows back, and in remote corners. It was like a conspiracy to keep it out of sight; it was not to be seen on the news-stands of the great hotels or the elevated stations, and Ray visited the principal railway depots without detecting a copy.

He blamed Mr. Brandreth for a lack of business energy in all this; he would like to see him fulfil some of those boasts of push which, when he first heard them, made him creep with shame. Mr. Brandreth had once proposed a file of sandwich men appealing with succeesive bill-boards :

I.

HAVE YOU READ

II.

"A MODERN ROMEO?"

III.

EVERY ONE IS READING

IV.

"A MODERN ROMEO."

V.

WHY?

VI.

BECAUSE

VII.

"A MODERN ROMEO" IS

VIII.

THE GREAT AMERICAN NOVEL.

Ray had absolutely forbidden this procession, but now he would have taken off his hat to it, and stood un-
;covered, if he could have met it in Union Square or in Twenty-third Street.

XL.

In this time of suspense Ray kept away from old Kane, whose peculiar touch he could not bear. But he knew perfectly well what his own feelings were, and he did not care to have them analyzed. He could not help sending Kane the book, and for a while he dreaded his acknowledgments; then he resented his failure to make any.

In the frequent visits he paid to his publisher, he fancied that his welcome from Mr. Brandreth was growing cooler, and he did not go so often. He kept doggedly at his work in the *Every Evening* office; but here the absolute silence of his chief concerning his book was as hard to bear as Mr. Brandreth's fancied coolness; he could not make out whether it meant compassion or dissatisfaction, or how it was to effect his relation to the paper. The worst of it was that his adversity, or his delayed prosperity, which ever it was, began to corrupt him. In his self-pity he wrote so leniently of some rather worthless books that he had no defence to make when his chief called his attention to the wide divergence between his opinions and those of some other critics. At times when he resented the hardship of his fate he scored the books before him with a severity that was as unjust as the weak commiseration in his praises. He felt sure that if the

situation prolonged itself his failure as an author must
involve his failure as a critic.

It was not only the coolness in Mr. Brandreth's
welcome which kept him aloof; he had a sense of responsibility, which was almost a sense of guilt, in the
publisher's presence, for he was the author of a book
which had been published contrary to the counsel of
all his literary advisers. It was true that he had not
finally asked Mr. Brandreth to publish it, but he had
been eagerly ready to have him do it; he had kept
his absurd faith in it, and his steadfastness must have
imparted a favorable conviction to Mr. Brandreth ; he
knew that there had certainly been ever so much personal kindness for him mixed up with its acceptance.
The publisher, however civil outwardly — and Mr.
Brandreth, with all his foibles, was never less than a
gentleman — must inwardly blame him for his unlucky
venture. The thought of this became intolerable, and
at the end of a Saturday morning, when the book was
three or four weeks old, he dropped in at Chapley's to
have it out with Mr. Brandreth. The work on the
Saturday edition of the paper was always very heavy,
and Ray's nerves were fretted from the anxieties of
getting it together, as well as from the intense labor
of writing. He was going to humble himself to the
publisher, and declare their failure to be all his own
fault; but he had in reserve the potentiality of a bitter
quarrel with him if he did not take it in the right way.

He pushed on to Mr. Brandreth's room, tense with
his purpose, and stood scowling and silent when he

22

found Kane there with him. Perhaps the old fellow divined the danger in Ray's mood; perhaps he pitied him; perhaps he was really interested in the thing which he was talking of with the publisher, and which he referred to Ray without any preliminary ironies.

"It's about the career of a book; how it begins to go, and why, and when."

"Apropos of *A Modern Romeo?*" Ray asked, harshly.

"If you please, *A Modern Romeo.*" Ray took the chair which Mr. Brandreth signed a clerk to bring him from without. Kane went on: "It's very curious, the history of these things, and I've looked into it somewhat. Ordinarily a book makes its fortune, or it doesn't, at once. I should say this was always the case with a story that had already been published serially; but with a book that first appears as a book, the chances seem to be rather more capricious. The first great success with us was *Uncle Tom's Cabin*, and that was assured before the story was finished in the old *National Era*, where it was printed. But that had an immense motive power behind it — a vital question that affected the whole nation."

"I seem to have come too late for the vital questions," said Ray.

"Oh no! oh no! There are always plenty of them left. There is the industrial slavery, which exists on a much more universal scale than the chattel slavery; that is still waiting its novelist."

"Or its Trust of novelists," Ray scornfully suggested.

"Very good; very excellent good; nothing less than a syndicate perhaps could grapple with a theme of such vast dimensions."

"It would antagonize a large part of the reading public," Mr. Brandreth said; but he had the air of making a mental memorandum to keep an eye out for MSS. dealing with industrial slavery.

"So much the better! So much the better!" said Kane. "*Robert Elsmere* antagonized much more than half its readers by its religious positions. But that wasn't what I was trying to get at. I was thinking about how some of the phenomenally successful books hung fire at first."

"Ah, that interests me as the author of a phenominally successful book that is still hanging fire," sighed Ray.

Kane smiled approval of his attempt to play with his pain, and went on: "You know that *Gates Ajar*, which sold up into the hundred thousands, was three months selling the first fifteen hundred."

"Is that so?" Ray asked. "*A Modern Romeo* has been three weeks selling the first fifteen." He laughed, and Mr. Brandreth with him; but the fact encouraged him, and he could see that it encouraged the publisher.

"We won't speak of *Mr. Barnes of New York*"—

"Oh no! Don't!" cried Ray.

"You might be very glad to have written it on some accounts, my dear boy," said Kane.

"Have you read it?"

"That's neither here nor there. I haven't seen
Little Lord Fauntleroy. But I wanted to speak of
Looking Backward. Four months after that was pub-
lished, the first modest edition was still unsold."

Kane rose. " I just dropped in to impart these
facts to your publisher, in case you and he might be
getting a little impatient of the triumph which seems
to be rather behind time. I suppose you've noticed
it? These little disappointments are not suffered in a
corner."

" Then your inference is that at the end of three or
four months *A Modern Romeo* will be selling at the
rate of five hundred a day? I'm glad for Brandreth
here, but I shall be dead by that time."

" Oh no! Oh no!" Kane softly entreated, while he
took Ray's hand between his two hands. " One
doesn't really die of disappointed literature any more
than one dies of disappointed love. That is one of
the pathetic superstitions which we like to cherish in a
world where we get well of nearly all our hurts, and
live on to a hale old imbecility. Depend upon it, my
dear boy, you will survive your book at least fifty
years." Kane wrung Ray's hand, and got himself
quickly away.

" There is a good deal of truth in what he says "—
Mr. Brandreth began cheerfully.

"About my outliving my book?" Ray asked.
" Thank you. There's all the truth in the world in
it."

" I don't mean that, of course. I mean the chances

that it will pick up any time within three months, and make its fortune."

"You're counting on a lucky accident."

"Yes, I am. I've done everything I can to push the book, and now we must trust to luck. You have to trust to luck in the book business, in every business. Business is buying on the chance of selling at a profit. The political economists talk about the laws of business; but there are no laws of business. There is nothing but chances, and no amount of wisdom can forecast them or control them. You had better be prudent, but if you are always prudent you will die poor. 'Be bold; be bold; be not too bold.' That's about all there is of it. And I'm going to be cheerful too. I'm still betting on *A Modern Romeo.*" The young publisher leaned forward and put his hand on Ray's shoulder, in a kindly way, and shook him a little. "Come! What will you bet that it doesn't begin to go within the next fortnight? I don't ask you to put up any money. Will you risk the copyright on the first thousand?"

"No, I won't bet," said Ray, more spiritlessly than he felt, for the proposition to relinquish a part of his copyright realized it to him. Still he found it safest not to allow himself any revival of his hopes; if he did it would be tempting fate to dash them again. In that way he had often got the better of fate; there was no other way to do it, at least for him.

XLI

AFTER a silent and solitary dinner, Ray went to
see Mrs. Denton and Peace in their new lodging. It
was the upper floor of a little house in Greenwich Village, which was sublet to them by a machinist occupy-
ing the lower floors; Ray vaguely recalled something
in his face at his first visit, and then recognized one of
the attendants at Hughes's Sunday ministrations. He
was disposed to fellowship Ray in Hughes's doctrine,
and in the supposition of a community of interest in
Hughes's daughters. They could not have been in
better or kindlier keeping than that of the machinist's
friendly wife, who must have fully shared his notion of
Ray's relation to them. She always received him like
one of the family, and with an increasing intimacy and
cordiality.

That evening when she opened the street door to
him she said, " Go right along up; I guess you'll find
them there all right," and Ray mounted obediently.
Half-way up he met Mrs. Denton coming down, with
her cat in her arms. " Oh, well!" she said. " You'll
find Peace at home; I'll be back in a moment."

He suspected that Mrs. Denton fostered the belief
of the machinist and his wife that there was a tacit if
not an explicit understanding between himself and

Peace, and he thought that she would now very probably talk the matter over with them. But he kept on up to the little apartment at the top of the house, and tapped on the door standing wide open. The girl was sitting at one of the windows, with her head and bust sharply defined against the glassy clear evening light of the early summer. She had her face turned toward the street, and remained as if she did not hear him at first, so that there was a moment when it went through his mind that he would go away. Then she looked round, and greeted him; and he advanced into the room, and took the seat fronting her on the other side of the window. There was a small, irregular square below, and above the tops of its trees the swallows were weaving their swift flight and twittering song; the street noises came up slightly muted through the foliage; it was almost like a sylvan withdrawal from the city's worst; and they talked of the country, and how lovely it must be looking now.

He said: "Yes, I wonder we can ever leave it. This is the first spring-time that I have ever been where I couldn't feel my way with Nature at every step she took. It's like a great loss out of my life. I think sometimes I am a fool to have staid here; I can never get it back. I could have gone home, and been the richer by the experience of another spring. Why didn't I do it?"

"Perhaps you couldn't have done your work there," she suggested.

"Oh, my work! That is what people are always

sacrificing the good of life to — their work! Is it
worth so much? If I couldn't do my newspaper-
work there, I could do something else. I could write
another unsuccessful novel."

"Is your novel a failure?" she asked.

"Don't you know it is? It's been out three weeks,
and nobody seems to know it. That's my grief, now;
it may one day be my consolation. I don't complain.
Mr. Brandreth still keeps his heroic faith in it, and
even old Kane was trying to rise on the wings of favorable prophecy when I saw him just before dinner.
But I haven't the least hope any more. I think I
could stand it better if I respected the book itself
more. But to fail in a bad cause — that's bitter." He
stopped, knowing as well as if he had put his prayer in
words, that he had asked her to encourage him, and if
possible, flatter him.

"I've been reading it all through again, since it
came out," she said.

"Oh, have you?" he palpitated.

"And I have lent it to the people in the house here,
and they have read it. They are very intelligent in a
kind of way" —

"Yes?"

"And they have been talking to me about it; they
have been discussing the characters in it. They like it
because they say they can understand just how every
one felt. They like the hero, and Mrs. Simpson cried
over the last scene. She thinks you have managed
the heroine's character beautifully. Mr. Simpson

wondered whether you really believe in hypnotism. They both said they felt as if they were living it."

Ray listened with a curious mixture of pleasure and of pain. He knew very well that it was not possible for such people as the Simpsons to judge his story with as fine artistic perception as that old society woman who thought he meant to make his characters cheap and ridiculous, and in the light of this knowledge their praise galled him. But then came the question whether they could not judge better of its truth and reality. If he had made a book which appealed to the feeling and knowledge of the great, simply-conditioned, sound-hearted, common-schooled American mass whom the Simpsons represented, he had made his fortune. He put aside that other question, which from time to time presses upon every artist, whether he would rather please the few who despise the judgment of the many, or the many who have no taste, but somehow have in their keeping the touchstone by which a work of art proves itself a human interest, and not merely a polite pleasure. Ray could not make this choice. He said dreamily: " If Mr. Brandreth could only find out how to reach all the Simpsons with it! I believe a twenty-five-cent paper edition would be the thing after all. I wish you could tell me just what Mr. and Mrs. Simpson said of the book; and if you can remember what they disliked as well as what they liked in it."

Peace laughed a little. " Oh, they disliked the wicked people. They thought the hard old father of

the heroine was terrible, and was justly punished by
his daughter's death. At the same time they thought
you ought to have had her revive in time to seize the
hero's hand, when he is going to shoot himself, and
keep him from giving himself a mortal wound. The
cousin ought to get well, too ; or else confess before
he dies that he intended to throw the hero over the
cliff, so that it could be made out a case of self-defence.
Mr. Simpson says that could be done to the satisfaction
of any jury."

Ray laughed too. "Yes. It would have been more
popular if it had ended well."

"Perhaps not," Peace suggested. "Isn't it the
great thing to make people talk about a book? If it
ended well they wouldn't have half so much to say as
they will now about it."

"Perhaps," Ray assented with meek hopefulness.
"But, Peace, what do *you* say about it? You've
never told me that yet. Do you really despise it so
much ? "

"I've never said that I despised it."

"You've never said you didn't, and by everything
that you've done, you've left me to think that you do.
I know," said the young man, "that I'm bringing up
associations and recollections that must be painful to
you; they're painful and humiliating to me. But it
seems to me that you owe me that much."

"I owe you much more than that," said the girl.
"Do you think that I forget — can forget — anything
— all that you've been to us ? "

"Oh, don't speak of it!" said Ray. "I didn't mean that. And you needn't tell me now what you think of my book. But sometime you will, won't you?" He drew forward a little nearer to her, where they sat in the light which had begun to wane. "Until then — until then — I want you to let me be the best friend you have in the world — the best friend I can be to any one."

He stopped for some answer from her, and she said: "No one could be a truer friend to us than you have been, from the very first. And we have mixed you up so in our trouble!"

"Oh, no! But if it's given me any sort of right to keep on coming to see Mrs. Denton and you, just as I used?"

"Why not?" she returned.

XLII

Ray went home ill at ease with himself. He spent
a bad night, and he seemed to have sunk away only a
moment from his troubles, when a knock at his door
brought him up again into the midst of them. He
realized them before he realized the knock sufficiently
to call out, "Who's there?"

"Oh!" said Mr. Brandreth's voice without; "you're
not up yet! Can I come in?"

"Certainly," said Ray, and he leaned forward and
slid back the bolt of his door : it was one advantage
of a room so small that he could do this without getting out of bed.

Mr. Brandreth seemed to beam with one radiance
from his silk hat, his collar, his boots, his scarf, his
shining eyes and smooth-shaven friendly face, as he
entered.

"Of course," he said, "you haven't seen the *Metropolis* yet?"

"No ; what is the matter with the *Metropolis?*"

Mr. Brandreth, with his perfectly fitted gloves on,
and his natty cane dangling from his wrist, unfolded
the supplement of the newspaper, and accurately
folded it again to the lines of the first three columns

of the page. Then he handed it to Ray, and delicately turned away and looked out of the window.

Ray glanced at the space defined, and saw that it was occupied by a review of *A Modern Romeo*. There were lengths of large open type for the reviewer's introduction and comments and conclusion, and embedded among these, in closer and finer print, extracts from the novel, where Ray saw his own language transfigured and glorified.

The critic struck in the beginning a note which he sounded throughout; a cry of relief, of exultation, at what was apparently the beginning of a new order of things in fiction. He hailed the unknown writer of *A Modern Romeo* as the champion of the imaginative and the ideal against the photographic and the commonplace, and he expressed a pious joy in the novel as a bold advance in the path that was to lead forever away from the slough of realism. But he put on a philosophic air in making the reader observe that it was not absolutely a new departure, a break, a schism; it was a natural and scientific evolution, it was a development of the spiritual from the material; the essential part of realism was there, but freed from the grossness, the dulness of realism as we had hitherto known it, and imbued with a fresh life. He called attention to the firmness and fineness with which the situation was portrayed and the characters studied before the imagination began to deal with them; and then he asked the reader to notice how, when this foundation had once been laid, it was made to serve as a " star-ypointing pyramid" from which the author's fancy took its bold flight through realms untravelled by the photographic and the commonplace. He praised the style of the book, which he said corresponded to the dual nature of the conception, and recalled Thackeray in the treatment of persons and things, and Hawthorne in the handling of motives and ideas. There was, in fact, so much subtlety in the author's dealing with these, that one might almost suspect a feminine touch, but for the free and virile strength shown in the passages of passion and action.

The reviewer quoted several of such passages, and Ray followed with a novel intensity of interest the words he already knew by heart. The whole episode of throwing the cousin over the cliff was reprinted; but the parts which the reviewer gave the largest room and the loudest praise were those embodying the incidents of the hypnotic trance and the tragical close of the story. Here, he said, was a piece of the most palpitant actuality, and he applauded it as an instance of how the imagination might deal with actuality. Nothing in the whole range of commonplace, photographic, realistic fiction was of such striking effect as this employment of a scientific discovery in the region of the ideal. He contended that whatever lingering doubt people might have of the usefulness of hypnotism as a remedial agent, there could be no question of the splendid success with which the writer of this remarkable novel had turned it to account in poetic fiction of a very high grade. He did not say the highest grade;

the book had many obvious faults. It was evidently the first book of a young writer, whose experience of life had apparently been limited to a narrow and comparatively obscure field. It was in a certain sense provincial, even parochial; but perhaps the very want of an extended horizon had concentrated the author's thoughts the more penetratingly on the life immediately at hand. What was important was that he had seen this life with the vision of an idealist, and had discerned its poetic uses with the sense of the born artist, and had set it in

"The light that never was on sea or land."

Much more followed to like effect, and the reviewer closed with a promise to look with interest for the future performance of a writer who had already given much more than the promise of mastery; who had given proofs of it. His novel might not be the great American novel which we had so long been expecting, but it was a most notable achievement in the right direction. The author was the prophet of better things; he was a Moses, who, if we followed him, would lead us up from the flesh-pots of Realism toward the promised land of the Ideal.

From time to time Ray made a little apologetic show of not meaning to do more than glance the review over, but Mr. Brandreth insisted upon his taking his time and reading it all; he wanted to talk to him about it. He began to talk before Ray finished; in fact he agonized him with question and comment, all through;

and when Ray laid the paper down at last, he came
and sat on the edge of his bed.

"Now, I'll tell you what I'm going to do. I don't
believe in working on Sunday, and that sort of thing;
but I believe this is providential. My wife does, too;
she says it's a reward for the faith we've had in the
book; and that it would be a sin to lose a moment's
time. If there is to be any catch-on at all, it must be
instantaneous; we mustn't let the effect of this review
get cold, and I'm going to strike while it's red-hot."
The word seem to suggest the magnitude of the purpose which Mr. Brandreth expressed with seriousness
that befitted the day. "I'm simply going to paint the
universe red. You'll see."

"Well, well," said Ray, "you'd better not tell me
how. I guess I've got as much as I can stand, now."

"If that book doesn't succeed," said Mr. Brandreth,
as solemnly as if registering a vow, "it won't be my
fault."

He went away, and Ray passed into a trance such
as wraps a fortunate lover from the outer world. But
nothing was further from his thoughts than love. The
passion that possessed him was egotism flattered to an
intensity in which he had no life but in the sense of
himself. No experience could be more unwholesome
while it lasted, but a condition so intense could not
endure. His first impulse was to keep away from
every one who could keep him from the voluptuous
sense of his own success. He knew very well that the
review in the *Metropolis* overrated his book, but he

liked it to be overrated; he wilfully renewed his delirium from it by reading it again and again, over his
breakfast, on the train to the Park, and in the lonely
places which he sought out there apart from all who
could know him or distract him from himself. At first
it seemed impossible; at last it became unintelligible.
He threw the paper into some bushes; then after he
had got a long way off, he went back and recovered it,
and read the review once more. The sense had returned, the praises had relumed their fires; again he
bathed his spirit in their splendor. It was he, he, he,
of whom those things were said. He tried to realize
it. Who was he? The question scared him; perhaps he was going out of his mind. At any rate he
must get away from himself now; that was his only
safety. He thought whom he should turn to for refuge.
There were still people of his society acquaintance in
town, and he could have had a cup of tea poured for
him by a charming girl at any one of a dozen friendly
houses. There were young men, more than enough
of them, who would have welcomed him to their
bachelor quarters. There was old Kane. But they
would have all begun to talk to him about that review;
Peace herself would have done so. He ended by going home, and setting to work on some notices for the
next day's *Every Evening*. The performance was a
play of double consciousness in which he struggled
with himself as if with some alien personality. But
the next day he could take the time to pay Mr. Brandreth a visit without wronging the work he had carried
so far.

23

On the way he bought the leading morning papers, and saw that the publisher had reprinted long extracts from the *Metropolis* review as advertisments in the type of the editorial page ; in the *Metropolis* itself he reprinted the whole review. " This sort of thing will be in the principal Philadelphia, Boston, Chicago, Cincinnati, and St. Louis papers just as soon as the mail can carry them my copy. I *had* thought of tele-graphing the advertisement, but it will cost money enough as it is," said Mr. Brandreth.

" Are you sure you're not throwing your money away? " Ray asked, somewhat aghast.

" I'm sure I'm not throwing my chance away," the publisher retorted with gay courage. He developed the plan of campaign as he had conceived it, and Ray listened with a kind of nerveless avidity. He looked over at Mr. Chapley's room, where he knew that Peace was busily writing, and he hoped that she did not know that he was there. His last talk with her had mixed itself up with the intense experience that had followed, and seemed of one frantic quality with it. He walked out to the street door with Mr. Brandreth beside him, and did not turn for a glimpse of her.

" Oh by-the-way," said the publisher at parting, " if you'd been here a little sooner, I could have made you acquainted with your reviewer. He dropped in a little while ago to ask who S. Ray was, and I did my best to make him believe it was a real name. I don't think he was more than half convinced."

"I don't more than half believe in him," said Ray, lightly, to cover his disappointment. "Who is he?"

"Well, their regular man is off on sick leave, and this young fellow — Worrell is his name — is a sort of under study. He was telling me how he happened to go in for your book — those things are always interesting. He meant to take another book up to his house with him, and he found he had yours when he got home, and some things about hypnotism. He went through them, and then he thought he would just glance at yours, anyway, and he opened on the hypnotic trance scene, just when his mind was full of the subject, and he couldn't let go. He went back to the beginning and read it all through, and then he gave you the benefit of the other fellow's chance. He wanted to see you, when I told him about you. Curious how these things fall out, half the time?"

"Very," said Ray, rather blankly.

"I knew you'd enjoy it."

"Oh, I do."

XLIII.

WHETHER the boom for *A Modern Romeo* which began with the appearance of the *Metropolis* review was an effect of that review or not, no one acquainted with the caprices of the book trade would undertake to say. There had been enthusiastic reviews of other books in the *Metropolis* which had resulted in no boom whatever, as Kane pointed out in ironically inviting the author to believe that the success of the book was due wholly to its merit.

"And what was its long failure due to?" Ray asked, tasting the bitter of the suggestion, but feigning unconsciousness.

"To its demerit."

Mr. Brandreth was at first inclined to ascribe the boom to the review; afterwards he held that it was owing to his own wise and bold use of the review in advertising. There, he contended, was the true chance, which, in moments of grateful piety, he claimed that he was inspired to seize. What is certain is that other friendly reviews began to appear in other influential journals, in New York and throughout the country. Ray began to see the book on the news-stands now; he found it in the booksellers' windows; once he heard people in an elevated car talking of it; somehow it

was in the air. But how it got in the air, no one could
exactly say; he, least of all. He could put his hand
on certain causes, gross, palpable, like the advertising
activities of Mr. Brandreth; but these had been in
effectless operation long before. He could not define
the peculiar attraction that the novel seemed to have,
even when frankly invited to do so by a vivid young
girl who wrote New York letters for a Southern paper,
and who came to interview him about it. The most
that he could say was that it had struck a popular
mood. She was very grateful for that idea, and she
made much of it in her next letter; but she did not
succeed in analyzing this mood, except as a general
readiness for psychological fiction on the part of a
reading public wearied and disgusted with the realism
of the photographic, commonplace school. She was
much more precise in her personal account of Ray;
the young novelist appeared there as a type of manly
beauty, as to his face and head, but of a regrettably
low stature, which, however, you did not observe while
he remained seated. It was specially confided to lady
readers that his slightly wavy dark hair was parted in
the middle over a forehead as smooth and pure as a
girl's. The processed reproduction of Ray's photo-
graph did not perfectly bear out her encomium; but it
was as much like him as it was like her account of him.
His picture began to appear in many places, with ro-
manced biographies, which made much of the obscurity
of his origin and the struggles of his early life. When
it came to be said that he sprang from the lower classes,

it brought him a letter of indignant protest from his mother, who reminded him that his father was a physician, and his people had always been educated and respectable on both sides. She thought that he ought to write to the papers and stop the injurious paragraph ; and he did not wholly convince her that this was impossible. He could not have made her understand how in the sudden invasion of publicity his personality had quite passed out of his own keeping. The interviewers were upon him everywhere : at his hotel, whose quaintness and foreign picturesqueness they made go far in their studies of him ; at the *Every Evening* office, where their visits subjected him to the mockery of his associates on the paper. His chief was too simple and serious of purpose to take the comic view of Ray's celebrity ; when he realized it through the frequency of the interviews, he took occasion to say : " I like your work and I want to keep you. As it is only a question of time when you will ask an increase of salary, I prefer to anticipate, and you'll find it put up in your next check to the figure which I think the paper ought to stand." He did not otherwise recognize the fact of the book's success, or speak of it ; as compared with his paper, Ray's book was of no importance to him whatever.

The interviews were always flattering to Ray's vanity, in a certain way, but it was rather wounding to find that most of the interviewers had not read his book ; though they had just got it, or they were going to get it and read it. In some cases they came to him with poetic preoccupations from previous interviews with Mr. Brandreth, and he could not disabuse them of the notion that his literary career had been full of facts much stranger than fiction.

"Mr. Brandreth says that if the truth could be told about that book," one young lady journalist stated, keeping her blue eyes fixed winningly upon the author's, "it would form one of the most dramatic chapters in the whole history of literature. *Won't* you tell *me* the truth about it, Mr. Ray?"

"Why, I don't know the truth about it myself," Ray said.

"Oh, how delightful!" cried the young lady. "I'm going to put *that* in, at any rate;" and she continued to work the young author with her appealing eyes and her unusually intelligent flatteries, until she had got a great deal more out of him concerning the periculations of his novel in manuscript than he could have believed himself capable of telling.

He went to Mr. Brandreth smarting with a sense of having made a fool of himself, and, "See here, Brandreth," he said, "what is so very remarkably dramatic in the history of a novel kicking about for six months among the trade?"

Mr. Brandreth stared at him, and then said, with a flash of recollection, "Oh! *That* girl! Well, she was determined to have *something* exclusive about the book, and I just threw out the remark. I wasn't thinking of your side of the business entirely. Ray, you're a good fellow, and I don't mind telling you that

when I chanced it on this book of yours, it had got to
a point with us where we had to chance it on something. Mr. Chapley had let the publishing interests
of the house go till there was hardly anything of them
left; and when he went up into the country, this
spring, he was strongly opposed to my trying anything
in the publishing line. But my wife and I talked it
over, and she saw as well as I did that I should either
have to go actively into the business, or else go out of
it. As it stood, it wouldn't support two families. So
I made up my mind to risk your book. If it had
failed it would have embarrassed me awfully; I don't
say but what I could have pulled through, but it would
have been rough sledding."

"That *is* interesting," said Ray. "I don't see why
I shouldn't begin to pose as your preserver."

"Well, it wasn't quite so bad as that," Mr. Brandreth gayly protested. "And at the last moment it
might have been some one else. There's no reason
why I shouldn't tell you that the night you came and
wanted me to take old Hughes's book, I talked it very
seriously over with my wife, and we determined that
we would look at it in the morning, and perhaps post-
pone your novel. We woke the baby up with our
talk, and then he woke us up the rest of the night, and
in the morning we were not fit to grapple with the
question, and I took that for a sign and let them go
on with your book. I suppose these things were in
my mind when I told that girl what she repeated to
you."

"Well, the incidents are dramatic enough," said
Ray, musingly. " Even tragical."

" Yes," sighed Mr. Brandreth. " I always dreaded
to ask you how you made it right with Mr. Hughes."

"Oh, Mrs. Denton made it right with *him*," Ray
scoffed. " I told her how I failed with you, and she
went right to him and said that you had taken his
book and would bring it out at once."

Mr. Brandreth looked pained. " Well, I don't
know what to say about that. But I'm satisfied now
that I acted for the best in keeping on with your
book. I'm going to have Mr. Hughes's carefully examined, though. I believe there's the making of
another hit in it. By-the-way," he ended, cheerily,
" you'll be glad to know that *A Modern Romeo* has
come of age; we've just printed the twenty-first
thousand of him."

" Is it possible!" said Ray, with well-simulated
rapture. With all the talk there had been about
the book, he supposed it had certainly gone to fifty
thousand by this time.

The sale never really reached that figure. It went
to forty two or three thousand, and there it stopped,
and nothing could carry it farther. The author talked
the strange arrest over with the publisher, but they
could arrive at no solution of the mystery. There
was no reason why a book which had been so widely
talked about and written about should not keep on
selling indefinitely; there was every reason why it
should; but it did not. Had it, by some process of

natural selection, reached exactly those people who cared for a psychological novel of its peculiar make, and were there really no more of them than had given it just that vogue? He sought a law for the fact in vain, in the more philosophical discussions he held with old Kane, as well as in his inquiries with Mr. Brandreth.

Finally, Kane said: "Why do we always seek a law for things? Is there a law for ourselves? We think so, but it's out of sight for the most part, and generally we act from mere caprice, from impulse. I've lived a good many years, but I couldn't honestly say that I've seen the cause overtaken by the consequence more than two or three times; then it struck me as rather theatrical. Consequences I've seen a plenty, but not causes. Perhaps this is merely a sphere of ultimations. We used to flatter ourselves, in the simple old days, when we thought we were all miserable sinners, that we were preparing tremendous effects, to follow elsewhere, by what we said and did here. But what if the things that happen here are effects initiated elsewhere?"

"It's a very pretty conjecture," said Ray, "but it doesn't seem to have a very direct bearing on the falling off in the sale of *A Modern Romeo*."

"Everything in the universe is related to that book, if you could only see it properly. If it has stopped selling, it is probably because the influence of some favorable star, extinguished thousands of years ago, has just ceased to reach this planet."

Kane had the air of making a mental note after he said this, and Ray began to laugh. "There ought to be money in that," he said.

"No, there is no money in Hard Sayings," Kane returned, sadly; "there is only — wisdom."

Ray was by no means discouraged with his failures to divine the reason for the arrested sale of his book. At heart he was richly satisfied with its success, and he left the public without grudging, to their belief that it had sold a hundred and fifty thousand. Mr. Brandreth was satisfied, too. He believed that the sale would pick up again in the fall after people got back from the country; he had discovered that the book had enduring qualities; but now the question was, what was Ray going to write next? "You ought to strike while the iron's hot, you know."

"Of course, I've been thinking about that," the young fellow admitted, "and I believe I've got a pretty good scheme for a novel."

"Could you give me some notion of it?"

"No, I couldn't. It hasn't quite crystallized in my mind yet. And I don't believe it will, somehow, till I get a name for it."

"Have you thought of a name?"

"Yes— half-a-dozen that won't do."

"There's everything in a name," said the publisher. "I believe it made the *Modern Romeo's* fortune."

Ray mused a moment. "How would *A Rose by any other Name* do?"

"That's rather attractive," said Mr. Brandreth.

"Well, anyway, remember that we are to have the book."

Ray hesitated. " Well — not on those old ten-per-cent. terms, Brandreth."

" Oh, I think we can arrange the terms all right," said Mr. Brandreth.

" Because I can do much better, you know."

" Oh, they've been after you, have they ? "

The young fellow held up the fingers of one hand.

" Well," said Mr. Brandreth, " your next book be-longs to Chapley & Co. You want to keep your books together.   One will help sell the other. *A Rose by any other Name* will wake up *A Modern Romeo* when it comes out."

XLIV

For Peace Hughes and her sister, the summer passed uneventfully. The girl made up for the time she had lost earlier in the year by doing double duty at the increased business of the publishing house. The prosperity of *A Modern Romeo* had itself added to her work, and the new enterprises which its success had inspired Mr. Brandreth to consider meant more letter-writing and more formulation of the ideas which he struck shapelessly if boldly out. He trusted her advice as well as her skill, and she had now become one of the regular readers for Chapley & Co.

Ray inferred this from the number of manuscripts which he saw on her table at home, and he could not help knowing the other things through his own acquaintance, which was almost an intimacy, with Mr. Brandreth's affairs. The publisher was always praising her. "Talk about men!" he broke out one day. "That girl has a better business head than half the business men in New York. If she were not a woman, it would be only a question of time when we should have to offer her a partnership, or run the risk of losing her. But there's only one kind of partnership you can offer a woman." Ray flushed, but he did not say anything, and Mr. Brandreth asked, apparently from some association in his mind, " Do you see much of them at their new place? "

" Yes; I go there every week or so."

" How are they getting on? "

" Very well, I believe." Ray mused a moment, and then he said : " If it were not contrary to all our pre-conceptions of a sort of duty in people who have been through what they have been through, I should say they were both happier than I ever saw them before. I don't think Mrs. Denton cared a great deal for her children or husband, but in her father's last days he wouldn't have anybody else about him. She strikes one like a person who would get married again."

Mr. Brandreth listened with the air of one trying to feel shocked; but he smiled.

" I don't blame her," Ray continued. " Perhaps old Kane's habit of not blaming people is infectious. She once accounted for herself on the ground that she didn't make herself; I suppose it might be rather dangerous ground if people began to take it generally. But Miss Hughes did care for those poor little souls and for that wretched creature, and now the care's gone, and the relief has come. They both miss their father; but he was doomed; he *had* to die; and be-sides, his fatherhood struck me as being rather thin, at times, from having been spread out over a community so long. I can't express it exactly, but it seems to me that the children of a man who is trying to bring about a millennium of any kind do not have a good time. Still, I suppose we must have the millenniums."

"You said that just like old Kane," Mr. Brandreth observed.

"Did I? I just owned he was infectious. If I've caught his habit of mind, I dare say I've caught his accent. I don't particularly admire either. But what I mean is that Miss Hughes and her sister are getting on very comfortably and sweetly. Their place is as homelike as any I know in New York."

"As soon as we get back in the fall, Mrs. Brandreth is going to call on them. Now that Mr. Chapley and Mr. Hughes are out of the way, there's no reason why we shouldn't show them some attention. Miss Hughes, at least, is a perfect lady. I'm going to see that she doesn't overwork; the success of *A Modern Romeo* has killed us nearly all; I'm going to give her a three weeks' vacation toward the end of August."

Ray called upon Peace one evening in the beginning of her vacation, and found her with the manuscript of a book before her; Mrs. Denton was sitting with the Simpsons on their front steps, and sent him on up to Peace when he declined to join her there.

He said, "I supposed I should find you reading up the Adirondack guide-books, or trying to decide between Newport and Saratoga. I don't see how your outing differs very much from your inning."

"This was only a book I brought home because I had got interested in it," the girl explained in self-defence. "We're not going away anywhere."

"I think I would stay myself," said Ray, "if it were not for wanting to see my family. My vacation begins to-morrow."

"Does it?"

"Yes; and I should be very willing to spend my fortnight excursioning around New York. But I'm off at once to-night; I came in to say good-by. I hope you'll miss me."

"We shall miss you very much," she said; and she added, "I suppose most of our fashionable friends have gone out of town."

"Have they?"

"I should think you would know. We had them at second-hand from you."

"Oh! Those?" said Ray. "Yes. They're gone, and I'm going. I hate to leave you behind. Have you any message for the country?"

"Only my love." She faced the manuscript down on the table before her, and rocked softly to and fro a moment. "It does make me a little homesick to think of it," she said, with touching patience.

He felt the forlornness in her accent, and a sense of her isolation possessed him. When Mrs. Denton should marry again, Peace would be alone in the world. He looked at her, and she seemed very little and slight, to make her way single-handed.

"Peace!" he said, and the intensity of his voice startled him. "There is something I wanted to say to you — to ask you," and he was aware of her listening as intensely as he spoke, though no change of attitude or demeanor betrayed the fact; he had to go on in a lighter strain if he went on at all. "You know, I suppose, what a rich man I am going to be

when I get the copyright on my book. It's almost
incredible, but I'm going to be worth five or six thousand dollars; to be as rich as most millionaires. Well
— I asked you to let me be your friend once, because I
didn't think a man who was turning out a failure had
the right to ask to be more. Or, no! That *isn't* it!"
he broke off, shocked by the false ring of his words.
"I don't know how to say it. I was in love once —
very much in love; the kind of love that I've put into
my book; and this — this worship that I have for you,
for I do worship you! — it isn't the same, Peace. It's
everything that honors you, and once it *was* like that;
but now I'm not sure. But I couldn't go away without offering you my worship, for you to accept for all
our lives; or reject, if it wasn't enough. Do you
understand?"

"I do understand," the girl returned, and she nervously pressed the hand which she allowed to gather
hers into it.

"I couldn't leave you," he went on, "without telling
you that there is no one in the world that I honor so
much as you. I had it in my heart to say this long
ago; but it seems such a strange thing to stop with.
If I didn't think you so wise and so good, I don't believe I could say it to you. I know that now whatever you decide will be right, and the best for us both.
I couldn't bear to have you suppose I would keep
coming to see you without — I would have told you
this long ago, but I always expected to tell you more.
But I'm twenty-six now, and perhaps I shall never
24

feel in that old way again. I *know* our lives would be
united in the highest things; and you would save me
from living for myself alone. What do you say,
Peace?"

He waited for her to break the silence which he did
not know how to interpret. At last she said "No!"
and she drew back from him and took her hand away.
"It wouldn't be right. I shouldn't be afraid to trust
you"—

"Then why"—

"For I know how faithful you are. But I'm afraid
— I *know* — I don't love you! And without that it
would be a sacrilege. That isn't enough of itself, but
everything else would be nothing without it." As if
she felt the wound her words must have dealt to his
self-love, she hurried on: "I did love you once. Yes!
I did. And when Mr. Brandreth wanted me to read
your book that time, I wouldn't, because I was afraid
of myself. But afterwards it — went." ·

"Was it my fault?" Ray asked.

"It wasn't any one's fault," said the girl. "If I
had not been so unhappy, it might have been different."

"Oh, Peace!"

"But I had no heart for it. And now my life must
go on just as it is. I have thought it all out. I
thought that some time you might tell me — what you
have — or different — and I tried to think what I
ought to do. I shall never care for any one else; I
shall never get married. Don't think I shall be unhappy! I can take good care of myself, and Jenny

and I will not be lonesome together. Even if we
don't always live together — still, I can always make
myself a home. I'm not afraid to be an old maid.
There is work in the world for me to do, and I can
do it. Is it so strange I should be saying this?"

"No, no. It's right."

"I suppose that most of the girls you know wouldn't
do it. But I have been brought up differently. In
the Family they did not think that marriage was always
the best thing; and when I saw how Jenny and Ansel
—I don't mean that it would ever have been like
that! But I don't wish you to think that life will be
hard or unhappy for me. And you — you will find
somebody that you can feel towards as you did towards
that first girl."

"Never! I shall never care for any one again!"
he cried. At the bottom of his heart there was a relief which he tried to ignore, though he could not deny
himself a sense of the unique literary value of the
situation. It was from a consciousness of this relief
that he asked, "And what do you think of me, Peace?
Do you blame me?"

"Blame you? How? For my having changed?"

"I feel to blame," said the young man. "How
shall we do, now? Shall I come to see you when I
return?"

"Yes. But we won't speak of this again."

"Shall you tell Mrs. Denton?"

"Of course."

"She will blame me."

"She will blame *me*," said Peace. "But—I shall
not be troubled, and you mustn't," she said, and she
lightly touched him. "This is just as I wish it to be.
I've been afraid that if this ever happened, I shouldn't
have the courage to tell you what I have. But you
helped me, and I am so glad you did! I was afraid
you would say something that would blind me, and
keep me from going on in the right way; but now—
Good-night."

"Good-night," said Ray, vaguely. "May I—
dream of you, Peace?"

"If you'll stop at daybreak."

"Ah, then I shall begin to think of you."

XLV.

THEY had certainly come to an understanding, and
for Ray at least there was release from the obscure
sense of culpability which had so long harassed him.
He knew that unless he was sure of his love for Peace,
he was to blame for letting her trust it; but now that
he had spoken, and spoken frankly, it had freed them
both to go on and be friends without fear for each
other. Her confession that there had been a time
when she loved him flattered his vanity out of the pain
of knowing that she did not love him now; it consoled
him, it justified him; for the offence which he had accused himself of was of no other kind than hers. How
wisely, how generously she had taken the whole
matter!

The question whether she had not taken it more
generously than he merited began to ask itself. She
might have chosen to feign a parity with him in this.
He had read of women who sacrificed their love to
their love; and consented to a life-long silence, or
practised a life-long deceit, that the men they loved
might never know they loved them. He had never
personally known of such a case, but the books were
full of such cases. This might be one of them. Or it
might much more simply and probably be that she had

received his strange declaration as she did in order to
spare his feelings.   If that were true she had already
told her sister, and Mrs. Denton had turned the absurd
side of it to the light, and had made Peace laugh it
over with her.

A cold perspiration broke out over him at the notion,
which he rejected upon a moment's reflection as un-
worthy of Peace.   He got back to his compassionate
admiration of her, as he walked down to the ferry and
began his homeward journey.   He looked about the
boat, and fancied it the same he had crossed to New
York in, when he came to the city nearly a year before·
The old negro who whistled, limped silently through
the long saloon ; he glanced from right to left on the
passengers, but he must have thought them too few,
or not in the mood for his music.   Ray wondered if
he whistled only for the incoming passengers.   He recalled every circumstance of his acquaintance with
Peace, from the moment she caught his notice when
Mrs. Denton made her outcry about the pocket-book.
He saw how once it had seemed to deepen to love, and
then had ceased to do so, but he did not see how.
There had been everything in it to make them more to
each other, but after a certain time they had grown
less.   It was not so strange to him that he had changed ;
he had often changed ; but we suppose a constancy in
others as to all passions which we cannot exact of ourselves.   He tried to think what he had done to alienate
the love which she confessed she once had for him, and
he could not remember anything unless it was his

cruelty to her when he found that she was the friend
who would not look at his story a second time. She
said she had forgiven him that; but perhaps she had
not; perhaps she had divined a potential brutality in
him, which made her afraid to trust him. But after
that their lives had been united in the most intimate
anxieties, and she had shown absolute trust in him.
He reviewed his conduct toward her throughout, and
he could find no blame in it except for that one thing.
He could truly feel that he had been her faithful friend,
and the friend of her whole uncomfortable family, in
spite of all his prejudices and principles against people
of that kind. In the recognition of this fact he enjoyed
a moment's sense of injury, which was heightened when
he reflected that he had even been willing to sacrifice
his pride, after his brilliant literary success, so far as
to offer himself to a girl who worked for her living;
it had always galled him that she held a place little
better than a type-writer's. No, he had nothing to
accuse himself of, after a scrutiny of his behavior repeated in every detail, and applied in complex, again
and again, with helpless iteration. Still he had a
remote feeling of self-reproach, which he tried to verify,
but which forever eluded him. It was mixed up with
that sense of escape, which made him ashamed.

He lay awake in the sleeping-car the greater part of
the night, and turned from side to side, seeking for the
reason of a thing that can never have any reason, and
trying to find some parity between his expectations
and experiences of himself in such an affair. It went

art life

through his mind that it would be a good thing to write
a story with some such situation in it; only the reader
would not stand it. People expected love to begin
mysteriously, but they did not like it to end so; though
life itself began mysteriously and ended so. He believed that he should really try it; a story that opened
with an engagement ought to be as interesting as one
that closed with an engagement; and it would be very
original. He must study his own affair very closely
when he got a little further away from it. There was
no doubt but that when the chances that favored love
were so many and so recognizable, the chance that
undid it could at last be recognized. It was merely a
chance, and that ought to be shown.

He began to wonder if life had not all been a chance
with him. Nothing, not even the success of his book,
in the light he now looked at it in, was the result of
reasoned cause. That success had happened; it had
not followed; and he didn't deserve any praise for
what had merely happened. If this apparent fatality
were confined to the economic world alone, he would
have been willing to censure civilization, and take his
chance dumbly, blindly, with the rest. He had not
found it so. On the contrary, he had found the same
caprice, the same rule of mere casualty, in the world
which we suppose to be ordered by law — the world
of thinking, the world of feeling. Who knew why or
how this or that thought came, this or that feeling?
Then, in that world where we lived in the spirit, was
wrong always punished, was right always rewarded?

We must own that we often saw the good unhappy, and the wicked enjoying themselves. This was not just; yet somehow we felt, we knew, that justice ruled the universe. Nothing, then, that seemed chance was really chance. It was the operation of a law so large that we caught a glimpse of its vast orbit once or twice in a lifetime. It was Providence.

The car rushed on through the night with its succession of smooth impulses. The thought of the old friends he should soon meet began to dispossess the cares and questions that had ridden him; the notion of certain girls at Midland haunted him sweetly, warmly. He told that one who first read his story all about Peace Hughes, and she said they had never really been in love, for love was eternal. After a while he drowsed, and then he heard her saying that he had got that notion of the larger law from old Kane. Then it was not he, and not she. It was nothing.

BY MARY E. WILKINS.

JANE FIELD. A Novel. Illustrated. 16mo, Cloth, Ornamental, $1 25.

YOUNG LUCRETIA, and Other Stories. Illustrated. Post 8vo, Cloth, Ornamental, $1 25.

A NEW ENGLAND NUN, and Other Stories. 16mo, Cloth, Ornamental, $1 25.

A HUMBLE ROMANCE, and Other Stories. 16mo, Cloth, Extra, $1 25.

It takes just such distinguishing literary art as Mary E. Wilkins possesses to give an episode of New England its soul, pathos, and poetry.—*N. Y. Times.*

The simplicity, purity, and quaintness of these stories set them apart in a niche of distinction where they have no rivals. —*Literary World,* Boston.

The author has the unusual gift of writing a short story which is complete in itself, having a real *beginning*, a *middle*, and an *end.*—*Observer*, N. Y.

A gallery of striking studies in the humblest quarters of American country life. No one has dealt with this kind of life better than Miss Wilkins. Nowhere are there to be found such faithful, delicately drawn, sympathetic, tenderly humorous pictures.—*N. Y. Tribune.*

The charm of Miss Wilkins's stories is in her intimate acquaintance and comprehension of humble life, and the sweet human interest she feels and makes her readers partake of, in the simple, common, homely people she draws. — *Springfield Republican.*

The author has given us studies from real life which must be the result of a lifetime of patient, sympathetic observation. . . . No one has done the same kind of work so lovingly and so well.—*Christian Register*, Boston.

PUBLISHED BY HARPER & BROTHERS, NEW YORK.

☞ *The above works will be sent by mail, postage prepaid, to any part of the United States, Canada, or Mexico, on receipt of the price.*

BEN-HUR:

A TALE OF THE CHRIST. By LEW. WALLACE. 16mo, Cloth, $1 50; Half Leather, $2 00; Three-quarter Leather, $2 50; Half Calf, $3 00; Full Leather, $3 50; Three-quarter Crushed Levant, $4 00.—GARFIELD EDITION. 2 volumes. Illustrated with twenty full-page photogravures. Over 1,000 illustrations as marginal drawings by WILLIAM MARTIN JOHNSON. Crown 8vo, Silk and Gold, Uncut Edges and Gilt Tops, $7 00. (*In a Gladstone box.*)

Anything so startling, new, and distinctive as the leading feature of this romance does not often appear in works of fiction. . . . Some of Mr. Wallace's writing is remarkable for its pathetic eloquence. The scenes described in the New Testament are rewritten with the power and skill of an accomplished master of style.—*N. Y. Times.*

Its real basis is a description of the life of the Jews and Romans at the beginning of the Christian era, and this is both forcible and brilliant. . . . We are carried through a surprising variety of scenes; we witness a sea-fight, a chariot-race, the internal economy of a Roman galley, domestic interiors at Antioch, at Jerusalem, and among the tribes of the desert; palaces, prisons, the haunts of dissipated Roman youth, the houses of pious families of Israel. There is plenty of exciting incident; everything is animated, vivid, and glowing.—*N. Y. Tribune.*

It is full of poetic beauty, as though born of an Eastern sage, and there is sufficient of Oriental customs, geography, nomenclature, etc., to greatly strengthen the semblance.—*Boston Commonwealth.*

"Ben-Hur" is interesting, and its characterization is fine and strong. Meanwhile it evinces careful study of the period in which the scene is laid, and will help those who read it with reasonable attention to realize the nature and conditions of Hebrew life in Jerusalem and Roman life at Antioch at the time of our Saviour's advent.—*Examiner,* N. Y.

The book is one of unquestionable power, and will be read with unwonted interest by many readers who are weary of the conventional novel and romance.—*Boston Journal.*

PUBLISHED BY HARPER & BROTHERS, NEW YORK.

☞ *The above work sent by mail, postage prepaid, to any part of the United States, Canada, or Mexico, on receipt of the price.*

TESS OF THE D'URBERVILLES.

A Pure Woman, Faithfully Presented. By THOMAS HARDY, author of "The Woodlanders," "A Laodicean," etc. Illustrated. Post 8vo, Cloth, Ornamental, $1 50. *New Edition, revised and considerably expanded by the author, according to the latest English edition.*

A remarkably fine and moving story. It is marked by all those qualities of genius which we are accustomed to associate with the work of Mr. Hardy. It is full of poetry of incident and phrase. . . . A great story. Nobody should miss it.—*N. Y. Sun.*

In "Tess of the D'Urbervilles" Thomas Hardy exhibits the strongest, and in some respects the best, piece of literary work that has ever left his pen.—*Philadelphia Ledger.*

One of the few great novels of the century.—*N. Y. Mail and Express.*

Not only by far the best work Mr. Hardy has done; it is one of the strongest novels that have appeared for a long time. . . . A more tragic or powerfully moving story than that of Tess lives not in fiction; and the pity of it is heightened by the exquisite pastoral scenes in which it is mainly set. . . . The book is full of suggestion on questions which have never agitated men's minds more than at the present time. . . . It is certainly a masterpiece, and one upon which the reputation of the author may safely rest.—*N. Y. Tribune.*

Mr. Hardy has written a novel that is not only good, but great. . . . "Tess of the D'Urbervilles" is well in front of Mr. Hardy's previous work, and is destined, there can be no doubt, to rank high among the achievements of Victorian novelists.—*Athenæum,* London.

The best English novel that has appeared for many a day. . . . The book is the most ingeniously constructed and artistically developed that has been produced by an English novelist since George Eliot's time.—*Philadelphia Bulletin.*

Powerful and strange in design, splendid and terrible in execution, this story brands itself upon the mind as with the touch of incandescent iron.—*Academy,* London.

PUBLISHED BY HARPER & BROTHERS, N. Y.

☞ *The above work is for sale by all booksellers, or will be sent by the publishers, postage prepaid, to any part of the United States, Canada, or Mexico, on receipt of price.*